"In *Soul Prints* Marc Gafni has done the extraordinary: he has wedded the deepest currents of classical spirituality to the soundest insights of modern psychology. For the scholar there is a trove here for discovery and reflection; for the layman a compendium of insights that will further growth and community. Gafni emerges in this book as a modern master, learned and hip, at home in a variety of discourses and bringing his depth of scholarship and practical experience to bear on the fundamental issues of human identity. This book begins a great adventure."

—Peter Pitzele, Ph.D., author of *Our Fathers' Wells*

"A radical, profound, and important guide to enable each reader to find out why he is on this earth—and what he can do to make sure that he actualizes the person he or she is meant to be."

—Rabbi Joseph Telushkin, author of *The Book of Jewish Values*

"A stunning piece of work, so clear and true that it rings as obvious as Newton's Laws of Gravity, but is as earth-shattering today as Newton's laws were in his time. Rabbi Gafni's book touches the mind and the heart at once. A majestic journey to the heavens and back into the reader's soul, it reaches inside our own very humanity. A must-read for anyone anxious to learn what matters most— their own destiny, happiness, and soul."

—Jennifer Laszlo-Mizrachi, political consultant, Laszlo and Associates

"Rabbi Marc Gafni is a uniquely creative and exciting philosopher on the Israeli scene. Like Martin Buber, the philosopher of dialogue, he has built a bridge from the insights of original Hasidic and mystical texts to the most contemporary needs of tens of thousands of seekers. In learned lectures, on television, in Woodstock-like spiritual festivals, in books both popular and academic, he has mined the Bible for guidance in living our personal myths, which for him means a vision of humanity embodying both Divine fire and individual shadows."

—Noam Zion, Shalom Hartman Institute in Jerusalem, author
of *A Different Night: The Family Participation Haggadah*
and *A Different Light: The Hanukkah Book of Celebration*

"The most creative and talented spiritual teacher in Israel today."
—R. Leonid Feldman, Temple Emanu-El, Palm Beach, Florida

"Rarely has a uniquely gifted teacher been able to express himself in writing as well as before a class. Gafni has done it! His charisma, brilliance, erudition, charm, and creativity come across in *Soul Prints* as sharply as attested to by his many students. This is a contribution to a life of spiritual value to many thousands of all faiths."
—Avraham Infeld, President, Melitz Educational Institutions

"Rabbi Marc Gafni offers us a fascinating gift: a kaleidoscope of endless color and vision. As we turn the pages, Gafni's brilliance and creativity take us into a deep journey of the soul."
—Rabbi J. Rolando Matalon, Congregation Bnai Jeshurun,
New York City

SOUL PRINTS

Your Path to Fulfillment

MARC GAFNI

POCKET BOOKS

NEW YORK LONDON TORONTO SYDNEY SINGAPORE

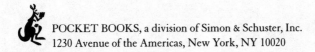

to my wife and partner, Cary

This book could not "be" without you.
Your love, wisdom, and clear vision were the womb
in which it was conceived. Your handling of
administrative chores, which are so foreign to
your nature, created the space for its gestation.
Your poet's pen and soulful eye helped craft many a phrase—
giving the book so much of the song it needed to be born.

Author's Meditation

May each page be a point of light
To illuminate the mind
Or if not the light
At least the wick
That holds the fire in line
And if not the wick then may it be
The oil to anoint the eye
But if not oil then at least the branch
That brought the olive to life
And if not branch then single seed
To plant the point of light.
Yes, let there be a single seed
within each page I write.

ACKNOWLEDGMENTS

It is a pleasure to recognize the colleagues, students, friends, and family who contributed directly and indirectly to this volume. I mention only a few. First, Fern Weissman—my beloved teacher and friend—who believed from the start that *Soul Prints* needed to be written. My colleagues and friends—Noam Zion of the Hartman Institute; Daniel Landes, director of Pardes Institute; Daniel Tropper, director of Gesher Educational Institutions; Avraham Leader of the Leader Minyan; Mimi Feigelson of Yakar; Ohad Ezrahi of Project HaMakom; Chava Rimon of *Chaim Acherim* magazine. All have been wonderful friends and support in the years of my teaching in Israel. Thanks to R. David Hartman for creating a beautiful space for contemplation and creation.

I need to single out for special mention Avrohom Infeld, president of the Melitz Institute, who has been a great friend, mentor, employer, and *mensch*. I am glad he is in the world.

To Wanda Keren, the woman who dreamed with me about making Israeli society a better place and much more—thank you. To Zivit Davidovich, my producer, who is more like a sister. To my friends, Efrat Dror and Ami Genegar of Hertzliya Studios; to Uri Shinar, Avi Nir, Merav Ofir, and, especially, Shai Avivi, from channel 2—my friendship and appreciation. Thanks to Menachem Schrader for challenging friendship. To Emanuel Green, for integrity and wisdom.

New friends, teachers, and colleagues in America include R. Zalman Shachter—a pathfinder whose footfalls make me feel less lonely in the world; and Peter Pitzele, Arthur Waskow, Jeff Roth, Art Green, Michael Lerner, Phyllis Berman, and Arthur Kurzweill, who have, each in his or her own way, become part of my spiritual family in the United States. Leonid Feldman, Joseph Telushkin, and

David Woznica have each in different ways been friends and colleagues whom I deeply appreciate. Rebbes essential to my early years, R. Mordechai Marcus, R. Yitzchack Adler.

Dos Lee Leader, Gedalia Gurfien, Michael Kagan, Yaakov Fogelman, Kate Breslaw, Shalom and Judy Brodt, Yehoshua and Emuna Witt, Don and Debra Seeman, Rachel Sabbath, Karen Abrams, Missy Feldman, Rachel Menkin, Shari Seeman, Steve Greenberg and new friend Gavriel Meir all enrich my life and thereby enrich my writings. To Roni Gili and family, to Eldad and Amit and to all the Holy Chevre of the Bereishit and Shantipl festivals. Jonathan and Jane Medved, Jacob and Chaviva Ner David, Rabbi Joe and Rolinda Schonwald, Marc and Chantal Belzberg, Jeffery Klien, Hillel Goldberg, Joseph Ehrenkranz, Shoshanna Cardin, Ely Evans, Lisa Goldberg, Suzy and Coby Rogovin, Boaz Jorabin, Yosefa Gelb, Valerie and Allan Adler, Suri Kasirer and Bruce Teitelbaum, Richard Joselit, and Avraham Trugman have each at pivotal points been good friends and supporters of the dream. I thank them. To Moti Bar Or for an important year of conversation and study.

Deep thanks to my friends who read portions of the manuscript— Jennifer Laszlo, Shoshana Cardin, Dinah Jacobs, Fran Immerman, Melanie Strum, Nigel Savage, David Frank, Rolinda Schonwald, Julian Sinclair, Marc Kirschbaum, Noam Zion, Mishael Zion, and Ilana Reitzes. Special thanks to Victor Mizrachi for his clarifications about physics, to Brad Kaplan for his close reading and editorial suggestions, and to Nedara Carlebach for her perceptive reading and enrichment of the Story section. Warm recognition to Robbie Gringrass for his help in drafting several paragraphs in the introduction and one story in chapter 7 which originated in the manuscript of the *Certainty* book. His pen and insight are a gift to all.

Soul Prints has become a reality through the vision of an exceptional group of people. Emily Bestler, my charming and wonderful editor at Pocket Books, and her able assistant, Kip Hakala—who always made things happen—have been superb. To Arabella Meyer for guiding me through the initial proposal. David Groff, who guided me through the final writing process, is a gift to any writer. My close friend Bob Marty at MPI is a fellow dreamer who believed that *Soul Prints* would make the world better. His innate goodness, contagious energy, and soul print have made this project happen. It is a privilege to be his partner. To his able administrator, Donna Benafatti, who knows that God is in the details—thank you. Mitchell Waters, my good friend and agent at Curtis Brown, has exceeded beyond imagination the role of book agent. His huge heart, wit, gentle patience, good cheer, and editorial insights have been indispensable in birthing this book.

To say I would not be who I am today without my parents, Claire Subar and Kehath Winiarz, is a major understatement—I recognize, appreciate, and thank them for the early years. My brothers, Yossi Winiarz and Dovid Winiarz, and their wives, Chaya and Miriam, along with my fourteen nephews and nieces, are an inspiration. My mum- and dad-in-law, Gary and Cheryl Kaplan, along with Brad and Ellen Kaplan, are among the most decent and wonderful people to walk the earth—I thank you for everything. To my sons, Eitan and Yair—I love you more than you can know. I pray to God that you will always love each other. To Rachel—in pain and in hope.

Finally and most important, to the so many wonderful *Talmidim* (students) who have come to learn, to ask, to quest, and to teach— you are G-d's faces. It is to you that I offer up my life in love.

CONTENTS

CONTENTS

PART FOUR: YOUR SOUL PRINT STORY

INTRODUCTION

———◆———

THE SPIRITUAL SIGNATURE

There once was a very stupid man. When he got up in the morning, it was so hard for him to find his clothes that at night he almost hesitated to go to bed for thinking of the trouble he would have upon waking. One evening, he finally made a great effort, took paper and pencil, and as he undressed, noted exactly where he put everything he had on. The next morning, very well pleased with himself, he took the slip of paper in his hand and read, "cap," and there it was; he set it on his head. "Pants," he read, and there they lay, and he got into them. So it went until he was fully dressed.

"That's all very well—but now where am I myself?" he asked in great consternation. "Where in the world am I?" He looked and looked, but it was a vain search. No matter where he looked, he could not find himself.

That is how it can be with our souls, no matter how smart we think we are. Sometimes, even when we try hard, we cannot locate the name and nature of our spiritual selves. If only each of us could write the name of our soul on a slip of paper, and be reminded every morning of the identity of our profound and distinctive essence—then we might be able to face the world awake and full of joy.

In fact, your soul does have a singular identity—what I call your "soul print."

What is your soul print?

Your soul print is your spiritual signature. It is the contour and content of your soul—its character. It is more specific to you, and you alone, than the handwriting of your name scrawled on a check or a letter. It is even more singular to you than your genes and chromosomes.

Just as in the physical world you have a fingerprint that is unique to you, so in the realm of the spirit you have a soul print that belongs to you alone. That print, like the print of your finger, is an identification marker of the deepest kind, with curves and swirls all its own—all your own.

Your soul print exists not only within, but also without—in how your soul touches the world. When you pick up a pen, brush your hand across a banister, turn a doorknob, shake a hand, touch someone's face, you leave behind an imprint of yourself—your fingerprint. Even after you've let go, a part of you remains. It is the same with your soul print. The people and places touched by your soul are imprinted with your mark, with your essence. Everywhere you walk in the world, you leave behind the beautiful, valuable, matchless print of your soul.

How can you make out the markings of your soul print? How can you discern your own spiritual signature, both in yourself and in the inscription you leave upon the world? In this book, I want to go with you on a journey to the center of your soul. I want to help you achieve access to the precise and gorgeous nature of your spirit. I hope we can learn together how living our soul prints can bring us happiness and profound connection to ourselves, to others, and to God—whatever our understandings of God may be.

Identifying your soul print requires detective work. Just as with the right tools you can pick up the finger's unique and subtle markings, with the right spiritual tools you can pick up the soul's markings. I wrote this book to be such a tool. It is in effect a soul print map, pointing out the trails of your soul. For your soul print is your unique path, and the more you walk a path the more a path it becomes. With each step the path and print of your soul will deepen, becoming more defined, more inviting—not only to yourself but also to others. The more defined the path of your soul print, the more people will walk with you. Finding your soul print path is the ultimate way to transcend loneliness and estrangement from yourself, others, and God.

In *Soul Prints,* our journey together is divided into four stages.

The first section of the book introduces the soul print. The second section defines the nature of soul print consciousness.

The third section explores your soul print calls—that is, your soul's vocation and how you can fulfill it. The ability to respond to the unique call of your soul print is essential in achieving joy and fulfillment in the world. It is for this achievement that we were created. The Italian Renaissance mystic Moses Luzatto taught us that God created us (whether directly or through a guided evolutionary process) in order to grant us what the bible calls the *Tov*— the Good. If we can profoundly realize our soul prints, then we can access that Good.

The fourth section of *Soul Prints* talks about the Soul Print Story, exploring the magic that comes from living your own authentic, unique, and Sacred Autobiography. Once you live your own story, you will no longer feel the desperate need to live in someone else's—and that is the source of all the jealousy that causes so much unhappiness in our lives. Through telling, reclaiming, and renewing your Soul Print Story, you attract to yourself allies and resources that help you live your story in the world.

As you read through this book, you'll encounter little exercises or pieces of "homework" that I call Soul Print Practices, designed to help you further integrate soul print consciousness into your life.

Like most homework, the Soul Print Practices are not absolutely necessary, but they do add a dimension of depth and clarity to your experience.

Creating a profound connection with your own soul print may seem intimidating, even impossible. But trust me—your soul print is sinewy, smart, strong, and very eagerly waiting for you to connect with it further.

If the concept of a soul print sounds a bit too amorphous for you—if you're saying, "I get the metaphor, but how can I really get to know my soul better?"—then I suggest one method to help you limn the terms of your own soul. It is a method implicit within the term "soul print" itself. That is, *print, write.* Find your soul print through your writing, for your soul print is your spiritual signature. This book invites you to leave your soul print all over its pages. Write along the length of the page, mark up the margins, leave your soul print imprint like tracks upon the ground. Books often display quotations from the famous like ornaments—what Nietzsche, Aristotle, or Emerson said about this and that. I'll be doing that too, but I also invite you to put your own quotes in the margins. If you choose—and you don't have to—you can be the wisdom master who writes the truths, your truths, on the page.

PRINT OF OUR CULTURE

Through the idea of the soul print, this book will make some radical claims about the nature of our lives and the meaning of life. That is no small ambition, to be sure. They will be by their nature "wisdom claims," not scientific claims. (Not, of course, antiscientific claims—I personally am wildly in love with science, especially physics.) However, as wisdom masters always knew, the realm of the human spirit is not subject to the empirical probing of the laboratory.

The wisdom claims I make in *Soul Prints* come from two distinct sources. The first source is my teachers and my partners in study—the men and women who feature in the stories of the

Bible, as well as the masters of biblical, Talmudic, and Kabbalistic myth. Over a lifetime of study, I have spent many thousands of hours, often until the touch of dawn, studying and teaching the wisdom traditions. Often I feel the presence of the wisdom masters hovering over my shoulder. We argue, engage, and study together. When I am unclear or lost, they wait for me. When an idea crystallizes and I grasp their intent, they are pleased. I hope you will feel those masters' presence as well. Their tales and wisdom have much to teach us.

Throughout *Soul Prints,* you will be reading myths—biblical, Talmudic, and mystical myths that I believe support, illustrate, and deepen our discussion. I was raised on such stories, and I believe they can be so resonant that our soul prints will vibrate with their meaning. As I worked to define the term "soul print," much of my soul print intuition and most of my language was drawn from these myths.

In my philosophy, my practice, and my passions, I am a Kabbalist. Kabbalah is the psychological-mythical interpretation of the biblical books passed down and unfolded over many, many generations. In the Kabbalistic understanding, biblical myth claims do not dwell on the questions of whether Moses did or did not actually live, but rather on the fact that he lived larger than life. Biblical myth is about wisdom and not history. Yes, Moses is a historical figure, but he is also much more. As we will see, the story of Moses serves as a metaphor for much deeper truths and understandings about self and world. It is as if the tale is a garment that accentuates the curves of a deeper inner truth.

One of the great, subtle, and pervasive crises occurring in our society is that we have lost our connection to core biblical myth. We have lost our core myth. The result is a myth hole at the heart of Western culture. And that is dangerous, for as Nietzsche said more than a century ago, "Every culture that has lost myth has lost, by the same token, its natural, healthy creativity. Only a horizon ringed about with myths can unify a culture." In effect, the mod-

ern dogmas of secularism and fundamentalism have demytholo-
gized our world, depriving us not only of the Greek myths of
Hermes and Cupid, Adonis and Aphrodite, but the myths of
Abraham, Moses, Sara, and Rachel—the core biblical myths that
form the basis of secular humanism and the biblical religions.
Those myths are centered in the original biblical canon—including
the Prophets and Writings and the five books of Moses, as well as
the psychological and mystical commentaries (Talmud and
Kabbalah) that form the essence of what is called *Torah*—which,
literally translated, mean "the Guide." They are—if you will—the
soul print of our culture. To heal our culture and ourselves, we
need to reweave our myth.

In *Soul Prints,* we will be using biblical myth sources in much
the same way that the Swiss psychologist Carl Jung—and in his
wake, the mythologist Joseph Campbell and many others—has
employed the world's various myths. Jung was particularly interested in Greek myth. He understood the obvious truth that had
been for a time ignored—that myths are not (and were never
meant to be) historical or scientific accounts of reality. Thus, history and science have nothing to fear from them. Myths are profound psychological understandings about the nature of our
human journey in the world. As Jung himself once said, "We do
not believe in the reality of Olympus, so the ancient Greek gods
live on in us as symptoms. We no longer have thunderbolts of
Zeus, we have headaches. We no longer have the arrows of Eros,
we have Angina pains. We no longer have the ecstasy of Dionysus,
we have addictive behavior. Even though we no longer recognize
the gods we experience their powerful forces."

Myths limn the underlying patterns of our lives. They allow us
to grasp otherwise elusive understandings of our world. Myths
may be literally untrue—for example, that a snake cunningly
brought about the downfall of humanity—but they are always psychologically and spiritually authentic. Myths are a finely woven
braid of stories, customs, rites, and rituals that inform and give a

foundational sense of meaning and direction to a person, family, community, or culture.

The critical difference between Greek and biblical myth is that Bible stories are not about gods but people. More specifically, biblical myth gives us stories of people who, just like you and me, wanted to live with meaning and to feel that their lives mattered. In the course of their lives, the biblical myth characters made many a mistake—from King David, who was overwhelmed by his desire for Bat Sheva, to Moses, who fell prey to his own anger. Yet they lived heroically. Their heroism arose from the fact that they never lost their core connection to the grounding source of life. Today we call that ground Energy, a personal God, the Force, and the like. All of these designations capture a part of the biblical understanding of God. Biblical myth is the product of the heroic human search for a life that matters. A life that matters, in biblical myth, is a life in which people live their soul print stories and respond to their soul print calling.

The core biblical "wow" idea is this: The human being is created *Bezelem Elohim*—in the divine image. What this means is that every human being is infinitely unique, dignified, and valuable. Our lives are about finding and living that uniqueness, affirming that dignity, and expressing and sharing our value in the world.

Because biblical myth has been largely ignored in much if not most of modern spiritual search literature, Buddhism and polytheism provide the underlying narratives for most soul quests today. Such myths are important and beautiful sources, to be sure; in *Soul Prints,* we will turn to them for profound illumination. Yet in many ways, biblical myth resonates more deeply with the natural contours of our Western psyche. Our core ideas of democracy, capitalism, human rights and dignity, science, individualism, and community derive from the lived truths of the Bible's stories. If culture were a great river running through history, then at its source would be the biblical story, the fount of our culture and psyches.

Wisdom is much like a symphony orchestra. Many instruments

play beautiful music, all of them essential to the sound of the symphony. Buddhism, Greek myth, and biblical religion are all instruments in the symphony of wisdom. But to be a member of the orchestra, you need to specialize in one instrument—your soul print instrument. For those of us in the West, our soul print instrument is biblical myth. Many of us have retreated to polytheism and turned to the East because we have come to believe that biblical myth is irrelevant to our lives—that is, unless we've chosen to adhere to a rigidly dogmatic religious faith. So we do not reach to the Bible for the stories that reverberate in our psyches and set our spirits humming to a deeper rhythm. We have fenced off the Bible from the primal power myth possesses.

And for good reason. Understandably, we often associate the Bible with a kind of fundamentalism that ignores science, enlightenment, and all that is valuable in civilization. For religious fundamentalists, biblical myth exists to establish or buttress some set of external dogmas, or to fulfill a set of ritual requirements. Of course, each cluster of fundamentalists claims it possesses the exclusive truth, promising heaven to all who believe precisely what they believe. If we surrender to the notion that the Bible belongs only to fundamentalists, then we allow a small group of people who purport to represent the Bible to hijack the greatest book ever produced by civilization. And when we let ourselves be estranged from the Bible, we've lost one of the most important sources of guiding wisdom available in the world.

We need to peel the hijackers' fingers from the Book and let its pages again pulsate with vitality, vision, and wisdom. Biblical consciousness is more than a set of laws. Nor is it only an ethical map. It is a spiritual-psychological worldview. It's a unique understanding of the world's workings, telling us of what it means to be and become in the universe. I invite its gorgeous, wise, and deeply compassionate consciousness to inform the pages of *Soul Prints*.

A second source of authority for this book is spoken of best by that greatly afflicted mythical figure, Job. Job tells us, "Through my flesh I vision God." (Or, as nineteenth-century poet John Keats reformulated Job's insight, "I am certain of nothing but of the holiness of the Heart's affections and the truth of Imagination.") For the mystical reader of biblical myth, to "vision God" is to understand being, for God and being are one.

Kabbalists read Job's words with a pronounced emphasis on the word *my*. "My flesh" means not only my physical form, but also the body of my life experience, my heart's affections, and my imagination. The verse is thus taken to mean that we access the epic of being through the drama of the psyche. Each of us can access the psyche only through our singular psyche—that is, through our unique story.

In our modern era, authentic philosophy cannot be divorced from the person of the philosopher. Gone are the days when we bow to the idol of objectivity—the impartial, disinterested thinker who claimed to logically reveal divine truth. Radical truth is to be found, albeit paradoxically, in radical subjectivity—in the holiness of the heart's affections and the truth of the imagination.

ABOUT YOUR GUIDES

Let me tell you a little about myself, since we'll be spending a lot of intimate time together in these pages.

I've been deemed a bit of a maverick. I qualify as an Orthodox rabbi, twice ordained. I prefer to define myself as "postdenominational," for I've learned that if you're going to meld worlds then you can't be molded into only one. I don't have a beard like many of the Orthodox, but I always cover my head with a *kippah* as a sign of respect to God. I drive a car, rent movies with a passion, use a mobile phone—but do none of these on the Sabbath. Although one of my greatest delights is presiding over weddings, until recently I was single. I left home at thirteen, married very young, and went through the pain of two very wrong choices in marriage before the Universe introduced me to my wife, Cary. I am a student and teacher of spiritual tradition, a father, a husband, and a deeply flawed yet joyful, hopeful, and striving human being. I am privileged to have taught thousands of people, all of whom I love very much. I have wonderful students who honor me with the title of Rebbe, teacher. They think me wise, brilliant, and compassionate. Usually I think they're crazy to think that, although occasionally I catch a glimmering of what may have led them astray. I am grateful to them for the honor.

I was drawn to Jerusalem twelve years ago. I translated my name, Winiarz—Polish for winemaker—into its Hebrew equivalent, Gafni. I have become a passionate Israeli even as I remain a proud American who celebrates Thanksgiving every year in his Jerusalem home. Some maintain that my personal history makes me unsuited to be an Orthodox rabbi, while others argue that my experience as well as my capabilities are the ultimate qualification. Perhaps they're both right. For me, the struggle with the mistakes of my past has only deepened my knowledge of and faith in God, as well as in myself.

All I know for sure in my life is this: I cannot live without my God and my religious observance, and I cannot be true to myself without teaching. In the end, my soul print calls me to be a Rebbe, not because I have chosen it but because it has chosen me. I've tried to leave. I spent three years marketing hi-tech, peddling the joys of software interfaces and the ubiquitous Internet. But that work could not compare with the intellectual and spiritual inspiration, and the sheer ecstasy of panic and deep intimacy with God, that overwhelmed me whenever I stepped up to the lectern to teach. I suppose I feel called. Simultaneously, I also often feel so radically inadequate that I'm embarrassed by my own reflection in the mirror. So here I am: a postdenominational, overqualified, and "disqualified" Orthodox rabbi, trying to make sense of the world by embracing all of its paradoxes and imbalances as well as my own.

With all of that baggage, I go riding off in search of meaning. I don't ride a motorcycle: I go in search of my Zen through my books. For me, study isn't a professorial kind of thing—it's time-travel, argument, and flying to the stars. Rashi, the medieval French writer of brilliant epigrams parsing almost every world of Bible and Talmud—keeps interrupting me. The Ishbitzer—revolutionary mystical master of nineteenth-century Poland—grabs me and whispers into my ear. Nachman of Breslav—tortured, joyous, and controversial teacher—sits me down and tells me a story. And Isaac Luria—the "Lion" of Renaissance mysticism—simply fixes me with his burning eyes and pierces my soul. Moses and Jacob engage Buddha and the bhodisattvas. Jung meets the great spiritual leader Baal Shem Tov on dusty rural cobblestones.

Sometimes I think I really don't read biblical myth—I see it as a 3D movie. Better yet, it is I who am the movie, playing every one of the characters. For me, bible-study isn't ritual; it's a personal quest into a world of complexity, pain, love, betrayal, and the towering characterizations of archetypal humans. Those humans are not objects of observations but living guides who invite us into passionate conversation.

The Kabbalists teach that one of the ways you hear the truths of your own voice is by engaging in conversation with guides. The men and women of biblical myth are such guides. They are real people who lived and loved, while at the same time they are larger-than-life symbols of the best—and occasionally the worst—that can exist in us. In the unique art of biblical myth study, we receive ancient wisdom through the prism of our souls. The truth of mythical stories cannot crowd out our own stories or thwart the full expressions of our distinctive soul prints. Rather, we are invited to integrate the ancients' wisdom into the words of our singular song.

As you explore the call of your soul print, I hope that you'll be sustained, nourished, and motivated by this book's tales from the biblical/mystical treasure chest. I hope that they will help you live your soul print more fully and spur you to tell your own stories.

THE LANTERN SWINGER

Do you remember taking those standardized tests in high school where you had to show what you know by filling in the right multiple-choice circle with a number-two pencil? (I didn't know a single kid, myself included, who didn't believe that his value as a person would somehow be enhanced if he succeeded in blackening enough of the right circles.) You may have done well on all your formal tests, from your kindergarten IQ assessments to your Graduate Record Exam. And now, years later, you may be stunningly successful in your field of professional endeavor.

Still, I suspect that like so many of us, you wonder why your number-two-pencil success hasn't led you to a happier and more fulfilling life. Conversely, perhaps you've performed poorly on standardized tests, and worldly success has eluded you, and you've come to realize that there is more to your life than our society can measure. No matter how you rate yourself by the world's standardized measures of success, I urge you to acknowledge what I suspect you already believe in your soul—that those tests have nothing to do with who you really are. They have nothing to do with your soul print. No test—from PSATs to the employee assessment you get when you're due for a raise—can calibrate your uniqueness, gauge your gorgeousness, or comprehend the singular contribution that your soul print can make in the world.

"The light of God is the soul of the human being," wrote Solomon the wisdom master, king in Jerusalem—my home—thousands of years ago. Solomon is talking about the unique expression of divinity that is you and no one else in the entire world, the expression that I call the soul print. To live your soul print is the purpose of your irreplaceable existence. Soul print is the light that you—and only you—were born to shine in this world.

Sometimes when I feel myself being seduced by the desire to achieve and accomplish, and worry that my unique light may be growing dim, I am reminded of the legend of the Spuyten Duyvil train station.

Some of you may know about a small bridge that stretches between the Bronx and Manhattan. It is called the Spuyten Duyvil Bridge. This bridge receives trains coming down from Westchester, which cross it and ride alongside the Hudson River to lower Manhattan. What is special about the bridge is that it is constantly opening and closing in order to allow ships, large and small, to circle Manhattan. During high school, I spent a lot of time wandering the magical area of overgrown grass, abandoned railroad cars, and open space between the banks of the Hudson and the local train station.

One day in 1904, a train was coming down from Westchester, wanting to cross the bridge. In those days, there would be a lantern swinger who stood at the bridge to let the train know if it could pass. When he heard the call of the train's whistle, he would swing his lantern if the bridge was up. If the conductor didn't see the lantern swinging, he would understand that the bridge was down and safe for passage.

That Friday morning at about three A.M., a train crashed into the water. It was a serious accident, a great tragedy, People died, others were injured, and the route was closed for eighteen months after the crash. Of course, everyone wanted to know who was responsible.

Suspicion naturally fell on the lantern swinger. After all, he was the one responsible for swinging his lantern if the bridge was up and could not be crossed. He, however, protested his innocence with such vigor that the case, which had been brought to court, could not be decided.

After six months of hung juries, his lawyer decided to make a dramatic break from courtroom practice at the time and call the lantern swinger to the stand.

"What is your occupation?" the bailiff asked.

"I am the Lantern Swinger," he responded with alacrity.

"Where were you early on the Friday morning in question?"

"At my post," he responded calmly.

"Did you see the oncoming train?"

"Yes, I did."

"Were you inebriated?"

"No, sir, I never drink."

"Then tell the court what happened when you saw the oncoming train. Did you or didn't you swing your lantern?"

A hush fell over the courtroom. Only the absent sound of bated breath and reporters' pencils could be heard.

Strangely, strangely, the lantern swinger, who up to this point had remained completely poised, began to stutter. "Y-y-y . . . yes. I d-d-d-did swing the lantern," he finally blurted out.

The jury did not know what to make of his stutter—was it a sign he was lying? They argued for a long time, but finally they decided to believe him. He was acquitted. As the last person filed out of the courtroom and the defense attorney was left alone with his client, he exploded. "I've been defending you for six months!" he shouted. "I've worked day and night! I've barely seen my wife and children, and you told me you were innocent. Then why the stutter of a guilty man? We nearly lost our case! Were you lying to me all these months?"

The lantern swinger looked sadly at his attorney. "I never lied to you . . . you just always asked me the wrong question," he said. "You asked if I swung my lantern. You forgot to ask if the lantern was lit."

We live in an age of competence and skill. We have read all the books on parenting and maintaining loving relationships. We are well trained in our chosen fields. Plumber, neurologist, mother, father, electrician, sales rep, marketing guru, computer programmer—we are good managers of ourselves. We manage our time; we are even taught how to manage our relationships. We are experts at swinging the lantern. We know at just what angle to swing it, we know how to hold it and what kind of material it should be made from.

We forget, however, that for the lantern to illuminate our way at all—the lantern must be lit.

Only the fire of your unique soul print can light up your life and transform your existence from the routine fulfillment of obligation to the passionate unfolding of your unique story in the world.

Yes, we know how to go through the motions of living and even of loving. We have fun, make money, make love, raise families, go to church, go to therapists, frequent seminars, read literature of self-development. After all is said and done, however, there is only one essential question to answer: Is the lantern lit?

This book is about lighting the lantern of your soul.

FEELING THE TUG

Soul print consciousness gives a unique answer to a very important question: What is the meaning of life? In this chapter, I am going to unpack that question and sketch some of the ways that people try to answer it—so that we can move on later toward finding the particular soul print response I believe is so important to us.

What is the meaning of life? Throughout history, philosophers and theologians have struggled to answer that huge, abstract question conclusively. Everyone offers a different picture of what goal, if we achieved it, would make men and women happy, satisfied, or at least somewhat more fulfilled.

We are all conglomerates, constructions of the philosophies we are fed and choose to feast upon. We nourish each other through a symphony of resonance and dissonance, defining ourselves in agreement with the beliefs that have walked before us, or challenging them. And we have lots of beliefs around life-meaning to synthesize. For Marx and Engels, human meaning came from being part of the right economic system—which for them meant some form of a communist state. For Hegel, meaning came from participating in the progress of history—the unfolding of what he called the absolute spirit. For classical religion, the answer has been God—with an important side bicker over which is more meaningful, believing in God or doing good deeds: Is God most interested in right faith or right action? For mystical traditions of both East and West, karma is the central concern—cleaning out the accumulations from a person's past and getting off the wheel of suffering. For others, meaning has come from the drive to achieve bliss—nirvana, satori-enlightenment—through detachment, drugs, meditation, study, or prayer.

Certainly all this meaning-making is important and valuable. But I believe it is all too general and abstract to touch any primal place in our daily lives—to help us live our soul prints. Somehow, it seems that after reading all the popular and learned tracts, most of us still feel curiously untouched and disconnected from the possibility of meaning in our lives. We are left with a nagging sense that the truth of our lives should be simpler—even if it's an elegant, profound kind of simplicity we seek.

In the ancient rabbinical Talmudic learning tradition I was raised on, we would spend our days simply asking questions in different ways before rushing to answer them. The reward and approbation we received in study came not just from a clever resolution of some spiritual conundrum, but also for a *Gut Kashya*—that is, a great question. As my teachers always insisted, framing the question is half the answer. So let us rephrase our what-is-the-meaning-of-life question in several new ways.

Where is the meaning in your life? That is not an abstract philosphical query but a passionate question.

What is the quest you are on? How are you searching for meaning in your individual existence? What meaning might you be able to wrap your mind and heart around and say "Aha!"?

Or to reformulate the question again, this time a bit more prosaically, What makes you get up in the morning?

Remember this famous getting-up story?

A mother went into her son's room. "Time to get up for school, Bernie!"

Bernie pulled the blanket over his head. "I don't wanna go to school."

"You have to go," the mother declared.

"I don't wanna! The teachers don't like me! And all the kids make fun of me."

The mother pulled the blanket down. "Bernie, you don't have any choice. You have to go to school."

"Yeah?" Bernie said. "Give me one good reason."

"You're forty-five years old and you're the principal!"

If you aren't Bernie, if you don't have to get out of bed anyway, what is it in your life that would happily draw you into the new day? What is it that would make you feel good about yourself if you could choose any calling that the world offers? Amid all the entanglement and drama of your everyday life, what tug toward meaning does your wonderfully specific soul print feel?

It was Timothy's twelfth birthday. He had saved up enough money to buy himself a present. Nickels, dimes, and quarters—he went to the neighborhood store, put his change on the counter, and—wonder of wonders—had exactly the right amount to buy the big red kite on the wall behind the cash register. The happiest kid in the world, he went to Van Cortland Park in the Bronx and began to fly his new kite.

There were great winds that day, and he let out some string, and a little more string, and a little more, until the kite was so high and far away you couldn't even see it anymore. When you looked at the boy, all you could see was a happy kid running with string in his hand.

A very respectable and rational-looking man in a business suit came upon the boy and stopped him. "Son, what are you doing?" he asked.

"What do you mean, sir?" Timothy asked. "I'm flying a kite!"

"Flying a kite? What do you mean? I don't see a kite. You don't see a kite. How do you know there's a kite?"

Timothy looked at the man very gravely. "I know there's a kite, sir—because I can feel the tug!"

When we are kids, it is relatively easy to feel the tug, that precious pull of our youthful souls toward meaning. Our world was small, the rules fairly clear, and the joys of childhood abundant. What happens when we grow up? How often do we lose the magic of the tug—the tug that tells us that life is exciting and worth living even if we can't always see the flying kite, the goal of our soul's efforts? Did we drop the string of meaning a long time ago because we didn't think there was anything there?

When you are truly connected with the nature of your soul print, when you know how you can leave its inscription on the world, then you feel the tug. You can get up in the morning and embrace the day.

SEX, MONEY, POWER, AND MEANING

What experiences tug at our soul prints and move us forward in the world? What are the primal passions that beckon us, irresistibly shaping and forming, consciously and unconsciously, the paths of our lives?

Just as philosophers and God-seekers find differing answers to the big meaning-of-life questions, so do thinkers draw different conclusions about the forces that stir us to seek personal meaning in our lives.

Sigmund Freud said we are driven by the libido—basically a technical synonym for the sex drive. Sexuality, said Freud, expresses the fundamental life force that courses through our lives and catalyzes civilization. Freud did not invent this idea. A fifth-century passage from the Babylonian Talmudic wisdom masters tells a proto-Freudian, once-upon-a-time tale:

It was a hot afternoon along the Euphrates . . . sexuality seemed to swarm through the village as surely as flies around the riverside. Problems propagated in the sultry air: affairs, jealousies, idolatries, and all sorts of questionable ecstasies. The communal leaders knew no other course of action but to gather in the shade and pray, pouring sweat and tears into each word until at last their voices broke through the heat, soared past the flies, and penetrated the heavens with their protest. "Master of the Universe," they cried, "have mercy on your children, and destroy this sexual drive that so enslaves us. Uproot this fester of indecency from our midst, and free us from these ecstasies!"

With open ear and arched eyebrow, God looked down and answered,

"I have hearkened to your prayer, but tell me my children . . . Are you sure?"

With unanimous nods and articulations of joy, the leaders responded, "Yes! Yes!" and collapsed from the fatigue of their efforts, exhausted but victorious.

Morning broke, and the leaders woke expectant. They searched the town for signs of release from the sexual drive. Indeed, an air of peace pervaded the sunburnt streets. No problems peeked from the windows, no bickering echoed from behind closed doors. In fact, they heard no noise at all.

They found their families lolling in bed, contented and calm. They checked the markets—empty stalls. They ventured into the barns; no chicken had laid an egg. No dog barked; no heart stirred in a heaving chest. The world was at rest, and it would not rise.

The leaders gathered again in their shaded alcove and prayed with a deeper pain than before, "Master of the Universe, restore our passions, lest we waste away to dust and tired dreams! Rekindle our drives!"

It was out of this tradition—one passed down in Freud's own rabbinical family for more than twenty generations—that the great doctor developed his notions of the motivating libido. Yet critics have spilled much ink to say that the fundamental human drive cannot be reduced to sexuality—essential as the urge may be. Indeed, the most blatant fallacy of the Freudian version of this position becomes clear when Freud claims that maternal love is really a manifestation of a mother's repressed sexuality. Freud went too far. Intuitively we understand that the wonder of a mother's love for a child cannot be reduced to a repressed sex drive.

After Freud, psychologists Abraham Maslow and Alfred Adler declared that the basic human drive lay in the attempt to achieve self-actualization or self-esteem. Yet these important teachers sometimes forgot to tell us what these terms really mean in our lives. What is self-actualization? How do you know when you're actually actualized? Are we all actualized by the same things? If we consider the drive for self-esteem as the motivating force in our lives, we face versions of those same questions.

Victor Frankel claimed we all shared what he called a drive for meaning. His major book, originally titled *Death Camps and Existentialism* and later revised and reissued with the more user friendly title *Man's Search for Meaning,* is truly wonderful. But when you read Frankel, you can conclude that any meaning that you might contrive could be the force that drives your life. This would seem to make the whole idea of "meaning" in Frankel's formulation, amorphous and convenient. After all, if you are the one mastermind making up the meaning of your life, couldn't you choose evil as your path? And if you're the one making up the meaning of my life, is it really meaningful after all? Playing make-believe may be entertaining, even comforting, but in the end, it is not real enough to satisfy our soul prints.

Another position, sometimes associated with Nietzsche, claims we are all pulled by the drive for power. According to this version, you build a large house not because you need it or even because it is a good investment. You build it as an expression of your power. You want to establish for all to see—and in the hopes of also convincing yourself—that you have a place in the world. Yet all the powerful people with their so often hopelessly unfulfilled and dissatisfied lives give lie to the idea that the possession of power can fulfill us. If the often-narcissistic autobiographies of the powerful have any redeeming value, it is that they shatter the false belief in a connection between power and fulfillment. Yes, we are driven to power, but is that our final destination? Where do we go from there?

Beyond the libido, actualization, the confection of meaning, or the achievement of mere power, what other urge might resonate with our spirits and help us live our soul prints in the world? What else might we identify as the primal drive which motivates our strivings in this world? How else might we identify that kite at the end of the string, tugging us toward a goal we might not always be able to discern?

What else might our soul print seek?

PART ONE

YOUR SOUL PRINT

1

◆

FROM LONELINESS TO THE GOOD

HOTEL ROOM REMEDIES

I began to rethink the whole meaning-of-life question some years ago when I found myself in a hotel in Denver, Colorado. You know how hotel rooms work. Along with the bed, television, and a lot of towels, if you look in the drawer next to the bed you will almost unfailingly find, at least in the United States, a Gideon Bible. My suitcase with my own set of books had missed its connecting flight; I was at the hotel tired, without loved ones or books around me, and I was feeling bereft. A hotel room far from home can be the loneliest place in the world. So I opened the only book in the room, the Gideon Bible in the drawer by the bed.

At the front, I was surprised to see a detailed index of how to use this Bible. If you're depressed, read Psalm 19, it said. If you're drunk, read Psalm 38. If you're feeling lonely, read Psalm 23. Well, I was feeling lonely, so I read Psalm 23. "The Lord is my shepherd, I shall not want," the famous psalm begins. "Yea, though I walk through the valley of the shadow of death, I will fear no evil. . . ." I read the psalm slowly, carefully, yet I have to admit I still felt lonely when I finished. Just as I was about to close the book, I saw a note scrawled at the bottom of the page. "If you're still lonely, call Lola."

When I recovered from laughing, I had one of those magic moments of grace where everything falls into place. Years of study, thinking, and teaching suddenly crystallized in a few simple and authentic sentences. Those sentences are the core of this chapter and their significance will be the lifeblood that courses through this book.

I realized that to a large extent what drives me, and I think what drives all of us, is a desire to move from loneliness to connection, from loneliness to loving. If you're still lonely, call Lola.

After all is said and done, after all of our grand self-actualization and accomplishments, our self-esteem and degrees, our meaning-making and our financial success—we still feel lonely. What drives us in the world is our attempt to move from our loneliness to a place of relationship, connection, and loving. Our soul prints seek to reach out to the prints of other souls—to touch them, and to be touched by them in turn. The more our soul prints connect, the sharper their signatures, and the more sustained and expansive our souls will be. Our soul prints are driven to other soul prints.

> The fleeting libidinal illusion of redemption—grand or tawdry as it may have been—is cruelly shattered when Lola leaves you alone again.

If the sexual revolution has taught us anything, it is that Lola may be wonderful but she cannot redeem us from loneliness. Making a soul print connection is not about actualizing the libido, as Freud would have it. Psychologist Rollo May was right when he declared that better sexual technique and more readily available sex partners are hardly enough to quench our thirst for intimate relationships. Indeed, the morning after Lola, one often feels loneliness that much more deeply. The fleeting libidinal illusion of redemption—grand or tawdry as it may have been—is cruelly shattered when Lola leaves you alone again.

While power is important, and libido and generalized meaning-making do propel us forward, my soul stirs in hesitation. Is that the root of it all? I don't think so. At my core, I have heard the call of the lonely, and I know of no greater force than its low and penetrating hum. The desire to move out of loneliness, to transcend alienation, sits at the center of our universe, enthroned as our most fundamental human drive. Nothing is more important to us than the need to share our lives with another . . . to imprint and be imprinted upon.

THE LONELY HOLE IN ONE

One of my favorite stories is about the soul's call to connection. It's also about golf.

A retired rabbi loved golf more than just about anything. Daily he was drawn to the green, addicted to his game, so much so that come Yom Kippur, the holiest day of the year, he feigned sickness, sent his family off to services without him, and snuck out to the empty green. It was a glorious day, and the vast green was his alone; he set aside his guilt and teed up.

A host of reproving angels gathered to gape at this sacrilegious rite. God came to join them, and with a slight smile playing on his lips, said, "Watch this!"

The rabbi swung, his form was superb, the ball flew, and with exquisite aim, it fell, divinely, into the hole.

The angels were in a rage. "What are you doing, O Lord, giving this heretic a hole in one!" they cried.

God winked. "Just wait."

Grumbling, the angels looked on as the rabbi's face lighted up with ecstasy. He turned to his right to exclaim, but only trees met his gaze. He turned to his left, but there were only trees there too. Behind him lay nothing but trees. A shadow passed over the man's face, as he realized the awful truth: There was no living soul he could tell.

Imagine that you've won the lottery, the great jackpot. What is the first thing you would do? You would run to the telephone, to call someone you love and tell her that you've won. It doesn't take much imagination to picture the overwhelming pathos of realizing that you have no one to tell, no one to call, no one with whom to share a stupendous moment.

Soul Print Practice

Have you ever experienced a situation when something significant happened to you, good or bad, and you had no one to tell?

If so, tell it now! Write in the margins of this page, or put it down on paper or in an e-mail and send it. Declare it to someone— a loved one, a stranger. Share it with me (info@soulprints.org). Make the soul print connection that you couldn't make when that "something significant" happened.

EXILE

We're all familiar with the philosophical conundrum, "If a tree falls in a forest and there's no one there to hear it, does it make a sound?" Let's rephrase it. "If something happens to you and you have no one to share it with, did it really happen?" If we are unable to tell our tale because there's no one to share it with, if we are left mute [of meaning] for lack of listening—then, in the language of the mystics, we are in exile. The basic plot of biblical myth story line revolves around trying to get to the Promised Land. In the Kabbalah—the mystical interpretation of biblical myth—exile is not related to leaving a geographical location. Land becomes a symbol for our emotional existential place in the world. Exile is about losing our place.

Loneliness is a form of exile. All of our accomplishments, successes, and achievements pale in significance when we lack the ability to share them with another. This understanding is in fact the core of the biblical myth. The Bible has a unique understanding of what drives us forward in the world. It is, as we have seen, an insight fundamentally different from Freud, Nietzsche, Adler, and Frankel, as well as different from the wealth of the philosophies of the East.

Let's look for a moment at the opening of the biblical tale—the creation story. First, note that this story is not meant to be taken literally. It is not a manual on how to create a world. Rather, the aim of the first two creation chapters is to establish the basic meaning structures of our world. Implicit in the creation story are the basic ideas of democracy, science, the idea that life has meaningful patterns, the sacredness of existence, the human being in the image of God, depth ecology, progress, and much more. In chapter one, one particular refrain becomes the mantra of the entire section. "God saw that it was good." At the close of every stage of creation's unfolding, God makes the finishing touches and inspects his work, always concluding with the chorus, "It was good." God saw the light of day and it was good, the gathering together of the seas and it was good, the earth sprouting forth and it was good. All of creation is characterized by this overarching Goodness. Good is the goal of creation—the desired end toward which all creatures and creations stretch.

However, a simple literary reading of chapter two yields that all of the good of creation is undone in one short phrase. Suddenly the universe exclaims, "It is not good." It is a very distinctive kind of not-goodness. In the exact words of the biblical myth, God says, "It is not good for the human being to be alone."

It was these words that the epic poet John Milton was reformulating when he wrote that to be alone is, "the first thing which God's eye nam'd not good." The text builds day by day as creation accrues, each day crescendoing with the exultant approval of "It was good," only to meet in the second chapter a depressing anticlimax: "It is not good." Moreover, not only is this the first time but it is the only time in the Bible when the unequivocal "not good" describes a state of being.

Chapter 1 of the creation story sets an elaborate table of goodness, stars and spheres, fish and fruits, and vistas of magnificence. Then chapter two coldly steps up to the feast and tumbles the table, draping the glory in a veil of nullification and defeat. Chapter two says, in essence, "The entire world, all of these works, are ultimately valueless, meaningless, if the man remains alone."

Indeed, all of the good in the world is not good as long as human beings are alienated from each other. Aristotle confirmed the biblical intuition when he wrote, "No one would choose a friendless existence on condition of having all the other things in the world." If the purpose of biblical living—the *telos*—is to get to the good, then the "not good" of loneliness remains the great challenge of every life. Overcoming loneliness and moving to connection, to loving, to union, is not merely an exercise in pop psychology fulfillment or personal gratification. It is the very goal of existence, of being and of becoming. It is what our soul prints seek.

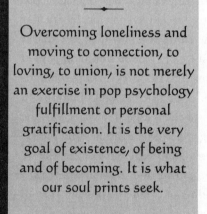

Overcoming loneliness and moving to connection, to loving, to union, is not merely an exercise in pop psychology fulfillment or personal gratification. It is the very goal of existence, of being and of becoming. It is what our soul prints seek.

If life is a great mansion, the rooms may be full of exquisite creations, but if there is no other person padding across the carpeted floor, then the rooms are essentially empty and the owner is alone. As Cat Stevens so plaintively sang, "I don't wanna live in no mansion, there are too many empty rooms."

The primal drive that propels us in biblical consciousness is the drive to move from loneliness to loving, from separation to union, from the pain of rupture to the rapture of connection.

Soul Print Practice

List seven of the most precious things you could have in the world.

What is number one? Number two?

If you have something other than relationship or connection at the top of your list, ask yourself if the value you put there is important to you in and of itself—or because it helps you in your relationships with people.

For example, do you want a large house in and of itself or because it helps you directly or indirectly in creating relationships?

If you did not put some form of relationships at the top of the list, ask yourself—Why?

Picture yourself receiving especially good news. Picture yourself receiving especially bad news.

Who would you want to share the news with?

Now call those people for "no reason" and tell them you love them! C'mon, go for it! I *promise* they will not think you lost it. On the contrary, they may think you have found it!

LEVADO

The original Hebrew word for "alone" is *levado*. When God uses it in the creation story, it can be rendered most accurately not as being physically alone but as "lonely." God is essentially saying to us, "It is not good for the human being to be lonely." As long as the human being is lonely, all of the good of creation cannot sate him. As long as the human being has no one with whom to share her experiences, as long as the human being feels alienated, separate from, and empty, then all of the objective goods of the universe will be irrelevant. That is the experience of loneliness—to feel apart from, severed from, alienated, and empty.

The goal of the universe is the Good. In fact, a close reading of mystic Isaac Luria suggests that this "goodness" is indeed the goal of God. God and Good are one. "Taste and see that God is Good," cries out one biblical myth epigram. In fact, Luria reads our text, "It is not Good for man to be alone," as referring not only to man but to God as well. For God himself to achieve the Good, he has to move out of divine *levado*—God's own loneliness—and create a world to be in relationship with.

What all this means in our human terms is that God is the force in the universe for the healing and transformation of loneliness. God is the force that tells us that we do not need to be alone forever. The universe is friendly. God knows our name; he yearns and even actively militates for our joy.

Standing against this fundamental goal of living is the shadow of the Not Good, a dark form engendered by the lonely existence of the human being. Mystically, a human loneliness is a reflection of divine loneliness. When we are alone, God is somehow more alone. The Zohar, the great work of the Kabbalah, suggests that we are less Godlike when we are alone. Our divine life force ebbs when we are disconnected. To be disconnected on a human level is to be cut off from the life source of the universe. A host of studies bears this out in the most powerful and concrete way.

To quote only one of many sources, Researcher Skeels did a long-term study of twenty-four children in an orphanage. Half of the children went daily to be cared for and loved by adolescent mentally handicapped girls at a nearby institution. Half did not! At the end of a twenty-year tracking study, he found that all of the twelve in the group of orphans that had not experienced the afternoon visits were either dead or in institutions for the mentally retarded. All in the group who had received loving attention were self-sufficient, most were married, almost all had successfully completed significant educational degrees. Wow! We know as well that an infant who receives perfect care but no regular human contact will often simply die.

The fundamental drive of the human being is to move beyond the "Not Good" of loneliness to the "Good" of connection. In order for human beings to benefit from and participate in all of the good of creation unfolded in chapter one of Genesis, in order to be fully alive, we must move beyond loneliness to connection, to loving, to union. A soul print is fully realized when it prints its essence, leaving its unique mark on life.

THE GIFTS OF LONELINESS

Before we proceed to the heart of soul print consciousness, we need, however, to remind ourselves that loneliness is not a pitiful human condition to which we can apply the often equally pitiful salves of pop psychology. Instead, *levado* is of great and grounding value to us. The experience of loneliness is, to the best of our knowledge, a uniquely human experience. In the words of poet W. H. Auden, it is "man's real condition." Novelist Thomas Wolfe calls loneliness "the central and inevitable experience of every man." Loneliness is an experience to be moved beyond but never skipped over.

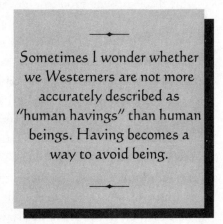

Sometimes I wonder whether we Westerners are not more accurately described as "human havings" than human beings. Having becomes a way to avoid being.

We have lost sight of the truth of our elemental loneliness because we cover the aloneness of our being with the illusion of having. In our modern culture, being is too often connected with having. Today, we have become shoppers and accumulators, defining ourselves by our consumption, attempting to smother our loneliness with *things*. Gandhi said, "There is enough in this world for everyone's need, but not enough for everyone's greed." Sometimes I wonder whether we Westerners are not more accurately described as "human havings" than human beings. Having becomes a way to avoid being. Moreover, we use having to validate our being, our personal worth and value.

Puritan thinking, a theology that still sits at the core of the American psyche, powerfully influenced the Western ideas of accumulation and consumption values. The Puritans taught that whether a person was saved or damned was a condition preordained by God. This belief created two huge problems for them— one pragmatic, and the other existential. Pragmatically, we can ask, if our soul's fate is preordained anyway, why should we work or expend effort in the world? Existentially, the idea is so disempowering as to be an unbearable belief to hold.

The Puritans solved both these problems in one ingenious move. They taught that prosperity was a sign that you are counted among those predestined for salvation. Of course, we know that this Puritan theology was really great at getting people to work. Indeed, what we know of as the Protestant work ethic is based on this theology. The problem, however, is that replacing being with success and having causes us to get really crazy when a piece of external success, completely beyond our control, doesn't happen our way. And of course, this syndrome pulls us far from the central soul print consciousness of the Bible.

To this day, we are closet Puritans when we implicitly associate success with goodness and secretly view failure as some sort of moral flaw. We have become Grand Acquisitors, oppressed by our own desperate need "to have." To be is to be successful, we too often believe. One of the most important signs of success is social status, which is largely determined by the admiration we receive and the power we wield; but status doesn't keep us from feeling lonely and being disconnected.

Soul Print Practice

When it comes to things that you want or need, do these sentences sound familiar?

I'll be happy when I have a degree.

If only I had more time.

If only I had a job that I liked.

If I had a deeper relationship . . .

If so, then turn your "have"s into "be"s:

I can be more hardworking . . .

I can be more time-effective . . .

I can be more resourceful . . .

I can be more loving . . .

The "have" sentences are focused on the outside world, circumstances exterior to yourself, while the "be" sentences work from the inside. They point the way to work you can do on yourself to be more. For eventually, when you can be more, you will have more.

We fear that admitting our loneliness would undermine our sense of success and status. Success is supposed to do away with vulnerability, and loneliness is the ultimate vulnerability. "If we are good, we must be successful—and if we are successful we certainly cannot be lonely"—that's our unconscious association. We are prepared to admit to many foibles—financial, sexual, and ethical—more readily than we would bare the truth of our loneliness. After all, we have a million friends and are, of course, always busy on Saturday night. Loneliness is viewed as a great curse—a notion supported ostensibly by biblical myth's proclamation, "It is not good for man to be alone."

The Kabbalists read the biblical myth on loneliness very differently. True, life's ultimate goals are loving and union. However, these are only attainable if we first embrace our loneliness. If we attempt to bypass our loneliness—to return to the oneness that characterized the Garden of Eden—then biblical myth suggests we will surely be burned by the flaming swords that guard the garden's entrance. Loneliness, suggests Hayim of Voloshin, an early nineteenth-century mystical writer, is not an expression of human debasement. Rather, it is an expression of human grandeur.

Loneliness reminds us of a great truth. "You are special, unique, and irreplaceable," proclaims the universe. There is absolutely no one else like you on the face of the planet. That is the starting point for any relationship. Loneliness is the common fate of humanity, which is transformed into grand destiny by the freely chosen human movement from loneliness to loving.

LONELINESS AND PSYCHOANALYSTS

Loneliness is not merely a psychological problem. As we've just seen, it is rather a grand metaphysical reality that needs to be appreciated before it is explained away or solved. Psychology, suggests contemporary philosopher Ernest Becker, tends to reduce human experience. It can disenchant the human being, estranging him or her from a sense of grandeur or ultimate value. We want to focus our love on the absolute measure of power and value, and the analyst tells us that our urge is based upon our early conditioning and is therefore relative. We want to find and experience the marvelous, and the analyst tells us how matter-of-fact everything is, how clinically explainable are all of our deepest motives and guilt. We are thereby deprived of the absolute mystery our soul prints require. The only omnipotent thing that remains is the psychologist who explained it away. And so the patient clings to the analyst with all of his might and dreads the termination of analysis.

Robertson has been in analysis for ten years, seeing his doctor four times a week. Finally, the analyst tells him that they've achieved all their goals, and he doesn't have to come back anymore.

The man is terrified. "Doctor," he says, "I've grown very dependent on these sessions. I can't just stop."

The doctor gives Robertson his home phone number. "If you ever need to," he says, "call me at any time."

Two weeks later, at Sunday morning, six A.M., the telephone rings in the doctor's house. It's Robertson.

"Doctor," he says, "I just had a terrible nightmare. I dreamed that you were my mother, and I woke up in a terrible sweat."

"So what did you do?"

"I analyzed the dream the way you taught me in analysis."

"Yes?"

"Well, I couldn't fall back to sleep. So I went downstairs to have some breakfast."

"What'd you have?"

"Just a cup of coffee."

"You call that a breakfast!"

Robbing humans of their rightful grandeur is the tragic shadow side of Freud's legacy. In some sense, it is Freud's ultimate rebellion against the biblical myth that nourished him and really a bit of an Oedipal story in itself— where the son and his psychology overtake the vigor and significance of the father figure of biblical myth.

Robbing humans of their rightful grandeur is the tragic shadow side of Freud's legacy.

Psychological myth reduces our deepest yearnings and needs to a set of uninspiring, pitiful human drives that are beyond our control and ignoble at their core. Biblical consciousness tells us that while the human condition might at times be tragic, it is never pitiful.

Loneliness is indeed a painful, absurd, and desperate experience. It is also the necessary starting point on the journey toward loving. It is potentially a stimulating, invigorating circumstance that can make you feel fully alive, pressing the entirety of your being toward self-actualization. It is only when you embrace the experience of loneliness that you begin to feel fully alive. Only then can you be freed from it. The ability to enter and move through and beyond loneliness is the daring invitation and challenge of biblical consciousness. It is not good for us to be alone; however, when we access our singular soul prints, we can reach for the good, can transcend our loneliness and touch connection, loving, and union.

FIGURES OF LONELINESS

We need to move beyond loneliness, but how?

The first step is to be aware that we are lonely. Go to a cocktail party and listen to people; after they have the first few drinks, you will hear people confessing all sorts of weaknesses and improprieties, but you will rarely hear them owning the real depths of their loneliness. There is something leprous about loneliness. It's as if people will be afraid to be around us for fear of contagion, which of course only accentuates loneliness.

I once traveled to Europe to be the keynote speaker at a weekend charity event. It was an extravagant gathering of elite young professionals from across the continent—a group that had more class and social graces than the audience for the New York Philharmonic on a Saturday night. As I got the chance to inquire about their interests in the charity, I started realizing the real reason why they had come. "Well, a friend of mine met her fiancé at this event last year," one told me. "There's this woman I met at a charity event in Munich and she said she would be here," another one said. "Petite brunette, accountant—have you seen her?"

I don't mean to suggest that these charming and truly lovely Euro-yuppies had no philanthropic interests. I mean that their primary concern there, although hidden or even denied, lay with their lingering loneliness. When I understood the inner dynamic of the event, I became incredibly sad.

At the end of the day, every lecture, charitable event, and seminar that is followed by some sort of mixer is primarily about the mixer.

But none of us wants to admit our deep soul yearning to be "mixed." Many of us are addicted to the kind of soma pills of denial ingested by Aldous Huxley's characters in the novel *Brave New World*. We have different names for our soma fixes—we call them Prozac and Ritalin. We are workaholics or consumerholics or sexaholics or religioholics—anything to ignore the absence of human connection we feel. We get addicted to recovery programs, therapy, and self-help seminars—anything to take the sharp edge off our loneliness. But we cannot begin our healing until we move beyond denial, identifying the dis-ease that we feel and calling it by its name.

Soul print consciousness creates an awareness and a vocabulary that will move us toward the healing of this pain. The first act of the human being in Genesis is to give names to the creatures in his world. We too need to give names to the creatures in our world. Magically, just by the act of naming, we are able to dispel some of the darkness we've denied. Then we can move toward the light. It was Jung who said, "One does not become enlightened by imagining figures of light but by making the darkness conscious." The elevation of the nagging sense of worry, sadness, and anxiety into awareness of loneliness is an indispensable part of transcending it. We need to pause for a moment to describe—to shed light on—some of our epoch's most common forms of loneliness.

The first figure of loneliness is the one we encounter at parties and other convivial gatherings. We all know that we can be at a gala with dozens of people, say hello, engage in conversation with most of those present, and still feel deeply lonely. This experience may even make us feel more acutely isolated than we would have been had we not attended the party at all. Being lonely is for the most part unrelated to being alone or with people. Nietzsche wrote, "In solitude the lonely man is eaten up by himself, among crowds, by the many." That feeling of walking around a crowded room trying to look like you belong and are having a great time is probably familiar to all of us. It is not a nice feeling. It comes from being so disconnected from our soul print that blending in seems the only salve.

The second figure of loneliness is the single person secretly desperate for emotional intimacy. I know many people like this, and for seven years, until not too long ago, I was one of them. Many lonely people will go to sleep tonight alone, not being able to share the comfort of another caring body. The intense pain that I felt after being divorced, upon coming home every night to an empty bed, is almost indescribable.

Certainly, for some people, a life that embraces solitude can be rich and sustaining. A person who is alone is not necessarily lonely. To live alone and not be lonely can mean you have made friends with yourself, which is a wonderful spiritual accomplishment. When one's *self*-affirmation and *self*-validation satisfy one's constant need for affirmation, what a place to be in! However, lack of loneliness while living by yourself may come from an entirely different place as well—that is, a disconnection from yourself and hence a lack of awareness of the loneliness that exists within you. In other contexts, psychologists call this kind of state "disassociation."

> Modernity has almost institutionalized loneliness by fostering a new breed of psychological and sociological beings. They are called "singles"—people who have not yet found someone with whom to share their singularity.

The vast majority of unattached people of all ages feel loneliness deeply. Modernity has almost institutionalized loneliness by fostering a new breed of psychological and sociological beings. They are called "singles"—people who have not yet found someone with whom to share their singularity. Whether never married or previously divorced, they are a creative, energetic, wonderful group of people who are also, by and large, in perpetual pain.

For them, loneliness is usually not an admissible state. As a result, almost no communal resources are devoted to creating forums for singles to meet. When young adults hit their mid-twenties, they are tossed into the world fully mature in terms of skill and earning power and told, "Find a partner." To admit that our children are lonely is not something the community is able to bear.

The third figure of loneliness is the married single. This is someone who has been married for some twenty years, sharing a living room, bathroom, and bed with a partner, yet still feels desperately alone. Perhaps even worse than being lonely and alone is the pathos of being lonely in the arms of another.

Finally, and perhaps most powerfully, there is the loneliness of feeling irrelevant, replaceable, insignificant. *The fourth figure of loneliness is the "insignificant" man or woman.* This kind of loneliness arises from a deep sense of alienation. Novelist George Eliot captures the feeling well when he invites us to imagine skipping a stone into a pond. It makes ripples, sometimes even elegant and beautiful ones; maybe it skips several times, creating a series of ripples. But in the end, it is destined to stop skipping, to sink from sight, as if it were never there.

Most of us have experienced one or more of these four figures in our lives. The first stage of moving beyond loneliness is to not deny these figures and confront their lurking shadows.

Soul Print Practice

List four figures of loneliness you have encountered recently in your life.

Think of ways you could "bring them to light."

For example: That elderly lady who lives by herself next door. Seek out her soul print, ask her stories about her life.

Or, if what you read in this book (or any book) enlightens you in any way, commit to share one idea with one of your figures of loneliness.

2

---❖---

THE SOUL PRINT BOX

DESCRIPTIONS AND DEFINITIONS

Fully grasping the nature of loneliness is hard, even when we use the figures of loneliness we explored in the previous chapter. These images fundamentally describe loneliness, and, as important as description may be, that is insufficient for our purposes. Description speaks to our emotions and it is a critical tool, but for the mind, we need to define loneliness; we need to move from description to definition. Only a definition will allow us to understand what loneliness means, providing us with the tools and strategies for moving beyond it into loving.

> ## Soul Print Practice
> Fill in the blank.
>
> Loneliness is _____
>
> Look again at what you wrote. Is it a description or is it a definition?

A definition needs to be something that captures the essence of what the lonely experience is, beyond describing it. It does not need to be jargon and can even be captured in a story. It does need to be able to capture in one clear sentence, as in "What is loneliness?" The best way I can do that is with the following true story about my son Eitan.

Eitan is a great scholar. He is as of yet unpublished, so you will not have read him; he's thirteen and I don't want to push him. Most of my revelations have come through discussions with Eitan and with his no less learned and insightful brother Yair, aged twelve. Before I share the story let me tell you that you may recognize it; it may have happened to you in some form. That is usually so with stories that have universal themes. A story is truly great when you realize that you're not hearing just the story of the person telling it to you—you're really hearing your story.

I woke up on the morning of my departure for a lecture tour of the United States—and almost immediately, I was running late. I had some semblance of breakfast, said some form of brief morning prayers, and grabbed my suitcase to go. Just as I was running out the door to the airport for my all-important and very precious tour, my son Eitan, then five years old, said to me, "Dad, can you take this box with you?" He held up a little blue shoebox balanced in his hands.

"Eitan, sweetie, do I need to take it now?" I asked him hurriedly.

"Yes, *Abba,* yes, Pappa," Eitan told me, "it's very important. Take it and tell me what you think of it when you get home."

He looked quite serious, and so I took the box, stuffed it in my suitcase, gave him a kiss, got into the car, and sped off into the whirlwind of the tour.

A long ten days later, I returned home close to midnight. Eitan, usually in bed by eight, was wide-awake, waiting patiently in the kitchen with a look of enormous gravitas on his face. "Eitan, honey, why are you up?" I asked him.

"What do you mean, Dad?" he asked. "I stayed up to hear what you think of my box."

A look must have crossed my face—I couldn't even lie—for Eitan said, "*Abba,* didn't you look at the box?"

I felt terrible. I ran back out to the car and dug through my lecture notes and clothes to find, beneath the piles, Eitan's box. I came into the kitchen to see a tear finding its way down Eitan's cheek. I sat down and gently said, "I'm sorry, Eitan. I had a crazy trip and I didn't get to look at your box. Come, show me what's in it?"

We opened the box together. Inside was a seashell, a faded picture of me from a Florida newspaper, a tile, a marble, and a lock of Eitan's baby hair. I was a little bit baffled. "What is all this?" I asked Eitan.

"Dad, these are my things," Eitan said to me as another tear ran down his cheek. "I gave them to you and you didn't even see them."

At that moment, I understood what loneliness truly means. We all have boxes and in those boxes are our things, our authentic stuff. Not our jobs or titles, not our salaries or public-status trophies, just our stuff. The unique patterns and swirls of the soul. Our soul print.

A soul print is made up of our dreams and destiny both lived and unlived, conscious and not yet conscious. It is made up of our past—all of our yesterdays into the earliest crevices of childhood and perhaps even before. It includes our successes and especially our failures. It is the partner we married and the partner we didn't. It is our fears, fragility, and vulnerability as well as our grandiosity and our larger-than-life yearnings. All these together form our uniqueness, our soul print.

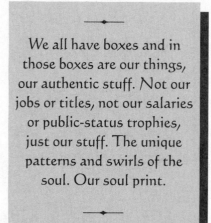

We all have boxes and in those boxes are our things, our authentic stuff. Not our jobs or titles, not our salaries or public-status trophies, just our stuff. The unique patterns and swirls of the soul. Our soul print.

Here is a definition of loneliness, and I hope now the difference between definition and description becomes clear. *Loneliness is the inability to share the essence of who I am, my soul print, with another.*

Eitan was my teacher that day. His few tears provoked a well of tears in me. I understood that I had done something very wrong.

Eitan had given me his soul print for safekeeping and I had been unable to receive it.

The parenting part of my soul print had been essentially cut off, occluded. Since then, I only pray I've gotten better.

Soul Print Practice

Make a Soul Print Box.

Put in it the five things that matter to you most.

Possibly the greatest value in the Soul Print Box comes from the process of making it. In spiritual searches, process is often the most important thing. Let's view your Soul Print Box as a treasure chest of sorts, which makes filling the box a treasure hunt. In a treasure hunt, the two words are inseparable—to find a treasure you must hunt for it, and if you hunt, you will surely find a treasure. The very process of "boxing" your soul print—pulling together the significant signs of your soul—will help reveal your soul print. I promise you, if you take the time to search your house for soul print articles, you will be making the time to search for your soul. And if you hunt, you will surely find.

What do you put in your Soul Print Box? Love letters, family heirlooms, photographs, favorite quotes, and your own soul print reflections on life? If any items are too big, represent them with an object or write them on a slip of paper.

To whom will you show it?

Sit down—on Sunday morning at a coffee shop, or late Saturday night in front of a fireplace—and share your Soul Print Box with someone important to you.

MYTHS OF THE SOUL PRINT BOX

People who have heard me tell my story of Eitan and his Soul Print Box have told me of similar stories that resonate for them. Classic stories that last a millennium and touch an eternal truth always appear in different versions in various cultural and historical settings. I would like to share two of those stories with you. I chose them because they add a dimension of depth to our definition of soul print and how it helps us transcend loneliness. While our first story was about parents and children, the second one is about people and God. It is from the Christian tradition, often told as "The Littlest Angel."

A four-year-old boy died and went to heaven. Although he became an angel, he was always getting into mischief, just as he had on earth. The time came when Jesus was about to be born. Everyone in heaven was celebrating—and preparing to present gifts to him. The littlest angel, however, being new to heaven, did not know what to give him. Finally, he decided to give him his treasure box. In it were things like the collar of his favorite dog, a shiny pebble he once found in a creek, a pretty feather, and the like. It was all stuff he had saved from when he was on earth, and Jesus, born to earth as a little boy, would like such things, just as he did. Or so he hoped.

The angels gathered around God as he examined the gifts that they intended to give to the infant Jesus. God looked approvingly on what the angels had brought—the precious heavenly equivalents of gold, frankincense, and myrrh. When God opened the treasure box, the littlest angel trembled in fearful anticipation. The other angels had given wondrous presents of heavenly gold and silver and all he could give was his old tattered tidbits from earth. The littlest angel, humiliated, began to cry.

God, however, smiled. He declared the treasure box to be his favorite present, and he turned it into the star of Bethlehem.

What this story understands so well is that the only gift we have to give to God is the gift of our deepest selves. Our deepest self is, of course, our soul print. God desires our soul print. It is one of the most daring ideas of the Kabbalah, that God becomes stronger through our living our truest selves, our soul prints. Our soul print is our divine stuff. It is our greatest gift and highest service.

Many prayers—Christian, Jewish, and Muslim—are written in acrostics that spell out the name of the writer. When I first noticed this at about fourteen years old, I was disappointed. Fresh from my first reading of Freud, I thought to myself, "It seems like even in prayer, ego is the driving force." Many years later as I began to unfold soul print consciousness in my mind, the deeper truth hit me hard. Those people signing their names in the acrostic of prayer weren't driven by ego; they understood that to pray is to live your soul print in the world. It is to press your soul to the lips of God.

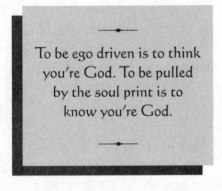

To be ego driven is to think you're God. To be pulled by the soul print is to know you're God.

To distinguish between soul print and ego is very simple. To be ego driven is to think you're God. To be pulled by the soul print is to know you're God.

In biblical myth, the word "knowing" as in knowing God or having carnal knowledge, is *deah*. The word *deah*'s first and primary application is actually as carnal knowledge. It appears to describe the relationship between the Bible's first pair of lovers and friends, Adam and Eve. According to a Kabbalistic description, God officiated at their wedding as all of creation gathered around in grandeur and celebration. This biblical myth brings me to a third version of the story of the Soul Print Box—the ultimate application of the Soul Print Box in romantic relationship and in marriage, and a story I have been telling at weddings for many years. I like to imagine that God told this story at the very first wedding. Existing in many different versions in different cultures, the myth provides for me the personal litmus test of how well my own close relationships surmount and transform loneliness.

There once existed a tribe in South America that received its main nourishment from milk. Yet somehow, as happens in the world, the source of milk one day dried up. The cows, struck by disease, died one by one. The tribe was left parched with thirst, with no way to slake their need. The famine persisted for three weeks, and many meetings of the elders were held, but no one could come up with a way to restore milk to the village.

One misty morning, however, after days of intense prayer and fasting, the villagers awoke to see a huge vat of steaming hot milk in the main clearing of the village. They were overjoyed at this gift of the gods and celebrations ensued. One morning, two mornings, three mornings, the vat kept reappearing, and with bellies full of the divine drink the villagers continued life, contented.

One young man from the village, around eighteen years old, was unsatisfied simply to receive the mysterious nourishment. As much as he needed the milk, he needed the knowledge of where this milk came from even more. And so, breaking with the village taboo against investigating the miracle, he got up early in the morning and waited. He was not disappointed, for within the purple mists of morning light he saw the most beautiful maiden his eyes had ever beheld descend from the heavens to place the vat of milk in the middle of the village.

The young man was overcome by her beauty and smitten immediately with love. The next morning he returned to watch her, and the third day and the fourth, and by the fifth day, he could endure it no more. He emerged from the bushes, grasped her graceful hand tight, and said, "I will not let you go until you agree to marry me."

Such a demanding marriage proposal seldom worked in this village or elsewhere in the world, but lo and behold, this divine creature of a woman agreed to marry the young man. That is, with one condition, which, she said, she would stipulate upon her return from one last journey to her home in the heavens.

She returned from the heavens a day later with enough milk to last a lifetime, and clutched to her heart was a golden box.

She agreed to marry the bedazzled young man, just as long as he promised never to open the golden box that she had mysteriously brought with her. For, she said with a touch of sadness, "If you do open this, I may very well have to leave."

The man agreed, and this mixed marriage between heaven and earth proceeded wonderfully. The young man and the maiden had children, built a home, and lived happily as the years sped by.

One afternoon, when his wife was away with the children, something snapped in her husband. Overwhelmed with unquenchable curiosity that had been gradually building for years, he rushed to open the box. He cracked open the creaking lid, slowly, a sliver, a slight bit more, until it was fully open. He stared, bewildered, and slammed it shut.

The man's wife returned. Now, for the men reading the story, keep this in mind. Women always know what men do while they're not home. She immediately understood that he had opened the box. She confronted him. "You opened it, didn't you? Now I may have to leave."

"What do you mean you have to leave?" the man cried. "Yes, I opened it—of course I opened it—but it was empty!"

"Indeed, I must now leave, I cannot stay," she responded sadly.

"But why?" he asked. "The box was empty! The box was empty!"

Shaking her head, the heavenly woman declared, "Don't you see, that is precisely why I must leave. For that empty box was not empty at all. When I took my final journey to the heavens before our marriage, I gathered all the sights, sounds,

> Your beauty includes everything that is you. It includes your weaknesses, your strengths, your pathologies, and your dreams. You can be in Times Square surrounded by the madding crowd, or in an office working as the mail boy, the CEO, or a mid-level exec; you can buy and sell and communicate with twelve different countries in one day; and yet you can still be lonely because you haven't shared your soul print.

and smells that were most dear and most precious to me from home. I gathered my hopes and my dreams, my fears and my memories, all the special moments of my life, and I placed them into that box. And you opened my box and thought that it was empty. I cannot stay."

When someone else opens our box and thinks it empty—that is the definition of loneliness. That is what produces the powerful experience of human loneliness, the inability for another to recognize the fullness of our experience, the complexity and diversity of our "stuff," the "things" that fill our box, that make it uniquely ours.

Soul prints give evidence to our individual beauty. Your beauty includes everything that is you. It includes your weaknesses, your strengths, your pathologies, and your dreams. You can be in Times Square surrounded by the madding crowd, or in an office working as the mail boy, the CEO, or a mid-level exec; you can buy and sell and communicate with twelve different countries in one day; and yet you can still be lonely because you haven't shared your soul print. You can be a married single. You can be in a relationship with someone, have three kids with her, yet still be lonely because although you've merged physically, you still haven't shared your soul print.

Soul prints are shared when we laugh and cry together. There's nothing more intimate than a couple crying together, whether tears of sadness or ecstasy. There is nothing more erotic than the passionate intertwining of two soul signatures. The magnum opus of the Kabbalah—the Zohar—teaches that we all need to bless each other. That is a strange idea on first hearing—but a beautiful gesture on second thought. We all have the power of blessing. So I bless you and ask that you bless that we all find our soul print and share it with the ones we love.

BEYOND THE FINGERPRINT AND DNA

Over the last century, rising tides of crime have helped introduce the new detective's tool—the fingerprint. Modern biology and biochemistry have led us to DNA prints, the unique gene structure that makes up the signature of every human being. At the dawn of a new millennium we need to understand that DNA prints and fingerprints are ultimately just reflections of something far deeper—the soul print. Your soul print is the true essence of who you are; your soul print is your unique story in the world. As the great philosopher Ugo Betti declares, "When I say 'I' I mean a thing absolutely unique, not to be confused with any other." absolutely unique, not to be confused with any other."

> Your soul print is the unique snowflake essence of your soul, which makes you who you are. Unlike a snowflake, however, it never melts.

Your soul print is etched with the lines of your pathologies and fears, your hopes and your dreams, your memories, angers, and all of those irreplaceable, fully special pieces that make up in a unique combination the woven fabric of your story. Those "things" cannot be reduced to gender or religious affiliation; they cannot be reduced to statistical data available about you. They cannot be fully understood by socioeconomic, cultural, psychological, or any of the other standards used to judge a person or to understand a human being.

Your soul print is the unique snowflake essence of your soul, which makes you who you are. Unlike a snowflake, however, it never melts.

Your idiosyncrasy is integral to your essence. It is strange, sad, and sometimes funny to realize that we spend so much of our energy and time trying to fit in and hide our idiosyncrasies—when what we should be doing is let them be revealed—viewed from the casing of our Soul Print Boxes, flaunted proudly as our soul print banners.

FOR YOUR SOUL PRINT TO BE KNOWN

Remember what we said about all of those babies who can't survive without living connection? Well, at least in this sense, I don't think any of us ever grow up, because our survival is often as dependent upon love and recognition as it is on food or shelter.

There is a myth about a man named Honi the circle drawer. Honi was the most notoriously audacious, impudent, and passionate teacher of his generation. He was both a mystic and a folk hero beloved of the people. One day he happened upon a man planting a carob tree. Upon hearing from the planter that the tree would not yield fruit for seventy years, Honi could not understand why the man was wasting his time planting. Honi was a mystic seeking the eternal in the now—he could not appreciate what he saw as an irrational concern with the distant future. The man told him that just as his ancestors planted the carobs he ate now, so did he plant for his descendants.

Shortly after hearing the carob-planter's words, Honi fell asleep—a Rip Van Winkle kind of sleep—and awoke a full seventy years later. He saw a man picking the fruit of the carob tree. "Are you the man who just planted this tree?" he asked.

"No," the stranger responded, "my grandfather planted it."

Realizing he must have slept for seventy years, Honi stumbled toward home. His son had already passed on, and his grandson was master of the house. He came in crying, "I am Honi!" but no one believed him. He went to the Academy and found them discussing the brilliance of the Great Honi, who had been a master in this very Academy seventy years earlier. "I am Honi!" he declared to them. He shared with them teachings of great brilliance, and while the masters listened to him and appreciated his words, they did not believe that he was Honi.

Honi prayed for mercy and asked God to take him. He lay down beneath the carob tree and fell into the great sleep of death.

The biblical myth masters concluded the story with an epigrammatic statement, *"Havrutah U'Metutah*—Companionship or Death."

How do we understand this strange, almost absurd tale? Honi

awakes after sleeping for seventy years and wants to return home. Home is his family and home is the Academy. Home, however, does not recognize him. The scholars see him as a man of immense wisdom and learning. They surely would offer him a position as a master in the Academy. Yet when he says, "I am Honi," he is not believed. He cannot transmit to them his Honi-ness. They honored him, say the storytellers—"but not according to the honor due to him."

Facing profound loneliness, Honi is not caught up in his own ego needs. It is not that they would have made him a better job offer if they knew he was Honi. The honor due to him is not a quantitative issue. The essential phrase that shows his loneliness is the honor "due to him." Honi wanted not more honor but his honor—to be seen for himself. The issue at stake is loneliness. He felt unseen for who he was. He was unable to communicate his most essential name—his soul print—to the people that made up his home, his world.

To be lonely is to experience a moment of death. The masters' comment, *"Havrutah O'Metutah*—Companionship or Death," equates friendship with life force. "To feel completely alone and isolated leads to mental disintegration just as physical starvation leads to Death," writes Erich Fromm in his classic work *Escape from Freedom*. We can be completely alone and isolated even when surrounded by people. So Honi prays for mercy and is allowed to go gently into the night. All of our lives sounds the great cry, "I exist. I have a name." To exist is to have people know that "I am Honi."

In the biblical myth tradition of central Europe, the most famous inheritor of Honi, another mystical master and folk hero, was a figure named "Israel son of Eliezer." He was referred to by the people as the Baal Shem Tov, which literally translates as "Master of the Good Name." A person who fully realized and shared his soul print, he became a master of his name, which is to say he became himself—which in biblical myth is the highest spiritual achievement. Moreover, as a folk hero, he was fully received by the people.

What is unique about biblical mysticism is its audacious invitation to all of us to become a Baal Shem—a master of our own name. In *Soul Prints,* we will return repeatedly to the idea of name, as well as to the tales of this mystical master the Baal Shem Tov. In fact, all of the stories told by the Baal Shem and his disciples form a genre that could be fairly called Soul Print Stories.

When I was fifteen I used to cut many of my high school classes in Riverdale, New York, and take the #100 bus to Yeshiva University in Washington Heights, where Joseph Soloveichik, one of the last great European masters, was lecturing in Talmud and philosophy. I was totally taken by all of his writings—the more obtuse the better—all of which I had practically memorized before the end of high school. I would linger outside of his apartment waiting for a glimpse of his face. I felt for him the intense if unrequited love of a disciple for a master. Years have past since then, Joseph Soloveichik has died, and many of those who claim his legacy have profoundly disappointed me. But he wrote one sentence that burrowed its way into my soul and stayed with me all through the years: "To be, is to be singular, unique, and consequently lonely."

Today I would be so bold as to add to Rabbi Soloveichik's proverb: "To be is to be received; to communicate my soul print to another, to move from loneliness to loving. To give people my Soul Print Box and know they have received it is the greatest human joy."

> "To be is to be received; to communicate my soul print to another is to move from loneliness to loving. To give people my Soul Print Box and know they have received it is the greatest human joy."

3

THE PROMISE OF MERE JOY

HAPPINESS UNEXPECTED

Once we become seekers of the authentic soul print connection, we transcend loneliness and can achieve that simple, authentic feeling I like to call "mere joy." But we won't find happiness in the ways we've learned all our lives. Popular Western concepts of joy are captured in the declaration by America's founding fathers that all people deserve the inalienable right to life, liberty, and the pursuit of happiness. The problem with that notion, however, is this: Happiness cannot be pursued. When we pursue happiness, it always runs away from us. Instead, we must pursue goals other than happiness, and as a natural by-product of their pursuit, we will be happy.

A Zen master enters a village and sees people scurrying about. "Where are you running?" he asks.

"To make a living," they respond.

"Why are you so sure that your living is in front of you?" he probes. "Maybe it's behind you and can't catch up. Do not run to make a living, be still and live."

Another version of that story from the Talmudic tradition adds a clever and important twist.

A student came to his master and said, "Teacher, you taught me that if I run from honor, then honor will pursue me. Well, I have been running from honor for many years now and honor is still not pursuing me."

"The problem," replied the master, nodding sagaciously, "is clearly apparent. When you run from honor you are always looking over your shoulder to see if honor is pursuing you—so honor is confused, not quite sure which way you are going."

Joy, like honor and serenity and so much else we ache and sweat for, is only available to us when we actively seek something else instead. A passage in a fifth-century document records a debate between the biblical myth masters on the pursuit of happiness. The Babylonian Talmud discusses several wisdom texts that seem to hold contradictory views on joy. One set of passages denies the possibility of achieving true joy, while the second set of texts is far more encouraging and positive about our chances of accessing happiness.

The resolution of the debate is achieved by explaining that the two different sets of texts are in fact talking about two different sorts of joy. The first is happiness as a detached value—a towering ideal, a castle that rests on an ever-retreating horizon. The second is happiness as a by-product—the ever-present companion that walks with life's meaningful goals. The Talmudic conclusion in a nutshell: Happiness as a detached value is not achievable, and joy pursued as an ideal, for its own sake, will never be attained. Happiness can only be realized as the by-product of the pursuit of some other goal. It can never be the primary goal.

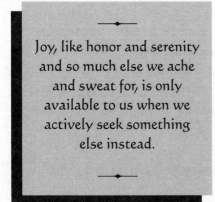

Joy, like honor and serenity and so much else we ache and sweat for, is only available to us when we actively seek something else instead.

What is the primary goal that you must pursue in order to achieve happiness as a by-product? Happiness is the by-product of the realization of your soul print. In the normal course of living, you are happy when you are living your soul print and you are unhappy if you are not living your soul print.

The happiness that is a by-product of soul print living is called by the myth masters "the joy of *mitzvah*." Although the word *mitzvah* is usually translated from the Hebrew as "commandment," the Kabbalists, ever sensitive to the nuances of Hebrew language, understand *mitzvah* to derive from a root word meaning "intimacy." For us soul print seekers, that is a very valuable translation of the word, for it connects joy with intimacy. Intimacy is both personal and interpersonal. It happens when you realize your soul print and when you intertwine it with another.

The imperative of biblical consciousness is not "be happy." Rather, it is "choose life"—which in the biblical myth means choose your life. Live your soul print in the world.

"Joyous is the believer," proclaim the biblical myth masters. The Kabbalists would interpret this declaration to mean, "Joyous is one who believes that he has a unique destiny," a soul print. To believe is not to believe that "it" is true, but that "I" am true. When you live your soul print, you experience your truth and are thus freed from the need to affirm your truth by believing in an external set of dogmas.

"He who is prosperous," teaches the Babylonian wisdom master called Ben Zoma, "is he who is joyous in his lot." Usually we understand Ben Zoma to mean, "Happiness is to appreciate what you have—unhappiness is to appreciate what you don't have." That is generally sound advice. However, while appreciation is an absolute prerequisite for happiness, it is insufficient by itself to make a person happy. We can learn from that sort of appreciation, and, as we will see, move past it into a more sustaining "mere joy." However, appreciation is a very good place to start.

Soul Print Practice

Bring happiness to one person each week, for no apparent reason.

Even if you haven't fully realized your soul print, you can touch happiness by acting happy. Playing the part is not necessarily fraudulent. It is sometimes the best path to get there. It's critical to get to happiness, because it's much easier to access and fulfill your soul print calling when you're happy than when you're depressed.

Do smile stretches. Smile! Smile the biggest smile you can. Then make it even bigger. Now hold it. Happiness is like a muscle: The more you work it, the stronger it is.

An ancient biblical tradition calls us to say one hundred blessings of appreciation. A blessing is a moment of appreciation, of consciousness—a soul print moment. You can aim to do that in your own life, in your own way. Identify or create one hundred "soul print moments." Those moments might include:

1) A conversation in which you feel heard.

2) A phone call to someone to say "hi," even though you don't need anything from that person.

3) Playing with your kids, or someone else's—with all your heart.

4) Giving your kids, your lover, or your coworker fifteen minutes of real listening.

You don't have to seek a hundred blessings right away. Five or ten would do just fine. Yet the number one hundred is deliberately high to teach us to always have our eyes open.

As you will find, blessings can burst from the most unlikely hiding places. Blessings can cover moments of gratitude, appreciation, and wonder. Blessings can be questions, requests, thankyous, or acknowledgments.

Acknowledge wonder. In doing so, you receive the soul print of the world itself.

Make a list of the seven wonders of your world. These are places where you experienced your greatest joy—for example, the summit of Mount Shasta after a challenging climb, or that Italian restaurant where you first fell in love.

Focus on this two-thousand-year-old biblical myth soul print meditation: "Source of all blessings are you who sustain me and enliven me—thank you for bringing me to this moment."

When we go beyond appreciation, the realization of the soul print unpacks a more subtle interpretation of Ben Zoma's epigram. Because your soul's signature is unique to you, to be happy is to be living "your lot"—your unique unfolding in the world. One evening over dinner with Cary and me, our friend Karen uttered something precious that we carry with us. "I'm the happiest I've ever been in *my* life," Karen said. The italics were hers. To be able to say, "I am happy in my life"—there is no greater gift in the world.

Imagine the difference between clothes tailored for you and clothes that you borrow from a friend that do not quite fit. That jacket, those pants can do for a day or so, but you will not feel fully comfortable in them, and you surely will not have that joyous feeling of putting on garments tailored to the measure of your life. If you feel as if you live your life in someone else's shoes, that you are fully replaceable, that if you leave there will be someone else sitting at your desk next week doing precisely what you do, then you will feel valueless. Such devaluation of self is the root of almost all depression.

Your soul print fits you more perfectly than any tailored suit of clothes. To get up in the morning knowing that you are already clothed in your own uniqueness, that you are doing something in the world totally distinctive to you and you alone, which no one else in the world can quite like you do—that is mere joy.

LIVE YOUR DEPTH

To live your soul print is to live your depth. Or, as American Poet Laureate Stanley Kunitz urges us, "Live in the layers, not on the litter." In every realm of our lives, we need to have a passionate desire to experience the depths, to live in the layers, for the opposite of the holy is not the unholy but the superficial.

Ultimately, living deeply is more fun. It feels better; it invigorates you, and it gives you vital energy for living in a way that superficial fun never can. Depth is a soul print characteristic.

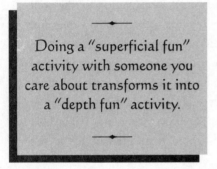

Doing a "superficial fun" activity with someone you care about transforms it into a "depth fun" activity.

There are two ways to distinguish surface fun from deep fun. The first is effort. No form of deep fun—reading a good book, creating a gorgeous meal, having great sex in the context of an equally great relationship—is attainable without effort. My wife calls this kind of effort "washing the dishes"—for behind every gorgeous dinner table is a kitchen that needs cleaning. These are the challenges that create the context for [experiencing] the depths of fun that will make your soul print quiver with delight.

Not even the seemingly easy "Eureka" joy of self-discovery is effortless. You may break through to a spiritual level where joy flows effortlessly, but only after you have expended untold energy and effort. If you read the memoirs of mystics throughout the ages, you will hear them tell of their most dazzling mystical encounters, those stunning moments of satori enlightenment. They almost unanimously write that these moments came soaring out of nowhere, unexpected, in the very second when they had stopped trying to attain them. Even this climax experience of effortless illumination was called forth only by discipline and dedicated practice. Two more valuable areas of endeavors—creative success and physical exercise—are models of the idea that you require effort to achieve the depths of joy. Both are opportunities for deep fun, engagement, and flowing joy. Yet the breakthrough moments in both—the burst of inspiration and the runner's high—happen only after the investment of much energy and effort.

The second way to distinguish depth fun from surface fun is aftertaste. How do you feel when the fun is over? If you're engaged in depth fun, then usually you'll feel an afterglow, a feeling of satiation and satisfaction. Sometimes the afterglow is even visible. Even if you have writer's cramp or your hamstrings are sore, you feel like the walking definition of fulfillment.

If, however, you're engaged in superficial fun, then you may well have had a great time doing your fun stuff, but you'll usually feel somewhat empty afterward. You'll be nagged by a sense of unfulfillment, maybe even discomfort, and a little bit of anger or disappointment. You'll feel a kind of negative afterglow. The most obvious example is the dreaded hangover—the sickly creature that creeps in on its hands and knees after your revelry departs. The very potion that took you so high the night before turns out to be the poison that lays you low the next morning.

One of the nicest aftertastes of fun, and the best and most subtle kind of fun, often comes from doing a good deed. One afternoon, sitting in a café, I caught a precious glimpse of that wonderful phenomenon—a good deed done. I saw a teenage girl dashing down the crowded street, toting a purse too big, black, and out of style to be her own. I wondered if she would find the bag's owner amid the mass of people. Several minutes later, I had my answer. I saw striding down the street the most brilliantly illuminated face you could imagine. A glow of pride, the aura of a good deed done, decorated the face of the girl. My eyes savored the aftertaste of her joy.

The motives we bring to fun can transform even the most superficial pleasure into an occasion for mere joy. Whom you are doing an activity with makes all the difference in the world. For example, going to see a superficial fun movie by yourself, because you are bored and want to escape yourself—that can be a wholly different enterprise than going with your lover. Doing a "superficial fun" activity with someone you care about transforms it into a "depth fun" activity. The same activity with the same person can be transformed from a surface to a depth activity or back again, based on context and intention. Sometimes, of course, when we want only to relax, "superficial" is just what we need. Consider how, after resolving an argument with your partner, the two of you curl up on the couch, intertwined, to watch some bad television. That's mere joy, no matter how tired the rerun.

Even more pointedly, consider the difference between spending two weeks on vacation and spending your life on vacation. The same two weeks with precisely the same activities and people may be fabulous on a special vacation and horribly joyless on a "life vacation." The formula for explaining the difference is simple and poignant. If you engage in superficial fun in order to cover your sense of emptiness, then when the fun wears off you always feel empty. If you engage in the same fun activity in order to reveal life's fullness—then the fun will make you feel enriched, and enlivened. Superficial fun has become depth fun. Fun as escape never works and often backfires. Fun as celebration is one of life's true pleasures.

Soul Print Practice

First, consider this list of what my son calls "the polar bear opposites"—the aftertaste of different kinds of fun:

1) A great meal (balanced, organic) vs. junk food (laced with chemicals, wrapped in plastic).

2) Great sex with a committed partner vs. great sex with someone whose name you don't know.

3) Great book vs. trash novel.

4) Making a sale of a product you believe in vs. making a sale of a product you do not believe in.

5) Producing an in-depth television show about a topic you care about vs. appearing as a square in *Hollywood Squares*.

Now, add to this list.

Write a few words describing your aftertaste feelings following depth fun and superficial fun.

Imagine that life itself has an aftertaste. Describe two different aftertaste scenarios at the end of your life—one good and the other less so.

List the activities or steps that you need to take to get to the positive afterglow feeling.

Always try to keep in mind before you bite, what the aftertaste will be!

THE JOY OF DEPTH

Depth is only attainable if you are living your soul print, not trying to live someone else's. If you're essentially on the wrong track, wearing someone else's shoes, leaving someone else's marks, living someone else's print—then there is a level of depth you can never achieve. And what you do achieve will give you far less satisfaction than if you walk a mile, or a lifetime of miles, in your own shoes.

I've said that happiness is a by-product of inner depth. The word "inner" here is critical. The Hebrew word for inner, inside, or interiority, is *panim*. It has a second meaning as well: "face." It is very significant that in biblical Hebrew, these multiple meanings are contained in one word, *panim*. "Face" and "inside" are the same word. Therefore, to be face-to-face is to try to get inside the issue—to have an in-depth encounter. To be intimate. To be connected to soul print.

The face, say the wisdom masters, is the symbol and expression of our distinctiveness. Each person's face is infinitely unique and special. Face is soul print. You "lose face" in life when you are not living your soul print. When a person feels her own depth, she is granted a dimension of inner peace, which is the essential prerequisite to authentic joy, and she brings that depth to the surface. We've all heard people say, "Her face was radiant!" Or, "You're shining!" When inner joy pervades, it emanates from the light of the face.

If we search for depth and not merely beauty, we realize that as we get older and our bodies lose their luster our faces begin to shine. There is little more beautiful and worthy of contemplation than the face of an elder. "I want to grow old without face-lifts. They take the lift out of a face, the character. I want to have the courage to be loyal to the face I've made." The speaker is Marylyn Monroe, who never came face-to-face with the wrinkled visage of old age. We do not know if she would've lost face or been loyal.

Face is a symbol for soul print. There are forty-five muscles in the face. By and large most of them are unnecessary for the biological functioning of the face. Their major purpose, it would seem, is to express emotional depth and nuance. They are the muscles of the soul. To be faceless is to lose perception of soul print. The poet Rilke describes the fear of the faceless:

The woman: she had completely fallen into herself, forward into her hands. . . . It cost me an indescribable effort to stay with those two hands, not to look at what had been torn out of them. I shuddered to see a face from the inside, but I was much more afraid of that bare flayed head waiting there, faceless.

Just as hope lights up a face, despair can rob a visage of its dignity and life.

Ultimately, however, face is not about hope or despair. It is the primary expression of singularity. The Talmudic myth masters write, "Just as their faces are different so is their essence."

In the paradox of living, face is the part of our body that we leave most exposed. Face, which contains the secrets of all our intimacies, we leave on the outside.

When we want to cover up soul or hide our fear that perhaps we are soulless after all, we try to lift our face. We somehow understand that our face is not surface. We intuit that the lifting of the face might have some effect on the soul. Cosmetic surgeons tell us that the overwhelming majority of optional cosmetic surgery is facial. Face-lifts to raise our sagging spirit?

And yet sometimes an external change is important to help us reconnect to our soul print energy, much in the same way that clothes that fit just right help us feel gorgeous—they help us access our soul print. A woman in my congregation once told me she was undergoing a face-lift because she felt that her body had betrayed her spirit. She could bear the betrayal on all levels except that of face. Face for her needed to be an expression of her insides.

And as much as the surface reflects the insides, the insides also come to reflect the surface. No doubt, looking younger and more energized can also help someone feel that way. The symbiotic relationship between the insides and the outsides, the inner face and the surface, is one of the defining tensions of life.

A SOUL PRINT MAP: FIVE SOULS, FIVE STAGES OF GROWTH

The Kabbalistic teachers speak of five souls that unfold over the course of a person's lifetime. The five souls, carefully understood, express five stages in a person's journey from the exile of loneliness, home to the joy of connection. If we consider these stages of the soul's growth in terms of our evolving realization of soul print in our lives, we can glimpse the deeper intent of the mystical masters and work to develop a Soul Print Map. Like all maps, this one gives us identifying characteristics that will make it easier to find our way on our soul print journey. Although these levels may unfold in a linear fashion—in that, as we get older, higher levels of the soul unfold—they often do not follow such a pattern. A person may sometimes straddle two levels, go to a later level before an earlier level, or skip a level for a time only to come back to it later.

The first soul stage is called *nefesh*. This stage is the beginning of life. This is the stage of infancy and early childhood. Although the unique soul print is not fully visible at this stage, there are already first hints. You will often hear parents talk about a good baby, an angry baby, or a particularly verbal or quiet baby. Even in infancy the first glimmerings of soul print begin to shine through.

At this basic level of the soul—one usually identified with the biophysical organism—there is already an experience of loneliness. However, as long as the biophysical organism is satisfied and we experience the physical and emotional presence of primary caretakers, our loneliness is dissipated and we continue on happily. Later in life, we may have friends from whom *nefesh* presence is precisely what we need. It is enough to redeem us from our loneliness and make us feel safe.

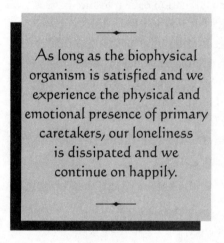

As long as the biophysical organism is satisfied and we experience the physical and emotional presence of primary caretakers, our loneliness is dissipated and we continue on happily.

The second soul print level is called *ruach,* roughly translated in English as either "wind," "spirit," or even "storm." At this stage, physical satisfaction is no longer enough to make us happy. We begin to feel a sense of dis-ease but we are not sure why. A vague dissatisfaction—like a wind—passes a chill through our tranquility. We feel, often subconsciously, an ache for cosmic specialness. We want to feel unique. It is often a stormy time. This is the soul stage where sibling rivalry manifests itself. We want to be the primary value in the eyes of our parents, who are still our entire world. We so want to be heroes that we run around in the capes and costumes of supermen, ecstatic over experiencing our own grandeur. The *ruach* level manifests again in our teenage years, explaining why teenagers are almost never satisfied or happy and at the same time they live like an open window, primed for deepening spiritual experiences. These are the *ruach* years, but they can revisit us later in life, particularly at that time known as the "midlife crisis," when the satisfactions that filled us once now leave us empty. Being nourished and provided for is no longer enough. Neither is being successful. Loneliness crouches at our doorstep. We desperately need to assert our uniqueness and singularity.

The third soul stage on the journey is *neshama*. The soul print matures beyond adolescence and begins to reveal its deeper and more profound contours. *Neshama* literally translated means "breath." It is also the most common word used in classical Hebrew for "soul." Breath is a path to soul print. Here we become aware of our breath—that is, of our singular and therefore lonely existence. We are consciously lonely for the first time, which presses us to identify and then connect to our soul print. We use our loneliness as a portal to our singularity. This level follows closely and often chronologically overlaps with the *ruach* level.

The best image for me in understanding how loneliness brings us to singularity is captured in a wonderful Norwegian folk tale.

A father handed his son a piece of smooth oak, and said to him, "This is your board. For every mistake you make, I will hammer in a nail."

By the time the boy was thirteen, the board was covered corner to corner with nails, some rusted, some shining new. The father took the board to his son and said, "For every good thing you do to fix all of these wrongs, I will take one nail out."

And it was not too long before the father took the last nail out and proudly showed his son the clean piece of oak. Yet when the son saw the board, his eyes brimmed with tears. He turned to his father and said, "But father, what about the holes?"

The story ends here. However, the father might have answered, "The holes are what make the board beautiful."

On the *neshama* level, the holes of our loneliness become the access roads to our uniqueness. Our soul prints are both formed and revealed in the holes of our lives. It is now that you begin to search for your soul mate—that is, the person who cherishes your soul print, not just its distinctive lines, but the empty spaces between the lines.

> ### Soul Print Practice
>
> How can you connect to your *neshama?* How can you catch your breath? Remember, *neshama* means "breath."
>
> As you read this, you are breathing. As long as you live, you breathe. Thus you are constantly connected to your *neshama,* but are you consciously connected to it?
>
> Become mindful of your breath.
>
> Do it right now.
>
> Catch your breath.
>
> Inhale deeply . . . hold your breath a moment . . . now let it go. Repeat this mindful breathing ten times.
>
> You are consciously connecting to your *neshama.* How does it feel? Your nervous system relaxes, slows, and calms. Your mind clears.
>
> The next time you see something that takes your breath away—a breathtaking vista, for instance—know that at that time the doors are open to your deepest insides. You will feel like you are home. That is the place and time to do a soul print meditation.
>
> The next time you are angry, stressed, confused, or troubled, connect to your *neshama.* Breathe ten deep breaths.

The fourth stage of the soul is called *chaya,* or "life energy." It comes at times when we feel most alive, often at times of our greatest successes or our most dramatic failures. Giving a brilliant lecture or getting fired from a job would both fall into the intensity of this kind of soul-awareness stage. You feel fully alive both in the skids of sharp turns and in the free fall of racing downhill. It is in

these moments of utter selfhood that our most important relationships are either cemented or shattered. If at these summits and
depths you are able to transmit your unique, essential soul print to
another, then you will enter a new level of living. If you cannot, or
if someone else seeks advantage from your openness or vulnerability, then you may experience your loneliness as betrayal of the most
devastating kind. *Chaya* is not a level we can hold with constancy. It
comes in moments of grace—when we feel and share our own
depths.

The fifth and final level is called *yechida* and is reached very
rarely by the very rare individual. *Yechida* derives from the
Hebrew root *yachad*. In the magic of biblical Hebrew, the root of
yachad means "singular," "special," "alone," as well as "together."
This is the highest place where in our aloneness we merge with the
all—we are together. Aloneness becomes All-Oneness. It is where
the contradictory drives—to stand out and to merge—become one.

Here is a description of this state from a thousand-year-old
Kabbalah passage:

> When one unites with God who is the Alpha of the world, he
> becomes ADAM . . . man must separate himself from . . .
> things to the extent that he will ascend through all the worlds
> and be in Union until his existence will be merged . . . and
> then he will be called ADAM.

The key to the passage is that in the ultimate place of merging,
where the initiate becomes part of the All-Oneness, he also finds
himself. It is there that he is called by the name Adam. Adam, the
name of the archetypal human being, is the ultimate name, and as
we know, name is the symbol of soul print. Aloneness dances with
All-Oneness.

Another description of this state comes from the Zen tradition of
Japanese Buddhism:

One day it happened: I did not shoot the arrow, it shot it-self. Did I bend the bow or did the bow bend me? Did I strike the target or did the target strike me? All of this, the bow, arrow, target, and myself, were merged one into the other. Furthermore, I felt no need to separate them.

All distinctions between subject and object disappear. The archer and the arrow become one. The solitary archer, who represents aloneness, merges with All-Oneness.

The litmus test of genuine singularity is this: Does it lead to Union? For our wonderful singular soul prints, all authentic uniqueness merges us with the One. Loneliness resolves itself grandly as the uniqueness of the soul print crystallizes, even while it sensuously melts into the all. We cannot hold this place with any constancy—yet in its grip we feel mere joy and taste eternity.

REFLECTIONS OF YECHIDA

In Kabbalah, *yechida* derives from the highest, that is to say, the deepest, and barely accessible spiritual realm called *keter*. *Keter* is

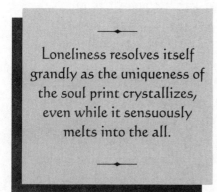

> Loneliness resolves itself grandly as the uniqueness of the soul print crystallizes, even while it sensuously melts into the all.

the place of silence—the place where we can go to experience our deepest soul print. It is not an encounter I can fully describe—it is somewhat like love, an orgasm, or your favorite ice cream flavor—so let me describe it through a scenario we are all familiar with—a date.

You're on a date and you have been for three hours. You realized in the first five minutes or less that this was not a good idea. You have made all the polite conversation you can muster, about her work, her family, her family's work—but nothing between you clicks—and you have not one word left to say. You are in the car, ready to drop her off. You are seven minutes away from her house. They are seven of the most uncomfortable, even painful, minutes of silence you can imagine. You are enduring what I call Silence of Absence. Silence of Absence arises when words can no longer cover up the emptiness of the moment. A yawning chasm stretches between you and the person next to you—a void unbridgeable by words.

Re-imagine the same scene. However, this time the three hours have flown by as one extended moment of magic. The conversation was alternately funny, deep, and light, with flirtatious undertones limning every sentence. She is driving you home. There are seven minutes left. Silence settles on the car. No one talks for seven of the most lovely, even ecstatic, minutes of silence you can imagine. This is what I call Silence of Presence. Silence of Presence occurs when words won't do—when the moment is too full to be captured in the confines of language. In such a moment, you are fully present, your soul print leaving its mark on every second you share. Silence of Presence is an experience of powerful soul print revelation. You and your companion are at once separate and merged, with each other and with the world. You are each alone yet you each taste All-Oneness. Ecstasy.

Ecstasy is one soul print stage beyond mere joy. You have reached a peak level where you are connected to your own soul print even as you feel it being witnessed by a person or force beyond yourself.

THE AFTER-SILENCE

A second moment of *yechida* ecstasy occurs after the mystical recognition and reunion of first meetings. Here also, Silence of Presence shows its face. To continue with our metaphor of dating, this usually occurs on what I like to call the confession date. When we're going out with someone, we all put on our best face. You know what I mean. We wear our best clothes, deliver our most clever lines, and beam our award-winning smiles. Yet we all know that it is truly tragic if we marry after only showing our best face, because our best face is far from the whole story and maybe not even the best part of who we are.

Moving beyond loneliness, you remember, is when we're able to share our "things," our intimate Soul Print Box of self. Everyone's box, however, has a bit of Pandora-stuff in it, and in a relationship, Pandora always finds her way out. That is why the Confession Date is so important. The Confession Date is usually somewhere around date five, six, or seven, when the chemistry seems like it just might be cosmic, that this person might just be the one. We may or may not have met each other's families. We may or may not have slept with each other yet, depending on lifestyle and religious understanding. In any case, we've not really been fully ourselves yet. We understand with the intuitive wisdom of the heart that we have to break through this or it's just not worth it.

The Confession Date may begin in a restaurant, with both people looking at the menu, and then someone abruptly says, "You know, I never told you, but I killed my cat. Accidentally, of course."

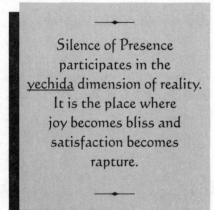

Silence of Presence participates in the <u>yechida</u> dimension of reality. It is the place where joy becomes bliss and satisfaction becomes rapture.

"You did? Well, let me tell you something. I used to shoplift when I was sixteen."

"Oh, you did? Well, you know . . ."

At this point, the talk usually shifts to sexual misdeeds— every couple according to its understanding of the offense. This conversation often takes quite a while as they go down an unwritten list of sometimes funny, occasionally very serious, and often poignant confessions.

After each admission, the confessor might furtively look up to see if the other person is still at the table. If at the end both people are emotionally present and engaged, then a very gentle and deep silence sometimes rests between them. Glimmerings of grace, a flicker of eternity, silence of presence, reflections of *yechida*—a beautiful soul print moment.

The confession date—like other encounters where two or more people risk being authentic—becomes a clasp, connecting your past alone to your present together, entwining your souls. You realize for the first time that another person is beginning to like you, indeed to love you, for who you really are.

Silence of Presence participates in the *yechida* dimension of reality. It is the place where joy becomes bliss and satisfaction becomes rapture.

4

———◆———

SOUL PRINT WITNESSING

BEWARE OF LABELS AND LETTERS

When Janis was a student of dance therapy at New York University, she did her internship at Bellevue Hospital, on the locked psychiatric ward. After she held her first session, which was quite successful, she hurried to leave the ward to get to class. She went up to the guard and asked to be let out. He looked at her with a slightly surprised smile and asked, "What do you mean? I'm not going to let you out!"

Janis was a little bewildered by his answer but tried to explain. "I'm a student at NYU and have to get to class. Can you please let me out?"

He laughed at her again incredulously. "Yeah, right! And I'm at Harvard. I can't let you out!"

Janis suddenly realized she was stuck in a locked ward, and that anything she said would not be believed. Her pleas would be thrown right back at her. She was locked in the guard's conception of her as a patient! She tried to reason with the guard a few more minutes, but to no avail. She felt anxious, trapped; everything she said to the guard just plunged her deeper into trouble.

Finally, she decided to turn back and look for her supervisor, the doc-

tor in charge. When she found him and told him what had happened, he looked at her, suppressing a smile, and asked, "But, Janis, why were you asking a patient to let you out?"

It happens to us practically since birth—we affix labels to others and to ourselves. Sometimes those labels are meant to hurt; at other times, they are complimentary labels intended to praise. Positive or negative, every label builds walls. When we hold onto our labels and self-definitions ("I'm not good at this, I could never do that.") we refuse to treat ourselves as full humans with infinite potential. When we give them to other people or types of people ("She's bad with numbers," "He's Jewish and so he's tight with his money."), we estrange ourselves from other people's soul prints.

The most often mentioned ethical guideline in biblical myth— appearing no less than thirty-six times—is "deal kindly with the stranger." A stranger is anyone whose soul print is blocked from view by the label of his place of origin, be it family, nationality, or religion.

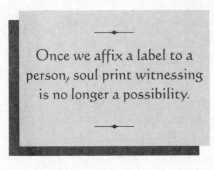

Once we affix a label to a person, soul print witnessing is no longer a possibility.

Our challenge is never to let external labels transform the other into a stranger.

We so often get lost in our perceived limitations. One of our culture's responses is to try to salve our collective discomfort with labels and complexes. Narcissist, neurotic, character disorder, borderline personality with schizoid tendencies, anal retentive, learning disabled—these are just a few of the terms we use to separate ourselves from others, diminishing ourselves in the process. Labels, of course, can clarify, shedding light on otherwise difficult-to-grasp symptoms. Yet too often, when they are used as judgments they occlude further soul print connection.

Labeling happens all the time, even when we don't think we are doing it. We label ourselves as well in subtle and pernicious ways. "There is no possible way I could ever do that," someone might say about an ambition or desire. That kind of sentiment is also a label that estranges us from ourselves. Such comments are certainties that lie. We hold them because they allow us a comfort zone in which we do not need to challenge our self-perceptions or stretch to the fullness of our soul prints. Labels are the archenemy of soul prints. Relying on them is like trying to take someone's fingerprint when he's wearing a Band-Aid. Labels control and suffocate the soul instead of nurturing the soul print. If we are not willing to move beyond our artificial comfort zones, we cannot grow—and we cannot truly engage in soul print witnessing.

Soul Print Practice

Make a list of five positive I CAN _____ statements.

I CAN _____

I CAN _____

I CAN _____

I CAN _____

I CAN _____

Make a list of five negative I CAN'T _____ statements.

I CAN'T _____

I CAN'T _____

I CAN'T _____

I CAN'T _____

I CAN'T _____

How many of your statements (positive or negative) did you hear from someone else? At what stage of your life were you when you heard them? Write a one-paragraph description of your feelings the first time that you heard each one of them.

Make of list of people you have labeled positively.

Make a list of people you have labeled negatively.

If possible, then let the people you labeled negatively know that you were wrong to label them.

Go back to a label that was put on you, whether by doctors, parents, teachers, or friends. Rename it. Reframe it. See how it could expand into the rich truth of your soul print.

In postbiblical Hebrew, the word *teivah* means "a letter," the basic building block of a word. In biblical Hebrew, however, *teivah* also denotes an enclosure, or a box. Not accidentally, the Hebrew language captures the fascinating correspondence between the two meanings. Like enclosures, words can protect, but they can also "box us in." To live the soul print, we need to break the boxes open and command our unique inner potential.

Once we affix a label to a person, soul print witnessing is no longer a possibility. Witnessing involves seeing, hearing, and understanding. A person who has been labeled becomes effectively invisible. To witness other people is to see their life and their growth. If we are not growing, then we are not truly alive. At some point, of course, growth—at least in our accessible sensory field—stops. This point is death. I remember having an epiphany regarding my own death in my early twenties. I realized that my only fear of death was a fear of not having lived. That is to say, not having lived my soul print. Jung says it this way: "in the final analysis we count for something only because of the essential that we embody, and if we do not embody that, life is wasted." I would add only one word to Jung's dictum—we count because of the "unique" essential. If we have lived our lives unfolding our soul prints, then when the time comes, we can indeed go gently into the dark night.

WOULD THE TRUE MESSIAH PLEASE STAND UP?

There was once a monastery that had seen better days. In decline for many years, it had now reached the stage where only five aging monks remained.

One day the abbot of the monastery met the local rabbi during a walk in the woods and shared his plight with him. How was he to attract new postulants to his monastery? The rabbi listened with patience and sympathy, but he was unable to suggest anything the abbot had not already tried. As the abbot bade the rabbi a sad farewell and began to trudge back to his dying monastery, the rabbi's eyes suddenly lit up with a mischievous glint. "There is one thing I can tell you," he called to the abbot. "It's nothing very certain, but it may help. I have it on good authority that one of the members of your monastery may be the Messiah."

Before the abbot could ask for an explanation, the rabbi was gone.

Returning to the monastery, the abbot shared the rabbi's cryptic message with the monks. Confused and unclear about the meaning of the rabbi's words, the monks tried to put his message to the back of their minds. But during their daily chores, the same question began to arise unbidden in each monk's thoughts: If the Messiah may be one of us, I wonder who it is?

It must be the abbot, each one thought in turn. He has been our leader for so many years. He's held us together through all these hard times, and surely, whoever is the Messiah will have to be a great leader. Maybe it is indeed the abbot. But then, some of them wondered, what about John, the scholar? Day and night, he studies the holy texts. Maybe hiding underneath his scholarly veneer is the deep divine knowledge a Messiah requires.

The monks' musing went on. What about Thomas, the jester of our group? We all know the healing power of laughter, and there is no greater doctor of happiness than Thomas. Maybe Thomas is the Messiah? And what about Luke? Luke is always organizing things, making sure we have what we need, keeping the monastery running.

Perhaps Luke is the one who will bring about the harmonious order of the world to come?

But on the other hand, maybe . . . maybe it's me.

Uncertain as to who was the Messiah, the monks began to look at each other differently. They began to treat each other with a great deal more respect and to treat themselves with a great deal more respect too. Soon a new atmosphere of admiration and revelation began to settle on the monastery, such that people were drawn to visit this place of wonder and infinite possibility. Some of the visitors would stay and talk with the monks. Some stayed the weekend, some stayed the week, and others simply stayed. The monastery became more thriving, more prosperous, and—above all—a more sacred place than ever before.

The biblical word for "community" is *Edah,* deriving from the Hebrew word *Yiud,* meaning unique destiny. We form a community whenever we let go of the labels we use to define both other and self, and in their place create space for the full and free emergence of our soul prints. This is the life and liberty that we need to view as our inalienable right. The purpose of community is not to control—that is the function of labels—but to care for and nurture the soil of every person's unique destiny.

Edah also means "witness." In biblical myth, community is the crucible for witnessing each other. The epigram of the prophet Isaiah, "You are my witnesses," is usually taken to mean that the human being is God's witness. In the soul print understanding of what I call *edah*-consciousness we are all called to witness the God in each other. In this kind of community, we try to see each other with God's eyes. We need only to imagine how we might like God to see and understand us despite all of our foibles—and then turn that same perception outward on the world. When we become witnesses, then our communities—like that of the monks in the story—will thrive and prosper. We become our own messiah. In the language of the mystics, we are engraved on the divine throne of glory.

SOUL PRINT FLASHES:
TO FIND YOUR FACE UPON THE THRONE

Neither in environment nor in heredity can we find the exact instrument that fashioned each of us. As Vladimir Nabokov writes in his autobiography *Speak, Memory,* "the anonymous roller . . . passed upon my life a certain intricate watermark whose unique design becomes visible when the lamp of art is made to shine through life's foolscap." The art of living is shining light on that certain intricate watermark.

It is in that shining that we experience the core certainty of our beings. Every person's image is etched onto the divine throne. Indeed, we could say that divinity is the composite of all the soul prints that are, were, and will be. In the Kabbalistic rendition, the names that are, were, and will be all make up the name of God. One suggestive image is the art of Georges Seurat, one of the leaders of the Pointillist movement. In Pointillism, each painting is made up of an astounding multitude of individual points, which the perspective of distance transforms into beautiful landscapes and images. It is in this sense that biblical myth understands every human being to be part of the divine image. We are all points in the divine portrait.

Imagine that each of us must face a kind of trial—like the character in Albert Brooks's movie *The Judgment* had to, after death. There is only one witness and one item introduced as evidence. You are the only witness and the evidence is the impress of your soul print. Does it match the impress on the divine throne? If it does, we are in heaven.

Soul Print Practice

Create a place of witnessing. Plan an event, a talent show of sorts, where everyone shares a unique talent, expressing a piece of his or her soul print.

It doesn't need to be a show; this practice works great around the dinner table or in the living room.

For the adventuresome, next time you have a dinner party, ask your guests to bring something along that somehow expresses their soul—whether it be a poem, a picture, a performance. Not only will your "witnessing" of their soul expression be an affirmative experience, but the very opportunity for them to express themselves in front of others will bring out aspects of their soul that may have been hidden even to themselves.

One way of discovering your soul print is by actively expressing it in the world. Use your friends' witnessing as an opportunity for discovering the print of your soul.

Or for the less formal, go around the table and ask each person what experience that week has touched his or her soul. Share.

One of the ways to avoid getting caught in label-making is to catch and hold our soul print flashes. This effort is called by the Kabbalists "arousal from above"—indicating that it is a heavenly gift and not something we have earned down on earth. We often have soul print flashes even before we have truly connected to our soul print. We catch a glimpse of ourselves or we get a momentary inside look at someone else. To have faith means to be faithful to these flash-instances of greatness.

One of the most fascinating literary images in biblical myth is that of Jacob's ladder. Jacob—whom we will meet again shortly in another chapter of this book—is a true soul print hero. He sets out to seek his destiny, and the very first night of his journey he has a vision. He beholds a ladder stretching to heaven, decked with angels ascending and descending its rungs.

Why were these angels so busy going up and down the ladder?

The myth masters tell us that the angels had come to finally meet the face they had seen so many times before. Where had they seen the face before? It was sculpted on the heavenly throne of glory. It was a common sight to them in heaven, but now they beheld the face on earth. So they were climbing the ladder to glimpse Jacob's face on the throne—and then eagerly descending to compare it to Jacob's face on the ground, pointing and peeking, whispering with each other over the incredible likeness.

In his vision, Jacob became the mirror image of his higher self— what the poet William Butler Yeats called the "face before the world was made." It is a moment of grace. What is remarkable about this episode is that Jacob is going in the wrong direction. He is leaving the Promised Land. He is not even venturing on some epic-hero's quest into the underworld or wilderness. He is going into exile, beginning the low ebb in the tide of his life. In fact, his life as he knows it is falling apart. Yet just like Jacob, even in the midst of our confusion and disorder, we can have an epiphany. When we empty out our illusions, we see ourselves as we could be, in all of our splendor and glory. Jacob touched his soul print, fleetingly, for one awesome moment. Afterward, the maelstrom of inauthenticity swept him away. Will he be able to reconnect to his image on the throne of glory? That—as we shall see—is the source of great suspense in the biblical soul print myth of Jacob.

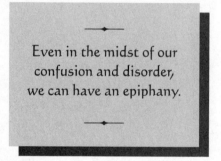

Even in the midst of our confusion and disorder, we can have an epiphany.

The goal of biblical myth is to help us find that "face we had" by fully living the authentic soul print. When we succeed in returning to it, however, we are always deeper and more beautiful than we were when we set out.

PART TWO

SOUL PRINT CONSCIOUSNESS

5

◆

SOUL PRINT RECEIVING

Why are there lonely people in the world? Why are alienation and uncertainty such a hovering presence in the lives of so many of us? Now that we have a definition of loneliness, we can begin to answer the question and in doing so chart effective strategies for moving from loneliness to loving. Our definition, you remember, is one sentence: *Loneliness is the inability to share my soul print with another.* Soul print consciousness tells us there are three possible answers to the question.

1) You are lonely because you have a "reception problem": you are unable to find another who will receive your soul print.

2) Or you are lonely because you have a "perception problem": You do not perceive your self as unique; you do not believe you have a soul print. Your soul print remains unrecognized, even and especially by yourself. You may have a number of excellent receivers who are both willing and able to receive your soul print, but you remain lonely because your receiver can accept only the soul print you have shared. If you do not recognize your own soul print, it is surely impossible for you to transmit it to another.

3) Or you are lonely because you have a "transmission
   problem": You have someone to receive your soul print,
   and you perceive yourself as unique, but you have not
   learned how to communicate it to another.

Throughout this book, we will be addressing the three ways we
can transcend our profound loneliness through the work our soul
prints call us to: *receiving* the soul prints of others, *believing/
perceiving* our own soul print, and *communicating* our soul print to
others. Of course, the three approaches often overlap with each
other. One person may read a section and think it deepened her
ability to receive, while another person may read the same section
and say, "I'd really like to share that story with my lover because it
will help me communicate my soul print." Still a third person will
read the same section and feel that it powerfully connected her to
her own soul print.

Our goal is to create a soul print language that enlivens and deepens our understanding of soul prints, nourishing them within ourselves and empowering their realization in the world. The Soul
Print Practices will be more important than ever in solidifying a
sense of our own soul prints and developing methods of communicating them to others and receiving their soul prints in return.

RECEIVING ANOTHER

Our primary promise to our fellow humans is to receive their soul
prints. Our great hope is to be received by another.

What does it mean to receive? What is the art of receiving? It is not
by accident that *Kabbalah,* the name of one of the most important
mystical traditions in the world, is a Hebrew word that means "to
receive." Receiving lies at the core of mystical practice. If biblical consciousness is, as we have posited, about the move from loneliness to
loving as the primary human drive and *telos* of existence, then it
makes sense that biblical mystical knowledge is called *Sefer*

HaKabbalah, the Book of Receiving. For to receive another is the highest fulfillment of biblical vision.

A friend of mine tells of the first time he attended a Kabbalah class. It was in Tiberias, one of the four mystical cities of Israel, a city where the Talmud and Kabbalah developed, and where Jesus stepped across the water in the tales of the Christian Bible. My friend entered the cloistered room of the Kabbalist and the teacher offered him an apple. He moved to take the apple, but the teacher's eyes indicated he was doing something wrong. Again, the teacher's hand extended to give him an apple, again he reached out to take the apple, and again the teacher indicated no. This back and forth occurred several times. The teacher asked, "You have come to learn Kabbalah, have you not?" Finally, my friend understood. The teacher extended his hands to give the apple, and my friend cupped his hands to receive it, in gratitude, awe, and love. The teacher nodded. "You have *received* your first lesson."

The most passionate and stunning act of soul print receiving I have ever seen occurred in a moment I accidentally glimpsed on a darkened side street of Jerusalem. A man and woman were walking arm in arm. They did not see I was looking. She must have been somewhere around a hundred and ten and he looked a few years older. Apparently—and I caught this all in a fleeting moment—her shoe was untied.

Seeing this, he stopped. They made eye contact for the briefest of seconds, and then he bent down, very slowly. I hardly knew a person could move that slowly. Gently, and somewhat painfully with his arthritic hands, he tied her shoe. It must have taken a full five minutes. All the while I watched paralyzed by awe in the shadows.

Her acceptance of that act of loving was an ultimate erotic expression. She was being received by him, and he by her. He was fully accepted by her. Had I, for example, noticed her untied shoelace and bent down to tie it, she probably would have pounded my back with her umbrella. I was not to be received in that way.

In their one act of receiving were the soul prints of a lifetime.

Infinite moments of joy, of laughter, pain, perhaps separation and tears, all merged together in that eternity of a moment. That was the mystic, the living Kabbalah, the esoterica of receiving.

Soul Print Practice

Every day is full of opportunities to share our soul prints with another and to receive another's soul print in turn. Most of those moments are ordinary; all of them are subtly profound. Here are some opportunities you can create for soul print sharing.

Name is a soul print expression. Don't be served without knowing the name of your server, whether it be a receptionist, bus driver, waiter, or the person who changes the sheets in your hotel room. Call these people by their names.

Call one person a week for no other reason than to say that he or she was on your mind.

When you have a list of calls to return, call back first the people you believe can do nothing to advance your career or otherwise augment your material position in the world. Calling back people you need to talk to is about furthering your agenda—which is a good idea but is not necessarily soul print receiving.

Make sure you have friends who are not related to your job or profession. This will not only broaden your horizons, but it will also invite you to move out of networking and shop talk mode into greater soul print consciousness.

Practice seeing your professional colleagues not only as objects but as subjects. Treat them not as stepping-stones but as genuine people. You may do this by sharing with them more of your real self. Make an internal commitment to remains friends with them even if they could never help you again (for example, a funder who has no money to underwrite you, or a highly placed official who was fired or retired).

BROTHERS EAST OF EDEN

There is probably no pain greater than that of not being received. Indeed, biblical myth suggests that the primal violence that so often wells up from humanity is bound up with the pain of rejection. We see this in the story of Cain and Abel, the archetypal brothers, who both offered sacrifice to God. God "turns to" the sacrifice of Abel but not to the sacrifice of Cain.

Some readers of this disturbing story claim that God does not actually reject Cain. They maintain that the story is about God's bond with Abel, not his dismissal of Cain. After all, nowhere in the text is Cain taken to task for any wrongdoing. Moreover, Cain's entire experience of rejection is in relation to Abel. The verse begins, "God turned to Abel." *Turned* is an unusual biblical word suggesting God's unique relationship with Abel. One of the most universal expressions of intimacy is special language or pet names shared between friends or lovers. The phrase "God turned" captures the unique contour of intimacy between Abel and God. Perhaps God has other words to characterize his relationship with Cain—and maybe in his jealousy Cain was unable to hear the endearments God whispered to him.

"To Cain and his offering God did not turn," the text continues. Of course God didn't turn—for "turning" characterizes the relationship he has with Abel. Cain experiences himself as being rejected because he is not like Abel.

Cain's great mistake is that he does not perceive his own unique soul print. He does not believe in Cain. That is just the beginning, however; biblical myth goes one critical step further in understanding our story. According to the original Hebrew presentation of biblical myth, there is a person whose name is Jealousy: Cain. *Cain* in Hebrew derives from the same root as "ownership" and "jealousy."

Jealousy has two meanings in our lives. In the first meaning, jealousy declares, "I want what you have—what I have is not enough. And even if I can't have what you have, the very fact that you have it makes me jealous." In a second meaning, jealousy says, "I want ownership of you—I want all of you to myself. I am jealous if you share any part of yourself at all, with someone else." Both forms of jealousy are symptoms of soul print dysfunction. Both kinds say, "I am only jealous of you when I cannot perceive and do not believe in my own soul print." In an interpretation by Italian Renaissance myth reader Ovadiah Seforno, God says to Cain, "Why are you jealous—*if you are good* you will rise." The emphasis on "if you are good" shows that your only competition is yourself. He doesn't say, "if you are better than your brother you will rise," or "if you are the best around, you'll soar." God says, "if you are good for yourself, if you are the best of yourself, if you live your soul print in the world, you will rise." But Cain cannot hear the divine voice within him and feels that he can only exist if he destroys Abel. Cain has no independent sense of identity; he defines himself in relation to Abel. He is disconnected from his soul print. That being the case, his rejection is inevitable.

There is another way to read the Cain and Abel narrative, however. In this telling, the party at fault is not Cain but God. The issue is not Cain's failure to perceive his own uniqueness but God's unwillingness to receive Cain's soul print. This reading focuses on the two brothers' sacrifices. The Hebrew word for "sacrifice" is *korban,* deriving from a root meaning "closeness" or "intimacy." Rejection is the dark opposite of intimacy. Not to be received means we have offered our most intimate selves only to have them rejected. Cain has offered up the best of himself. Indeed, Shimon son of Yochai, considered by many to be the most important figure in biblical mysticism, held God himself to be responsible for the tragedy of Cain and Abel.

This second and radical reading of the story is explored in a modern retelling, John Steinbeck's *East of Eden.* In the novel, Adam is a farmer. Overwhelmed financially, he is in danger of losing his land. At a Thanksgiving celebration, his son Caleb presents his father with $2,000 he earned trading commodities sold in Europe during World War II. His father explodes and casts aside his offering. Your money is tainted, he says to Caleb, earned as it was by taking advantage of the wartime situation. Caleb is broken-hearted. His life can be divided into the time before and the time after the rejection.

Adam in Steinbeck's novel had arguably good reason for not embracing the offering of his child. In the biblical text, God too might have had his reasons. The biblical myth masters suggest that he did. They point out that Abel offered up to God his *bettor meitav*—the *best* of his flock—whereas brother Cain merely offered up his standard crop—not bringing God his best. This reading of biblical myth rejects a conception of God that only receives us when we are at our best. The tragic story of Cain reminds us that receiving another means the ability to receive not just the best of who they are but all of who they are. To receive someone's soul print means to receive all of what they may have to offer, light and shadow together. Both God and the character of Adam in Steinbeck's novel need to be held accountable for their acts of rejection. After all, is not every offering we make in some sense flawed? And is not the beauty of receiving rooted precisely in our ability to receive flawed offerings? Soul print consciousness invites each of us, in our closest relationships, to receive our loved ones as they are and not only as we might want them to be.

Soul Print Practice

The opposite of receiving someone is rejection. Yet it is possible to decide not to exchange soul prints with a person without rejecting him or her. "We may not be suited to be life partners," you might say to someone, "but I still fully affirm your soul print and the time we spent together." Unfortunately, we often tend to reject former partners after a relationship doesn't work. One of the highest acts of soul print receiving is to be able to honor the time together even when it's over. We need to recognize those people as what the Kabbalists call *Ben Zug Lesha'ah,* literally translated as "partners for an hour"—in our language, soul print partners for a profound if limited time.

Send a note to a former partner whom you haven't talked to in a while expressing your affirmation of his or her soul print.

We can reject the soul prints of friends and acquaintances too—and do it with cruel casualness. How many of us recognize this scene? The front door shuts behind us as we leave a party, and before we've reached the car, we've fully critiqued the food, her clothes, his jokes. Or worse, we slander our hosts. We say, "Did you hear that he . . ."

Next time you find yourself in this situation, try to hold back. If you do feel like you need to make some such remark, and find it too difficult to restrain yourself entirely, then start by taking small steps. Keep yourself from gossiping until you get to the car. Then graduate a stage and commit not to gossip about your friends until you get home. When that works, commit yourself to waiting a day until you dissect anybody's dress, speech, or psyche.

I mention gossip here because it is one of the major sources of static in soul print reception. And yet it is so much a part of our lives, partly because it gives vent to our jealousy and partly because we enjoy it so much, that it is hard to go cold turkey. However, even just beginning to become aware of the challenge significantly expands our soul print consciousness.

Here is a modest yet challenging soul print practice. Make a commitment that for one hour every day you won't talk about other people—at all.

RECEIVING WHAT YOU CAN:
THE TALE OF THE DIRTY KOPEK

Why is it so hard to receive the soul print of another person? Why do we so often find ourselves playing God and rejecting others—with an angry glance, an ill-spoken word, or even with an indifferent shrug?

At least the beginning of an answer is found in the Zen-like Hasidic tale of the dirty kopek.

Shneur Zalman of Liadi, the master of a particular group of mystical initiates who lived in Europe in the mid-nineteenth century, and his two friends, master Menachem Mendel of Vitebsk and master Levi Isaac of Berdichev, had a common problem.

In their town lived an orphan girl who was to be married. There was no money available to make for her an appropriate wedding, much less to provide for her and her husband sufficient aid to get started in life. The mystics of the Kabbalah—which these men were—never allowed themselves to be carried away to the upper reaches of rapture and ecstasy to such an extent that they lost contact with the real life issues that plagued their congregations and disciples. The need for a wedding-couple fund was considered by all three of the masters a problem of solemn importance. It occupied all of their attention, and they all pondered deeply what the solution might be to the young couple's predicament.

Finally, Shneur Zalman said, "I have decided. I am going to go visit the miser who lives in that large house at the edge of Liadi."

"What!" exclaimed Menachem Mendel. "You know he will never give you any money."

"What's more, he will certainly humiliate you," Levi Isaac added. "You cannot let your honor be offended in such a way."

Yet Shneur Zalman insisted, and so his friends decided to accompany him in order to ensure that at least if he did not receive the money he would not be offended in some grievous fashion. The miser received them graciously, poured them drink, served them food, and made pleas-

ant conversation with them—until, that is, they ask him for a contribu-
tion to the fund for the young couple's start in life.

"You want money from me?" the miser declared gruffly. "Well, then,
I will give you something!"

Shneur Zalman's eyes lit up, and the other two masters raised their
eyebrows in surprise. The miser went into his study and soon emerged,
holding in his plump pink hand
one dirty old kopek—approxi-
mately the value of a penny. He
threw it at Shneur Zalman.
"Here, take this and be gone!" he
thundered.

> "To be a Kabbalist means
> to be prepared to receive
> what the other has to give,
> at the moment they give it."

Shneur Zalman's two friends
were almost ready to strike the
miser, so seriously had he offended
the honor of their master and col-
league. But Shneur Zalman held up his hand to forestall them. "No, no,
no," he said. He bent down and picked up the dirty kopek, cupping it
lovingly in his hands. 'Thank you, thank you so much, for this contribu-
tion to our fund!" he said to the miser. "I appreciate it."

With these words, Shneur Zalman left the miser's house, the masters
hurrying to follow him. The masters were astonished at Shneur
Zalman's behavior, but before they could protest they heard footsteps
behind them. "Wait!" shouted the angry miser. "I want to give you
more!" Once again, he took a dirty kopek from his pocket and threw it at
Shneur Zalman's feet.

This time Shneur Zalman had to physically restrain his friends, say-
ing, "No, no, no." To their utter bafflement, he bent to pick up the dirty
kopek from the ground, held it gratefully in his hands, and said, "Thank
you, sir! Thank you so much for your contribution. I accept and appre-
ciate it." The two other masters scurried to follow him a few more steps,
and once again the miser overtook them. This time he threw two kopeks
at their feet, for which Shneur Zalman thanked him profusely. This
happened again and again until by the time they had returned to Shneur

*Zalman's home, the miser had given them the entire sum that they
needed.*

*Shneur Zalman's two friends were at a loss for words. "What hap-
pened?" Menachem Mendel stammered.*

*"What did you do?" Levi Isaac asked. "What magic did you work on
this man? What spell did you cast?"*

*"There was no spell and no magic," replied Reb Shneur Zalman. "I
am a Kabbalist," he said, "and to be a Kabbalist means to be prepared to
receive what the other has to give, at the moment they give it."*

Consider this tale a veiled Kabbalistic critique of the Cain and
Abel story. Cain may not have been perfect, but God needed to find
a way to receive him—to embrace what he could offer at that
moment—even while inviting him to reach higher. That is the
essence of knowing how to receive. So often, we're unable to
receive because we want precisely what the other is unable to give.
How often in an argument, after both sides have hurled anger,
insult, even accusation, do things settle down, and one person turns
to the other with a tentative apology? Somehow the tentativeness of
the apology is insufficient for the other person and he flares up, saying, "After everything you've said, that's what you give me for an
apology? That's all you have to say?" The cycle of mutual recrimi-
nation and anger begins again. Indeed, all that the other person was
able to give at that moment was a tentative apology. In accepting it,
a different dynamic would have been introduced, a dynamic of
receiving could have escalated into full mutual apology, full rapprochement, and full embrace.

If you require a particular kind of apology, for example, and
don't receive it, then you will reject the other. If your need is for a
particular kind of friendship and that need isn't met, then you might
reject the other. The inability to accept what the other has to share *at
the moment he or she has it to offer* is ultimately one of the great
tragedies of our lives.

To receive another requires that you be able, for a time, to let go
of yourself. Receiving arises from your capacity to bracket your

needs—that is, to suspend them, to put them aside, and thus fully engage in the act of receiving the other. Indeed, this is precisely what each one of us needs from those people who are close to us. To receive is the most intimate and perhaps the only gift that is truly ours to give. When we put ourselves to the side for a time, we can be fully engaged in receiving the feelings, faults, and soul print of the face before us.

Soul Print Practice

When you accept a gift from a child—for instance, your daughter gives you a trinket of a necklace—you adore the gift not for its beauty but because of the beauty of the person who gave it, and the beauty of their act of giving.

When you receive a gift from another, try not to receive it from the adult whom you want to meet all of your expectations, but receive it from the child within them—the one you accept unconditionally.

A MASTER FROM JERUSALEM

A great mystical master lives today in Jerusalem. He is referred to as the master from Omshinov, after the Russian town from which his family immigrated. You can only see the Omshinover, as people call him, in the late hours of the night, at three, four, or five A.M. He is said to be beyond time. His assistant calls some twenty-five minutes before he's ready to see you, and you drive to his home to receive an audience. Based on the stories I've heard and from my own encounter with him, it is not completely clear that the Omshinover offers any great pieces of advice, insight, intuition that couldn't be gotten with less trouble elsewhere. Why, then, do people travel at all hours of the night from all over Israel, to visit the master of Omshinov?

I think the reason lies in the way he receives his guests. During the entire time in which you are in his presence, he is fully focused on your face. For the forty-five minutes I sat with him, he was absolutely intent upon me. His eyes did not waver. Not only did he refrain from looking at his watch, but it was clearly apparent that the only thing he was thinking about were the words I was saying. For him in that moment, my utterances were the most important thing in the entire world. When I left, I didn't take with me any great advice or a solution to the particular problem that I had brought to him. However, I did leave feeling fully received, and somehow that itself was the answer.

Tzadok the Priest of Lublin, an important nineteenth-century European holy man, taught that every human being is a secret. We all suffer the inability to communicate the mysteries that are within us to the uninitiated listener. To be initiated is to know the art of being fully present to receive the secret of another human being. Tzadok's concept becomes clearer when we consider its opposite— that ritual of society, the cocktail party. No one is really listening, and our soul prints all too often remain mute and invisible. To achieve the healing and transformation the world craves so deeply, we must all become initiates practicing the mystical Kabbalah of receiving in the temples of our daily lives.

BIBLICAL LEVADO MYTHS

Biblical myth is a gateway to untold depths of spiritual dimensions. As with every portal, in order to get through the gates you need the right keys. Over the years, I have developed a few devices to help me get past those locks. Whenever I approach a biblical text, I have learned always to carry a pocketful of key words. I believe these key words signal unique genres that weave throughout the text.

The biblical myths that focus on the key word *levado* lay the foundation for our work in *Soul Prints*. As I have sought ways to talk from a biblical perspective about how we can move from loneliness to soul print consciousness, I've uncovered a heretofore over-looked genre of biblical myth—what I call the *levado* myth. *Levado,* as we remember, is the Hebrew word for "lonely." Recall the regally set table of Genesis chapter 1, where God lavishly bestows material abundance, aesthetic enjoyment, and sensual fulfillment upon humankind, which God declared good. Yet, all of these "good" gifts prove to be of little value in the face of God's radical declaration that human loneliness is *not* good. The word *levado* single-handedly nullifies the good of creation and encapsulates an essential experience of existence. Thus, when that unusual word *levado* pops up in other biblical texts, it invariably signals a story that can deepen our understanding of loneliness and soul prints. Indeed, every one of the biblical *levado* myths is focused on one or more of the three moves from loneliness to loving—soul print receiving, believing, and communicating. These stories constitute what we will call the biblical *levado* myth.

The first *levado* story, which we have already studied together, is the story of the creation of relationships, as introduced in Genesis by God's declaration, "It is not good for man to be alone." The second and third stories arise from pivotal scenes in the lives of Jacob and Moses. In the fourth *levado* story, we will investigate a narrative where God himself experiences loneliness, uncovering what it might mean for God to be lonely—and how our soul prints might receive God's.

ACHING TO SHARE A SOUL PRINT

Jacob features in our second *levado* story. Jacob—later to be renamed Israel—is the son of Isaac and Rebecca, husband of Rachel and Leah, father of twelve sons and a daughter, and one of the more complex characters of biblical myth. He is also one of the most lonely. For as the Bible tells us, "Jacob was left *levado.*" Usually translated as "Jacob was left alone," we better understand it as, "Jacob was lonely." This phrase—and this translation of it—

matters to us, because Jacob's story conveys to us important wisdom about loneliness, soul print, and how we live our lives.

Where is Jacob at this point in his life? What is the backdrop for the drama of his loneliness? He is returning home to Canaan after twenty years in the foreign land of Padan Aram, home of his uncle Laban. Twenty years earlier, while still a young man, Jacob fled his home in Canaan, fearing the wrath of his big brother, Esav. Esav indeed had good reason to be angry, for Jacob, in an act of undeniable deception, had stolen from him the blessing of their father, Isaac—a blessing originally intended for Esav, the firstborn. We all seek the blessing of the father, sometimes so desperately do we want it that we engage in deception in order to receive it. This is the web that Jacob is wrapped in, the tangle of treachery that has led him far from home.

Over twenty years of exile, Jacob develops, matures. He comes home ready to unravel the web of his past, to reconcile with his brother, Esav. Yet, there is great suspense in the story. Will Jacob be able to receive the blessing that belongs uniquely to him and leave to Esav the blessing that is his? Blessing in biblical myth is more than the transmission of good wishes or spiritual protection. Blessing, particularly the blessing of the father, is a soul print expression. Each child is granted his own blessing, reflecting his unique destiny. For Jacob to steal Esau's blessing is the ultimate soul print violation.

> We often seek to receive the blessing of another because somehow we feel that our own soul print is incomplete, that our own story is not enough.

We often seek to receive the blessing of another because somehow we feel that our own soul print is incomplete, that our own story is not enough. When we are unable to feel deeply our own enoughness, we are driven to take the blessing of another. That is what is happening to Jacob.

Come daybreak, Jacob will meet Esav. Has Esav matured, has Esav developed, will Esav be able to forgive him? How does Esav remember the history between them? Images of his home wash over Jacob like the flow of the River Jabok at his feet. The images are of his mother and father, their complex relationship, the day of his deception, and a thousand other days of innocence and wonder. He sees flashes of his youth with Esav, running together through their father's vast fields, swimming in the brooks and streams of Canaan, twin brothers laughing and playing. These memories tease him with the chance they might spring back to life come sunrise.

A new family, two wives, concubines, twelve sons, a daughter, hordes of grandchildren, and an intense entourage of servants and their families surround Jacob. All that in twenty years! However— and this is the key to our story—his wives, children, indeed his whole household, know only the Jacob of Padam Aram, the land of his exile. They know only Jacob's exiled self. None of them know Jacob the child; none of them had ever met Esav, or Isaac or Rebecca. They do not recognize Jacob *levado*—they do not know Jacob in his loneliness.

On the night before meeting Esav, despite all of his attempts to explain to his loved ones the complexity of his childhood—what made him run and what moved him so to return—Jacob remains alone. He is unable to share with those closest to him the unique experiences of his youth. He sends his caravans before him and stays on the other side of the River Jabok alone, to sleep in the shadow of his loneliness, to be inconsolably *levado*. It is at this point that the text says "Jacob was left alone," Jacob was lonely. He is unable to transmit the intimacy of his being, his soul print, to those who share his life, his house, and his bed.

Jacob's *levado* story poignantly supports our definition of loneliness as the inability to share your soul print with someone else. It offers us a crucial *gauge* for soul print receiving, as well as a powerful method for soul print perception and communication. For soul prints are embedded in the folds of childhood. Although your early years don't entirely form your soul print—the soul print, like the fingerprint and DNA, is an inborn quality—your childhood certainly has a powerful impact on how your soul print unfolds in the world. That being the case, revisiting childhood usually provides a crucial lens for soul print perception. Your childhood may be the most transparent window to your soul print. It is almost always true that reconnecting with your childhood will reconnect you with your soul print.

Besides being a key in soul print perception, returning to the early scenes of your life is also a wonderful method for soul print communication. If you are having trouble sharing who you are today with a close friend or partner, try talking about who you were yesterday—your childhood. You don't need to start with the profound moments.

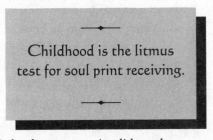

Childhood is the litmus test for soul print receiving.

Talk about the details. What comic books or mysteries did you love to read? Where was your favorite place to hide? Who was your best friend? Were you afraid of the dark?

Finally, as in the Jacob story, childhood is the litmus test for soul print receiving. If someone else is able to receive your adult self but cannot receive your child self, then you will remain lonely, for your soul print has not been received. Happily, of course, the reverse is true as well; when you are able to share your early years with a partner or friend, that is a signal that something very profound and special is happening. You have a right to feel wonderfully excited and blessed.

THE INTIMACY OF RECEIVING THE SOUL PRINT

I often tell my students that if they want to know whom to marry, marry someone who is able to hear the unique music of their soul. It is only this kind of relationship, with a life partner or even a close friend, that redeems you from loneliness. Almost invariably, a student will ask, "Well, how do I know if she hears my soul's music?" I cannot give a hard and fast answer to that question. However, I do suggest our litmus test. Like the milk maiden's box in the South American myth, or like my son's little treasury of significant items, imagine your life as a great gilded chest—the Soul Print Box of all your days. To make sure you are received, you need to share that Soul Print Box with another.

Some people may have stored their Soul Print Boxes in the attics of their memory, thrown away the key, and dare not even look up the attic stairs. Or some may use their chest as a centerpiece, a coffee table, a precious item on display. Wherever your chest may be, and whatever it may hold, take your friend or prospective partner there, and open up your childhood as if it were a music box. Let your companion dance to its song. If you can share with your beloved friend the unique symphony of your life, in all of its joy and trauma, complexity and simplicity, then you are being heard. The Soul Print Box cannot be full without the important mementos from our early years. In friendship, this is most clearly apparent when we meet the parent of a close friend. As intimately as we thought we knew our friend, our appreciation of his soul print invariably deepens after meeting his mum or dad or visiting the early scenes of his life.

I had such an experience with my wife, Cary, a few months after we married, when a twist of scheduling took us to visit Columbus, Ohio, the city where I grew up. The visit was nothing more than another site on a lecture tour. Having a residual distaste for the place from the not so pleasant years I had spent there as a child, I expected to do my lectures and leave as quickly as possible. Yet the moment we took that turn off Seneca Park Place onto Cassidy Avenue, to the brown brick house that I had lived in with my family till I was thirteen, I felt myself transported back in time. As we walked down street after street, I pointed out to my wife the props of the play of my childhood. In a cinematographic feat of memory, each detail came rushing back to me, as if excited to greet me after so many years away. Each particular was vibrant, emanating meaning. Many were sharp with pain. "That red mailbox there," I told Cary. "Andy Duberstein got grounded for five months for hitting it with his baseball bat. And those gray shutters—they were black, and you should have seen the beautiful girl who lived behind them. And there was a mulberry bush there—they must have cut it down." Finally, we came to the door of my old home, a door behind which lay a storehouse of scenes, so much sweetness, such frustration and pain, so much simple routine. The people who lived there were exceedingly gracious and let us slowly walk through the house undisturbed, room by room. Perhaps they sensed that it was soul print time for us.

"Memory . . . like an old musical box it will lie silent for long years," wrote Thomas Burke. "Then a mere nothing, a tremor, will start the spring, and from beneath its decent covering of dust it will talk to us." That afternoon, memories kaleidoscoped through me, seemingly unimportant details taking on gravity and preciousness I never expected. I was overwhelmed by the realization that if my memory has stored all of these trivial details with such accuracy and precision, then how much more so must it preserve those moments of major impact. If the landscape of Columbus, Ohio, was so deeply ingrained upon my mind's eye, imagine how rooted the spirit-scape of Columbus, Ohio, must be within my soul. I thought of Jacob the night before he met Esav, aching to reencounter the land of his youth, and I was glad I was able to share my past with another.

With the help of Cary's guiding questions, gentle prodding, and fully present witnessing, important gates were opened that day—not just the gate to memory but the gate between our soul prints. For our relationship it was wonderful—it allowed me to share a part of myself with Cary that I had never fully been able to communicate before this trip. It was one of our most beautiful afternoons together.

Soul Print Practice

Make a soul print date with your partner to walk down childhood lane. This can be done by sharing old pictures, memories, and mementos. If you want to get extravagant, make a soul print pilgrimage to the place where you grew up . . . walk your partner through your wondrous past.

Imagine your childhood as a great gilded chest, a Soul Print Box especially focused on childhood scenes. Open it. Visualize its contents, and begin to take them out, one by one, object by object, scene by scene, memory by memory. One particularly powerful visualization is to recall a favorite outfit that you wore, a special blouse or bow tie. Relish each detail.

Now introduce your friend or romantic partner to your childhood Soul Print Box. Create a special time or place where you can be inspired to share the intimacies of your past life. Allow no distractions. Ask some questions of the other person. Fix these memories in your head, discuss them with your friend or partner. What do these memories tell your friend about you? What have you and your friend learned?

Now ask your friend to introduce you to his Soul Print Box. Just as he has received for you, then retrace this process, as your friend opens his intimate treasury to reveal it to you.

FIRST, OWN YOUR LONELINESS

Imagine how Jacob feels as he steps back onto the land of his youth, unable to share the story of his childhood. Not only is he unable to share his soul print—he cannot even share his loneliness. Jacob, according to the mystical readers of biblical myth, remains disconnected from himself until his name is changed to Israel. His name change is an expression of a deeper shift in Jacob's consciousness. The verse "Jacob was left alone" can also be fairly translated from the Hebrew as "Jacob gave up on his loneliness." If your loneliness remains a vague dis-ease you are unable to articulate, it often undermines the possibility of creating true intimacy. Only when you own your loneliness and use it to claim your soul print can you begin to share your soul print with another and receive a soul print in return.

Fortunately, Jacob does the work required to open himself to his loneliness, his soul print, and to the possibility of having it received by others. He performs this work in a wonderful spiritual and startling way. After the text relates Jacob's loneliness, it tells how he wrestles through the night with a mysterious stranger. Who is the stranger? Answers abound. Kabbalists declare that the stranger is Jacob himself. "Strangers are we, errants at the gates of our own psyche," writes contemporary philosopher George Steiner. Jacob emerges from the night with a new name—Israel—which becomes the name of the nation he is destined to found. The powerful point is that Jacob enters the night, symbol of his loneliness—the "nail holes of the board" in the Norwegian legend we related earlier—and wrestles his way from loneliness to singularity, from aloneness to All-Oneness.

Jacob's new name is significant, since name is the outer casing of the soul print. His name becomes Israel—which is really two words, *Yashar El,* translated from the Hebrew as "divine integrity." The point is that by achieving soul print we realize our divine integrity. Integrity derives from the Latin word meaning "to integrate." Jacob has left behind his external name, integrated his loneliness, and transformed it into his realized soul print. In biblical mysticism, this is how one achieves rapture and merges with the divine. As we've already explored, in biblical myth it is by touching your uniqueness that you become part of the One. It is the move from Aloneness to All-Oneness, from loneliness to soul print.

In contrast to later forms of mysticism that would emphasize the need for self-annihilation in order to merge with the One, biblical myth understands the One as the personal divine integrity of the psyche. This occurs not by losing yourself but rather by integrating the pieces of your soul print. You claim your soul print and thereby affirm the integrity of your name. Then you are ready to move forward into sharing your soul print and receiving the soul print of another person.

It is not by accident that according to the reading of the Jacob myth by Renaissance mystic Isaac Luria, Jacob begins to develop an authentic relationship with his wife Leah only after his name is changed to Israel. In the Lurianic reading, Jacob is unable to create a deep relationship with Leah because he is uncomfortable with himself. Only when he realizes his soul print—that is, his Israel nature—can he create genuine relationship with Leah.

> To be intimate with yourself is to know your uniqueness; to be intimate with another is to share your uniqueness.

The intricacies of Hebrew word play deepen our understanding of the soul print receiving between Israel and Leah—and among all of us. As we've seen, *deah* is the template word in Genesis for intimate relations. *Deah* is also the Hebrew word for "opinion." Its meaning, however, transcends the superficial meanings of the English word "opinion"; it refers to the profound perspective on things that wells from a deep self-knowing. *Deah* is also the Hebrew word for "knowledge." But because *deah* also means intimate sexual relationship, to "know" someone in the biblical sense implies the highest intimacy.

It is therefore not an exaggeration to suggest that biblical myth's definition of intimacy is the giving and receiving of the soul print. To be intimate with yourself is to know your uniqueness; to be intimate with another is to share your uniqueness. Carnal knowledge that emerges from soul print sharing is gorgeous, sky-scraping, and holy; whereas carnal knowledge that bypasses the full range of *deah* is often sad—an ill-fated attempt to artificially fill the empty places that lust for more nourishing fare.

6

———◆———

RECEIVING THE UNKNOWABLE
SOUL PRINT

YOU NEVER KNOW

The goal of soul print consciousness is to fully receive the soul print of another through deep understanding and empathy. Yet how often in life are we simply unable to understand one another? Receiving each other becomes next to impossible because of distance, strangeness, hurry, deafness, carelessness, or inevitable difference in the languages of our soul prints. Try as we might, the soul prints of so many people are ultimately unknowable to us—just like the soul print of God.

Are we to give up, or is there a path of receiving that is true even when you cannot fully grasp the soul print of another? Is there a way to receive what seems so unreceivable, whether human or divine? This quandary inspires one of the more subtle ideas of St. Thomas Aquinas, the medieval writer who did so much to define Christianity, and Moses Maimonides, perhaps the most important Jewish philosopher of the last thousand years. Although their formal concern was our connection with God, their idea has important implications for human-to-human soul print receiving as well.

Our task, both wisdom masters assume, is—in some sense—to receive God. As Platonic philosopher Plotinus said, God is the lonely one. In biblical myth God is the protagonist in the third *levado* story. For just as the word *levado* is used to describe Adam and Jacob, it is used to refer to God. God is alone and God is lonely.

You don't have to read much of the Bible, or any other religious document for that matter, to realize that God has a serious soul print communication problem. God's essence—his divine soul print—remains unshared with most of humanity. How can we redeem God from divine loneliness? Clearly, the answer must be in accordance with soul print consciousness: We have to receive the divine soul print. However, for theologians like Aquinas and Maimonides and many others past and present, the very essence of God is his incommunicability. According to these medieval scholars, God is unknowable. In the language of one scholar, "If I knew him I would be him." Aquinas and Maimonides proposed an ingenious solution they called "the affirmation of not knowing"—that is, we recognize God in acknowledging that we do not know him. In the words of one of French writer Edmond Jabes's characters, "I know you, Lord, in the measure that I do not know you."

For years I thought the "affirmation of not knowing" to be a classic example of irrelevant if clever medieval sophistry. Two incidents occurred that changed my mind. The first took place at the small neighborhood grocer around the corner from my house. On a rare stormy day in Jerusalem, I made my way through the rain to the grocer to pick up some essentials for my bad-weather hibernation. My mood was about as foul as the gust of smoke that greeted me at the door. The source of the noxious fumes, I soon found out, was a swarthy-faced middle-aged man, loitering in *my* corner store! Shirt open to chest, large gold necklace and all, he stood there smoking his nine A.M. cigar. Fanning my way through his smoke, and coughing, I mumbled to the grocer my consternation at the torrential rains that had soaked me through and through.

The man with the gold necklace turned and looked at me—I promise—with the gentlest look you could possibly imagine. All of his features suddenly appeared handsome and majestic. The gold necklace seemed regal, the smoke sweet as an incense offering. "Don't you know," he said, "it's raining today because a holy man has gone to his world."

I felt like some gate had swung open inside of me. Something in my heart went soft—I just wanted to reach out and hug him for being so beautiful. It was an epiphany moment pure and simple. Only later when I got home and read the paper did I see that one of Jerusalem's great mystics had in fact died that morning—the Rebbe of Gur, a Hasidic master and leader of a thriving community with origins in the Eastern European town of Gur, a community that had been virtually wiped out during the Holocaust. This master had slowly, painstakingly, and with endless love, passion, and daring, rebuilt his community in Israel over the past forty years. The world felt so much darker without him.

If I said that I thought the man with the cigar and the gold necklace was an angel, I would be taking the easy way out. Indeed, he was not an angel but flesh and blood. And I had totally misjudged him. I thought him to be a boor—coarse and crass, involved only in his immediate needs. However, the shining beauty and Zen-like understanding on his face as he told me that a holy man had died, let me know how superficial my vision had been. I had assumed I knew him, and I had not truly known him at all. I had not received him.

The words of a modern spiritual singer, Shlomo Carlebach, flashed through my mind: "You Never Know—You Never Know—You never know." The intent of the refrain is the need to acknowledge that we never really can be certain of the nature of the person standing before us. That is precisely what Aquinas was saying about the lonely God. It is true we cannot understand God. But whether we are relating to God or to a human who is an intimate or a near-stranger, we can get to the end of all knowing—that is, the acknowledgment that we do not know.

We know that one major soul print danger is the temptation to judge, label, categorize, dismiss, or otherwise try to put another person in a box. People in boxes threaten us less. Instead, we must seek to receive another's soul print, even as we are aware that the other remains mysterious to us, ultimately unknowable, just like God. We are called to honor the soul print by gently saying to ourselves, "You Never Know—You Never Know—You never know."

TO KNOW YOU DON'T KNOW

Here is the second incident that made me come to accept the truth in my not-knowing. One Friday night in Jerusalem, I was the keynote speaker at a conference hosted by the Israeli government for all the editors of Jewish newspapers in the world. I had just arrived back in Israel from a lecture in San Francisco and was exhausted. Anyone who has ever been that tired knows that it is something like being drunk. When you're drunk, you go high or you go low. That night I went high. Speaking to the editors, I first taught them a song, then lectured for a while, drank a toast, sang another song, and then lectured and drank another toast and sang once more.

It was a truly beautiful evening and seemed like a strong and effective presentation, or so I thought. Truth is, it looked like everybody else thought so too. That is, except for one guy who sat in the third row—writing. Now I am a liberal Orthodox rabbi and I would never impose my Sabbath observance laws (which preclude writing) on anyone. Nevertheless, to write so openly despite the unspoken understanding that the Sabbath mood should be maintained, at least in the public spaces of the confer-ence, seemed a bit strange. What really made me crazy is that I was spilling my heart out giving this lecture and he was just sitting there in the third row, writing. The chutzpah!

By the time I ended my lecture, the man had succeeded in thoroughly annoying me. It was clear he was a superficial, self-involved journalistic bureaucrat. Surely, I thought, here was a symbol of the tepid, insipid sort of religiosity I was dedicated to overthrowing through spiritual revolution. Before I left the hall I sought him out, thinking to give him at least an oblique reprimand of sorts.

To my surprise, he greeted me with tears in his eyes. Before I had a chance to make a fool of myself, he said, "Please look at what I have written." He showed me sheet after sheet of musical notes. I cannot read a note of music and had no idea what this was about. Then, speaking English with a thick Bulgarian accent, he declared, "I have been the editor of a paper in Bulgaria for only a few months now. I got the job by chance. I have had nothing to do with the community. Since I was six years old, I have not heard a Jewish song . . . until you sang tonight. Something happened as you sang. I promised myself never to forget the songs of my people. But how to remember? So, I wrote down every note that you sang. I will sing them for the rest of my life." He smiled at me with fierce gratitude. "Thank you. I have come home."

I just stared at him, my heart too full, and my face too red, even to speak. I had spent the previous week in the United States lecturing on Kabbalah. I realized, sadly, that on this night I had not been a Kabbalist. I had not received him. My judgment of him had barreled past the truth of his soul print. The musical refrain of the spiritual folksinger kept playing in my mind: "You Never Know— You Never Know—You never know."

To acknowledge that you do not truly know another's soul print is to resist the siren's call to reduce that person to a box or a label. To know how much you don't know the other is sometimes the holiest act of receiving the other.

There are all sorts of ways to say "you never know." Sometimes you can redeem others from loneliness just by acknowledging them—by remembering their name or recognizing their face.

Soul Print Practice

Next time you pass someone in the street that you recognize but don't know well, don't turn the other way or look straight ahead or use your cell phone to avoid greeting him. Do just the opposite—clearly recognize your acquaintance, share the pleasure of seeing a familiar face, and if you don't know his name, ask gently.

One of the models for receiving without fully understanding is in biblical myth's response to an "open hand." An "open hand" is how biblical myth refers to the poor person on the street whose hand is open to receive your gift. Although most of us are not begging on the street with an open hand, are we not all pleading with an exposed and vulnerable heart to be received?

Always fill an open hand. When a person puts out an open palm to you, see it and remember the lines of her soul print.

Whenever you encounter a person with his hand extended for money, don't try to calculate, "Does he really need it, or doesn't he? Does he deserve it or not deserve it?" Admit the fact that you cannot fully know. There is a tradition of the Kabbalah that says if you give without checking too carefully whether the recipient "truly deserves it," then God may give to you without checking whether *you* "truly deserve it." Never walk by without giving something. Take notice of what happens to you when you close your heart and prevent yourself from giving. Pay attention . . . feel the constriction of your heart. Your heart has been attacked.

Don't label people or put them in boxes.

One way to see through a person's present circumstance to her soul print is to imagine her as a laughing baby. This image is a wonderful means for connecting to her soul print.

The next time you find yourself judging, boxing, or reducing someone else to a label, say to yourself, "You never know." These three words remind us that there is so much we do not know about other people, whose soul prints are sometimes too hidden for us to see. Pick a "you never know" melody. Use it like a mantra that permeates your consciousness. Whenever you are about to judge someone, let the melody mantra play in your mind.

Biblical myth law tells us that even when we are in the midst of the highest meditation on divinity—the *Shema* meditation—we must interrupt the rapture in order to greet a passerby. We greet them with the word *Shalom,* which, like the Thai greeting *Namaste,* is an affirmation of the God within the other. *Shalom* literally means peace, wholeness, or harmony. It is also one of the names of God as well as being a biblical greeting. In the Kabbalistic understanding of language, all meanings converge to convey a wider intent. *Shalom* thus means, "The divine point within me greets the divine point within you."

True, two people saying *"shalom"* to each other may not have fully received each other's soul prints. Certainly, they do not fully understand each other. Indeed, they may barely know each other. Yet through this point of human contact, the loneliness between the two of them is abated. For in the greeting *shalom* lies a kind of receiving. *Shalom* gives voice to this recognition—that you, the one I greet, have a wonderful and glorious soul print even if I have not yet been privileged to receive it in understanding. There is a level of receiving in the recognition itself. Thus the *shema,* the meditation on divinity, is interrupted to acknowledge a higher divinity, the soul print of the passerby.

Imagine you are standing by yourself in Times Square on New Year's Eve. The ball is about to drop. Surrounded by boisterous strangers, you feel terribly alone. Then someone taps you on your shoulder. You recognize each other, and you exchange greetings. The loneliness you felt has instantly been transformed into connection. Because of the initial experience of isolation, the connection is even more precious.

TO RECEIVE THE FACE OF A STRANGER

The basis of the law requiring one to interrupt rapture to give greeting is nowhere explicitly stated in the Bible. I believe its source is a stunning biblical myth vignette about Abraham and his guests. Abraham, the first hero of biblical myth, is the image of Plato's philosopher king—a powerful force in affairs of state whose major passion is for truth. In later Christian, Islamic, and Jewish traditions, Abraham becomes the first great spiritual master. In the text, God appeared to Abraham as he was sitting—perhaps in lotus position?—at the entrance to his tent. Abraham saw three strangers approach and said, "Wait a second, God, I have guests," and ran to greet the strangers.

The way the myth masters read this story, Abraham is in the midst of a meditation on the Godhead. No common activity. In the middle of rapture, he sees some strangers nearing. He breaks his meditation,

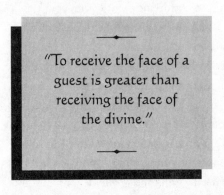

"To receive the face of a guest is greater than receiving the face of the divine."

says to God, "Don't go away—I'll be back soon," and goes to greet the visitors, inviting them to sit and have a drink with him. It is a pretty wild description. Can you imagine how you would respond if, in the middle of merging with the divine, you hear the doorbell? Could you see yourself saying, "Hey, God, hold on for a second, I have to get the door. There may be strangers there and I want to greet them and maybe even invite them in for a drink"?

Strange, indeed. One fourth-century Babylonian wisdom master explains Abraham's strange behavior with a startling and wonderful epigram: "To receive the face of a guest is greater than receiving the face of the divine."

Sometimes we greet a stranger without words and with no prior recognition of his face. Some of my best friends are people I will never talk to. They are people with whom I have exchanged a knowing look or a meaningful glance, in a crowded bus, in the market, or on a street corner. Although we do not know each other in any conventional way, in every one of those moments, I feel my soul print fully affirmed—fully recognized—even as it remains fully hidden.

Soul Print Practice

After shaking hands, Sephardic Jews have a tradition of kissing their own hand (as if kissing the trace of the person that lingers on their skin). Buddhists put their palms together and bow, saying *"Namaste"*: "The god within me welcomes the god within you."

Develop a receiving gesture for when you greet another person, whether it be a tip of the hat, a slight bow, or the placement of your hands upon your heart.

If such a gesture doesn't work for you, then try "the two-handed shake": When you shake someone's hand, shake with both hands, so that the shake turns into more of a split-second hold.

Remember, a good image for the soul print is the hand print. The next time you grasp someone's hand, remember that it can be either a mere formality or an opportunity for soul print connection. Imagine that as you receive the other's hand, he is allowing you, for a brief second, to touch his soul print. When people say, "I liked him from the first handshake," they are not referring to firmness of grasp but to an authentically felt moment of soul print connection.

Practice hospitality: Open doors in all directions.

The biblical hero of hospitality, Abraham, had a tent that was open to all four directions, welcoming wayfarers from all sides, of all sorts, at all times. In like manner, make a point of welcoming people from all different directions, from all sides of the social spectrum, from all faiths, all races, and all personality types.

When my wife, Cary, was a kid, one of her favorite stops in the neighborhood was the home of the Usdan family. People entering their house were greeted by a glass container filled to the brim with M&Ms. To her child eyes (and probably to her adult eyes as well), it was like an invitation to joy—a wonderful way to be welcomed in. So at our wedding when we received from the Usdans an identical glass container full of M&Ms, Cary's eyes filled with tears. Those M&Ms were much more than candies; they represented the art of receiving guests. Cary understood that the Usdans had passed over to us the gift of giving itself.

Food is a crucial element of hospitality. Always have some delectable on hand for an unexpected visitor. (If chocolates are a bit too much of a temptation for you, have a healthy alternative, like baby carrots, fruit, or nuts.)

Honor comings and goings: When people walk through your door, be a door chime; let your voice of welcome be the first sound that greets them.

There is a biblical tradition of escort. Walk your guests all the way out. In an apartment building, ride all the way down the elevator with them; in a house, escort them out to the street.

Consider going as far as taking up Abraham's tradition of ritual washing by pouring warm water over the hands (and for the daring, even the feet) of your guests.

BUY FLOWERS, GROW FLOWERS

There is something more we can do to receive others when we don't understand them. Something that moves beyond even that awesome acknowledgment, "You never know." We are called upon to perform little deeds—something, anything, that involves concrete action to honor the absolutely incredible and incomprehensible person in front of us. "Do something!" From the Bible to the Talmud to the Kabbalah, this refrain is one of the most powerful and important in biblical myth.

Get up and do something. For example, the old chivalry of buying flowers for someone—for your beloved or for anyone whose soul print remains elusive or somehow unknowable to you—can be no less important and sometimes more powerful than doing in-depth soulwork together. Flowers do not say, "I understand you." Rather they say, "Maybe I can't count all the colors, sights, and symbols that fill your Soul Print Box. Maybe I can't connect with your childhood dreams and fears. But I can honor them, because I honor you. And I promise not to make trinkets of them, not to trivialize, label, or categorize them."

The act of sending the flowers says, "I receive you through a small symbolic act of giving—even if I don't always have the tools to fully understand you." In the end, the understanding comes. You are no longer receiving an unknowable stranger but a beloved and mysterious friend.

A wonderful book called *Phoenix* contains a powerful story about how psychotherapist Milton Erickson understood and utilized the inordinate value of the little act of giving flowers. The book is about a pilgrimage of sorts undertaken by the authors, David Gordon and Meridith Meyers-Anderson, to visit the famed psychotherapist Milton Erickson at his home in Phoenix, Arizona. Erickson was the world's foremost authority on the utilization of trance states in therapy. His credentials, accomplishments, and contributions to the psychological world are stellar. In addition to all of this—or rather, at the source of all this—he was a soul of great depth, not that dissimilar from those we have been calling "myth masters." At age seventeen, Erickson was paralyzed by poliomyelitis and not expected to survive. His tenacity and strength of perception saved him. By concentrating on the slightest movement and how it was made, he laboriously learned how to move again, and built up his strength. Before going to college, he took a solo canoe trip down and back up the Mississippi River. Though his life's landscape was marred by attacks of pain and physical suffering, he managed to continue to write rigorously, teach, and help countless numbers of people. He applied his tenacity and Herculean strength of perception to his therapy. He was constantly adventuring over water and land, but especially through the human psyche.

Erickson's methods of psychotherapy very much resonate with the concept of the soul print. He approached each person in the belief that no two people are alike. In his words, "No two people understand the SAME sentence the same way, and so in dealing with people you try not to fit them to YOUR concept of what they should be. . . . You should try to discover what THEIR concept of themselves happens to be. . . ." Or as this book would put it, each person has a unique soul print. In dealing with people, you must seek to identify and receive their soul print as it is, not as you would have it be.

For Erickson, true interactions occur when you receive people "on their level," in accordance with their unique soul print. This belief translated into some of the most ingenious and effective therapy ever. He never developed a theory of psychotherapy or human nature. "Ever since I don't know how long, psychiatrists and psychologists have been devising theoretical schemes, disciplines of psychotherapy," he would say. "Psychiatrists have ALWAYS been propounding schools of psychotherapy. I think Freud did the worst job. Now, Freud contributed very greatly to the understanding of human behavior and he did a great disservice to the utilization of understanding human behavior. He developed a hypothetical school of thought that could be applied, according to Freud, to ALL people, of ALL ages, male or female, young or old, ALL degrees of education, in ALL cultures. . . ." It was for this reason that Erickson

never developed a theory of psychotherapy beyond his basic principle—that you receive each individual as a *unique* individual.
Erickson was a soul print therapist.

Erickson understands the biblical myth idea that *to give to
another is to receive another,* which in the end allows you—sometimes for the first time—to receive yourself. All this is accomplished with an awareness of our mutual mystery and unknowabil-
ity. In the following story taken from *Phoenix,* Erickson writes of
human uniqueness and mystery in action.

*Once while I was in Milwaukee, lecturing, a friend asked me, "My
mother's sister lives in Milwaukee. She is independently wealthy, very
religious, she doesn't like my mother and my mother doesn't like her ...
she stays alone in that big house, goes to church, has no friends there. She
just attends church and silently slips away. And she's been horribly
depressed for nine months. I'm worried about her and I'd like you to stop
in and do something for her. I'm the only relative she has that she likes
and she can't stand me. So call on her and see what you can do."*

*So, a depressed woman ... I introduced myself and identified myself
thoroughly ... asked to be taken on a tour of that house. In looking
around I saw she was a very wealthy woman living alone, idle, attending
church but keeping to herself, and I went through the house room after
room ... and I saw three African violets and a potting pot with a leaf in
it being sprouted as a new plant. So I knew what to do for her in the way
of therapy. I told her, "I want you to buy every African violet plant in
view for yourself ... those are yours. I want you to buy a couple hundred
potting pots for you to sprout new African violets, and you buy a couple
hundred gift pots. As soon as the sprouts are well rooted, for every birth
announcement you send an African violet; for every Christening; for
every engagement; for every wedding; for every sickness; for every death;
every Church bazaar." And one time she had two hundred African violets ... and if you take care of two hundred African violets you've got a
day's work cut out.*

*And she became the African Violet Queen of Milwaukee with endless
numbers of friends.*

It is not enough to say it; you need to do the deeds. There are many ways to buy flowers—or to encourage that as-yet unknown other to grow flowers, the way Erickson did. Leave behind notes. Cook dinner. Buy silly presents. Buy not-silly presents. Pick out great birthday cards, anniversary cards, get well cards, congratulations cards, no-occasion cards. (Better yet, make your own cards.) Imitate that great modern prophet, Stevie Wonder, and call for no purpose but to say I love you. For in the end, doing some little loving deed—for no reason other than the loving—gets the most done.

To be able to honor a soul print that you can't understand but are committed to, you need to move beyond words into the thousand little details of living. Is that the end of the story? No, it is not. The ultimate goal of receiving will be to understand deeply the soul print proffered to you. But the affirmation and recognition of another in all the ways we have just described is the surest path toward moments of full soul print sharing. And since, practically, you cannot fully receive every soul print that crosses your path, the expressions of honor and affirmation in little deeds and "you never know" moments go a long way toward moving our whole culture from loneliness to loving.

Love loves details.

Love loves details.

KEEPING GOD'S SOUL PRINT ALIVE

God is in the details too. As the Kabbalah teaches us, it is not enough to enter the cloud of God-unknowing through words alone. We need to do special things to honor God's unknowable soul print, for without our deeds God dies.

It is the turn of the last century, on the Lower East Side of Manhattan. A family of four live in a single-room flat on Ludlow Street. All day and into the night, mother and father work hard in a sweatshop factory. Every Friday, however, their table is set for a Sabbath meal. Their daughter, Sarah, and her brother go to services with their father, and every Sabbath Papa brings home a guest to share in the Sabbath meal. Now Sarah knows that they do not have much to eat and that the presence of the guest means less food for everyone. "Why, Papa?" she asks.

"It is written—charity saves from death," her father answers.

One day Papa comes back from the sweatshop alone. "Mama is sick," he says. For several long days, Papa goes every night to the two flats that serve as the makeshift hospital for the families of Ludlow Street. When Sabbath eve comes, Sarah takes her brother to services. She doesn't know it, but at dusk, her mother breathes her last.

Sarah dutifully brings home a guest for the Sabbath meal she has prepared. Long after the guest has left and Sarah and her brother have gone to sleep, she awakens to see her father weeping, sitting in a corner of the room. Sarah comes and sits on his lap. "Don't worry, Papa," she says. "Mama will get better."

He stares at her blankly. "What do you mean?"

"Mama will get well," Sarah says. "I went to services, Papa, and I brought home a guest for the Sabbath meal, and you always told me charity saves from death."

Papa smiles sadly. "My little one, you misunderstood. Charity does not save Mama from death. Charity saves God from death."

Erich Fromm talked about the little death of loneliness we all can suffer. So it is with divine loneliness. God dies a little death when we are unable to receive him.

Yet we cannot receive God because he is so unknowable! Trying to receive him is like fitting the entire sea into a seashell. As early-twentieth-century American poet Hilda Doolittle, better known as HD, wrote:

> but infinity? no,
> of nothing-too-much:
> I sense my own limit,
> my shell-jaws snap shut

We can acknowledge and honor God. We can even hum "you never know" with all the harmony of our souls. But we finite beings cannot fully receive the infinite.

So what can we do?

We can bring God flowers. Spontaneous and premeditated acts of kindness, little and large acts of caring, bring divinity to life in the details.

Meir Ibn Gabbai, one of the most important Kabbalists of the sixteenth century, introduced a critical term into Kabbalistic consciousness: *Avoda Tzorech Gavoha,* "God needs our service."

> We can bring God flowers. Spontaneous and premeditated acts of kindness, little and large acts of caring, bring divinity to life in the details.

But isn't God by definition beyond any sort of dependency—at least according to the Jews, Christians, Muslims, Buddhists, Hindus, and anyone else you can think of? How could God need our service? How can charity save God from death?

What could that mean? It means that God receives our service. To say "I need you" is to open yourself to receive an offering. The greatest gift you can give to a significant other is to receive an act of love. Remember the hundred-year-old woman we met in Jerusalem who allowed her husband to tie her shoe? In his small act of service, he received her. She received him in accepting his service. "Charity saves God from death" means that our giving is our receiving of the divine soul print. "God needs our service" means that God accepts and thereby gives, affirming our human adequacy, worth, and dignity.

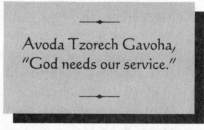

Avoda Tzorech Gavoha, "God needs our service."

True, we cannot fully receive the lonely God through understanding. However, we can acknowledge and love God by performing little deeds that declare "you never know." "We receive you in love," we can say to God. "We know that you are beautiful even though we don't fully understand you."

We express that receiving in little deeds of relationship to God. What deeds does God need most? What deeds show God that we have received him even without completely understanding him?

I have to say here that I never understood the Kabbalah's answer to this question until I had kids. Two of my children, Eitan and Yair, are boys close in age. As brothers, they both love each other deeply and fight with each other vociferously. One day while we were visiting in Florida, after a particularly bruising fight, they each came to make up with me—for I was mad at them for fighting. "Do you know what makes *Abba*"—Hebrew for "Dad"—"feel the happiest, the most loved?" I asked them.

"No, what?" Eitan and Yair asked, in their best make-up-with-*Abba* voices.

"When you love each other," I answered.

The boys grew quiet, thinking deeply about what they'd heard. Then Yair turned and gazed up at me. *"Abba,* I think that's what it means when we say God is our mother and father. It means that God is happiest and feels most loved when we love each other."

Wow! This was one of those moments of strange and beautiful sense. My sons and I realized that a great truth had just been spoken through us.

That night I was giving a guest lecture on theology to a local church group. You can guess what I talked about. Everyone was appropriately blown away—that is, except for one person. He stood up, clearly agitated. "God needs us? What a crazy idea! Didn't they teach us that God was perfect? Lacking nothing!"

Of course it doesn't take an advanced degree in physics to figure out that need implies lack. If you need something, then you're lacking something. How could God have needs? Isn't the whole point of God to be all-powerful? Doesn't God's needing us imply that we wield power over God?

Those are good questions and the Kabbalah certainly does not offer logical answers to them, for Kabbalah is not a logical wisdom; it is rather, a wisdom system that seeks to give voice to our deepest and most visionary knowing. And deep inside of us, we know that a person who doesn't need anyone else is actually less developed, less perfect, and less powerful than a person who has needs, and who can acknowledge those needs.

When I answered the agitated man at the Florida church group, I enlisted the aid of *Rocky.* In Sylvester Stallone's famous movie about the underdog boxer, the underlying spiritual message—and all movies that touch the national heart have a spiritual message of some kind—told us that talent isn't the only variable in life. Rocky is clearly not a better boxer than his opponent Apollo Creed. He has two qualities that are enormously powerful: determination and guts. Even those admirable characteristics are not necessarily enough for him to win. Indeed, the famous, triumphant Rocky music doesn't even start until after a pivotal scene, one that revolves around the parallel drama in the movie.

There is, if you remember, a second battle being waged by

Rocky—for the heart of Adrienne. Adrienne, who loves Rocky, has decided to leave the relationship. Rocky is wonderful and powerful, but he refuses to be vulnerable. At the movie's great turning point, Rocky cries out from the depths of his being. "Aaaaaadddrrriieenne!" He is saying, "Adrienne, I need you! I can't do it without you!"

At that moment, a new sort of power and perfection surges through Rocky. Immediately following we see a transformed Rocky, running, triumphant—and we hear his special music. He has acknowledged need, and he has become more whole. That is the God moment, the soul print moment, in *Rocky*.

The medieval philosophers, had they seen the movie, would have called that a moment of *imatatio dei*—the imitation of God. Rocky, in theological parlance, has become like God. Just as the all-powerful God, in opening himself up to need, becomes paradoxically even more powerful and more complete, so too Rocky, who is powerful, opens himself to need and becomes more powerful and more complete.

The Florida church group responded wonderfully that night. First, they all knew the Rocky theme music and hummed it out at the appropriate points. I promised them then that when I wrote a book I'd put the story in. So, you folks at the Southern Baptist Church in South Florida, thank you for helping to enrich our mutual understanding of our needful, powerful God.

PARTING WORDS OF RECEIVING

Sometimes we go through an entire lifetime being acquainted with certain people without ever being able to acknowledge the "you never know" surprise of receiving their soul prints. They die unreceived by us.

When I was a twenty-year-old rabbinical student, I was asked by a flourishing Manhattan congregation to officiate for the month of August while the other clergy were on vacation. On the second day of my shift, an older, dignified-looking man walked into my office and solemnly asked me to officiate at his wife's funeral that afternoon. Of course, I agreed.

When I walked into the chapel, I was handed a flower. Soon, I realized that everyone who entered received a flower. By the time the sanctuary was full, I thought I had never seen so many flowers in one place in my life. The chapel was bursting with color and fragrance.

Marilyn, the man's wife, had been an artist. Each person who rose to speak of her told of her greatness, her softness, and her talent. Finally, her husband rose to give his eulogy. He spoke poignantly, his voice transparent with grief. He told us how his wife was indeed an artist of great depths—such depths, he admitted, he had never fully reached the bottom of them, had never fully understood them.

He went on to say how she was always hinting to him to buy her flowers. Their aesthetics would inspire her, she told him. He knew the aesthetics she was after was the sight of him with a bundle full of color in his hands. Yet somehow in between his work as an arbitrageur, their great vacations, and their daily life in a penthouse apartment, he never got around to bringing her those flowers. That is, until that last Friday afternoon. He had been walking home, and on a whim, had stopped at the flower stand on the corner. He finally bought her that bouquet. He bounded up the stairs and burst into the house, gallantly ready to present his wife with the gift, but no one was home. After a number of frantic calls and a mad rush to the hospital, he was by her side. She had already slipped into a coma. He stood there holding the flowers. But she couldn't see him.

> Another person's soul print mysteries may be touched with the greatest acts of simplicity.

"All she wanted was flowers," he kept repeating. "All she wanted was flowers."

Another person's soul print mysteries may be touched with the greatest acts of simplicity.

PRESENCE IN ABSENCE

Abraham, the first father of the biblical myth, is married to Sarah. Yet he cannot truly see her. In a beautiful and complex reading suggested by biblical myth reader David Silber, we witness how Abraham gradually loses touch with his wife.

Even Abraham's care for Sarah at the beginning of their marriage is more bound up with what she can do for him than with his seeing her for who she is. His concern for her early on recedes as he becomes more enamored, of his maidservant Hagar and her son Ishmael. While Sarah remains his wife, Abraham believes that his destiny is bound up with Hagar and her son. As is often the case in life, the image of the wrong woman and the wrong destiny clouds a man's view of his life's true worth. Abraham is for a time emotionally estranged from his son, Isaac, and wife, Sarah. In a careful reading of the biblical myth, it becomes clear that while Abraham was able to effect a rapprochement with his son, Isaac, his relationship with Sarah is never fully healed before her death.

It is only upon her death that Abraham realizes what he has lost. For the first and last time in biblical text, Abraham cries as he eulogizes Sarah.

Sometimes we are tragically unable to receive a person in his or her lifetime. Death offers us a last opportunity. The paradox of human nature is that we so very often only experience presence in its absence. "You don't know what you've got 'til it's gone," as Joni Mitchell tells us; you didn't miss the water until the well ran dry. As long as the person was with us, we were unable to be sufficiently present to receive them. Yesterday we could've called, sent flowers, or reached out in so many different ways. Today a virtually untraversible chasm separates us. Yet we feel their presence more acutely than ever.

Biblical myth suggests that the eulogy is our last soul print receiving opportunity. This is because at the time of death, presence in absence is literally a felt reality. The eulogy should not be a glossy finish or a whitewash for a complex and colorful life. Nor should a eulogy be confused with an obituary. Obits often read like the deceased's last desperate attempt to circulate his résumé. Rather, a eulogy should be an attempt to do in death what we are so often unable to do in life—to portray as accurately and lovingly as possible the measure of the person's depths.

The eulogy usually takes place right around the time of burial, when Kabbalistic tradition teaches that the felt reality of the deceased is a reflection of a spiritual reality. Until the burial, we can still communicate easily with the person who has died. Mystically— if you are so inclined—or psychologically, the dead one's soul hovers above the proceeding. It waits, hoping for the last time in this existence to be received by those that person loved most. We ask forgiveness from the dead for not having understood them more fully in their lives. We acknowledge that we were not fully able to receive them. And we try to make amends. We bring flowers to their place of rest. To pay our respects is to honor the soul print.

Soul Print Practice

Is there someone in your life who has passed away whom you feel you were unable to receive while they were alive? There is no statute of limitations on a eulogy.

Write a one-page eulogy. Share with the person what they meant to you. Ask forgiveness for not understanding him or her in life. If you pray, you may want to include the eulogy as part of your prayer. Perhaps you will want to send it to someone who knew them. You may even want to go to the cemetery and leave it at the grave.

Or put it in your own Soul Print Box.

> Do something in someone's memory. On the anniversary of
> his death, light a candle. Give a donation in her name. Organize
> a charity or educational event in her memory.
>
> Now think about the living.
>
> On the anniversary of meeting a special friend, take him or
> her on a soul print date. Write a living eulogy—for *eulogy* itself
> means "good word."

APPLAUDING AN EMPTY STAGE

When I was eighteen or so, my college roommate's uncle died, and
I flew with him to the funeral in New Orleans. His uncle was a
well-known figure in the arts. A group of his friends decided that
he would not have wanted the usual funeral; they invited everyone
to gather at the first theater in which Jonathan had ever performed. There they would sit and tell the stories of his life, in a
final dramatic tribute to their friend.

The stage lights were lit, a chair was set center stage, and the
crowd slowly filled the theater's seats. The dramatic storytelling
went on for some three hours. While I learned a lot about what
Jonathan had done in his life, somehow it didn't work, and everybody knew it. Right as the ritual was about to close, a man who had
been sitting in the shadows, the custodian of the theater, surprised
everyone by asking to speak.

"When I met Jonathan, I was going through a divorce," he said.
"He was usually in a rush, as you all know. But he would always
stop to talk to me and find out how I was doing. I realized he was a
special man. And so I began to watch him."

The custodian went on to tell marvelous stories about Uncle
Jonathan. Stories he had gathered from the dust of his days, the
kind of stories that could only be told by someone who had spent
years picking up the odd change and occasional gems lost in the
corners of the crowds.

Everyone knew the Jonathan of the stage, the one who performed his life with passion, putting the spotlight to good use. But the custodian had studied the Jonathan behind the scenes, the one who worked in the quiet spaces, who walked in the shadows. And these stories from behind the curtain were what caught everyone's souls. They were the real art, the ultimate drama of the extraordinary made ordinary.

When the custodian finished, the room was silent, and then, spontaneously, one by one, everyone stood and applauded. From behind the curtain of life, Uncle Jonathan's voice echoed throughout the theater in the clamor of the applause.

Had someone walked in at that moment, he would have seen what seemed like a group of slightly deranged artists applauding an empty stage. But everyone there knew that the stage was fuller than it had ever been before. Presence in absence.

7

◆

SOUL PRINT CHALLENGES

THE LONELY LEADER

The more intricate the pattern of your soul print—the more difficult it is for it to be understood and received by others. The deeper,
the more nuanced your experience, the fewer people you can share
it with. That is the risk of depth. Yet when a profound soul print
sharing does happen it is all the more powerful and gorgeous. For
example, Moses, a man who was intimately close to his people and
his God, was also lonely, very much *levado*. In order to explore
some of the most complex challenges of soul print receiving, we
take up the tale of Moses, our next *levado* story.

THE LONELINESS OF THE LONG-DISTANCE PROPHET

What great ones do the less will prattle of.
—William Shakespeare, *Twelfth Night*

We begin the Moses *levado* story at the point when Moses feels
overwhelmed by the demands of leadership of his people. In these

early stressful days in the desert, Moses is confronted by his father-in-law, Jethro, who says to him, "It is not good"—*"lo tov"*—that you act *levado* . . . that you judge all the people alone."

Remember the foundational verse with which we began our exploration of the roots of the soul print in the idea of *levado,* where the God of Genesis declares, "It is not good for the human being to be *levado,* alone." Here in the Moses story is the only other place in biblical myth where the signature combination of *lo tov,* "it is not good," and *levado,* "to be alone" or lonely, is found. Apparently, the Moses story has something to add to our understanding of soul prints and how realizing our soul print can help us transcend loneliness and reach connection.

The entire "it is not good/loneliness" story of Genesis is replayed in the life of Moses. Moses, ostensibly the most successful personality in the Bible, is a lonely man. To understand why, we need to construct a vision of just who Moses is in the biblical literary narrative. Moses is certainly a leader, a revolutionary, a visionary. He is a father, a brother, a lover, and a husband also, but, more than any of these, Moses is a prophet. To be a prophet in biblical consciousness means to be possessed of unique spiritual experience. In a sense, the prophet experiences the world in a way that is qualitatively different than the average person. Not because the prophet is intrinsically greater, but because the prophet in biblical tradition has *prepared.* A prophet is one who has spent enormous amounts of time meditating, engaging in ethical action, perfecting his or her moral and rational virtue, in order to become a fitting vessel to receive the energy of prophecy. He or she has reached a different plane of consciousness.

Back when I was a boy, one day in Ms. Sullivan's geometry class I received a slim purple book called *Flatland.* Remarkably, I remember the early spring light cast through the window and exactly where I was sitting in the class. A square and a cube may stand in the exact same spot and see two totally different realities, according to the vistas afforded by their forms. And when they come into contact with one another, they won't necessarily see eye to eye, for their eyes open to different layers of reality.

So it is with the eyes of Moses. They have widened past common sight, allowing him to view the world as if through something like a "prophetscope"—the unique perspective of someone who has ascended the mountain. Moses experiences the world, spiritually, in a way radically different than the rest of his people. He is unable to share his experience of life, his unique vision of the world, his soul print, with the scores of people he encounters daily. He has realized his soul print to such a degree that he has left most of the world behind. Imagine, like a thumbprint upon a too small scrap of paper, a soul print that extends so far that it simply stretches beyond the sheet of reality. The paper can only pick up a portion of the print, leaving long lines unrecorded, unmet.

But there were other prophets at the time, you may argue, other people with long-lined soul prints. Couldn't they form a community of prophets, have colloquia or group therapy, share their secrets over aperitifs? Indeed, in Moses' day both Aaron and Miriam, his sister and brother, were prophets as well. And not only they but the community of seventy sages also experienced prophecy. Moses, however, is described by the text as the master of prophecy. Moses is the ultimate prophet. He has a unique experience of the spirit, unmatched by any other prophet of his day. While that may seem like a wonderful and astounding accomplishment, it can also be a profound burden, for it leaves Moses enormously lonely. He has climbed the stellar heights but stands there alone in splendid, but painful, isolation. The distance that greatness creates produces the greatest glory and the greatest pain.

Moses can't even share his vision of the world with his sister Miriam or with his brother Aaron. True, they are also prophets, but the nature of their experience is so fundamentally different from his that they are unable to grasp what he is going through. Moses lives in a reality that he's unable to share with anyone else. It is in that sense that the words "it is not good to be lonely" are uniquely applied only to Moses in the biblical text.

The Moses experience is not limited to Moses. In the language of the Kabbalists, there is a *Bechinat Moshe*—a Moses quality—in each of us.

Moses represents the radical uniqueness and singularity of human being-hood. Although demarcated by greatness, by vision, depth, and authenticity, his experience also engenders intense and powerful loneliness. If, as we said, every soul quality has its own potential shadow, then the potential shadow of singularity is loneliness. Often we can feel a powerful desire to abandon our singularity, thinking that it will be what enables us to "be with you." Every one of us has a unique arena of our life where "vision is true"— where we see heaven just a little clearer than the next guy. Early on in life when we try to share our unique "view of heaven," it is often rebuffed, ignored, or ridiculed. Our view of heaven might be a particular talent, understanding, or proclivity that expresses itself in a fully unique way in our being. It is our Moses dimension. It is our soul print. The Moses *levado* story invites us to take the risk and be faithful to our highest selves, to our realized soul print. In the end, it is only by living our soul print that we become people worthy of being loved—of being "there with you."

PRAY FOR ME

The second appearance of the *levado* word in the Moses story is when Moses gives his farewell speech as his people are about to cross the Jordan and enter the Promised Land without him. Moses says, "I said to you at that time I cannot myself, alone, carry you." Again, that key word, *levado*. Simply read, the text shows Moses giving his farewell oration, reviewing and commenting on his leadership. Moses is thought to be referring to that earlier time in his life that we just finished discussing, when he had what today's business consultants would call a severe time management problem. His load was too large for the length of his arms. He needed to learn to delegate responsibility. In stepped his father-in-law, Jethro, who had a knack for management. Jethro developed a new organizational flow-chart—a system that would form the basis of our modern judiciary.

This is a fair reading as far as it goes. It is insensitive, however, to the unique flavor of the word *levado* and its aura of existential loneliness. Mystical master Mordechai Lainer of Ishbitz suggests, based on the usage of the *levado* word by Moses, that there is a double meaning in Moses' speech—a subtle undercurrent of enormous poignancy, pathos, and even pain. On the second level of meaning, Moses is saying, "When you got into trouble, I prayed for you, interceded for you. I was your advocate as well as your adversary. I never left you alone. You sinned with the Golden Calf; you sinned when you refused to enter the Land. You fell time and again. But I did not leave you alone."

In the stories Moses mentions, those of the Golden Calf and the refusal to enter the Land, God was provoked to such great anger that he wanted to leave the people behind in the desert and take Moses and his family alone to the Promised Land. Yet Moses repeatedly interceded for the people, arguing, "No, God, I understand these people; you've got to understand them also. Give them another chance. Let them enter the Land you have promised. For if you won't forgive and guide these people, then erase me from your book. If you don't take them, I'm not going."

Now Moses' speech on the east bank of the Jordan River reminds the people of his loyalty: It's as if he's saying, "I carried you to the doorway of this country; I argued for your entrance." Yet ironically, tragically, this is the very entrance that Moses himself is being denied. God has told him, "You shall not enter the Land." The same punishment that God had wanted to mete out to the people is now placed upon Moses himself. Now Moses desperately waits for the people to intercede on his behalf, to argue for him just as he had argued for them. He waits for the people to pray to God and say, "Let our leader partake in the promise; let Moses enter the

Land with us, for we will not enter without him." He waits and he waits.

Of course, Moses' entreaty to the people is far more than an issue of quid pro quo, of "I prayed for you—now you pray for me." It goes far deeper than that; it goes to the profound level of soul print sharing and receiving. It is as if Moses is saying, "I understand you; I desperately want for you to understand me. I carried you and now I need you to carry me." We all want to get to the Promised Land, Moses maintains, but none of us can get there alone. At some point in the journey, we all need understanding arms to carry us.

It is not certain that Moses' entire soul print problem lies in the fact that he is unique and therefore lonely. Moses has a transmission problem. He is deeply connected to his soul print. He has people close to him who love him, his sister, wife, and brother; they want to receive his soul print. Moses, however, is not fully able to communicate his soul print.

Biblical myth tells us of Moses the stutterer, whose lips are uncircumcised. If Moses has a technical speech pathology issue it would be of little interest to the reader. But the mention of a speech impediment suggests a larger point: Moses, like all of us, needs to develop tools that will allow him to communicate his soul print.

THE CHALLENGE TO RECEIVE

It is sometimes embarrassing to ask for help. So we hint, allude, make oblique reference, hoping others will understand us, allowing us to open our soul prints to them, in all our souls' complexity, formidableness, and need. Sometimes the connection just doesn't happen.

Some years back, there was a particular theological conference scheduled to be held that I was not invited to participate in. It was a deliberate exclusion based on misinformation shared with the conference organizers by persons who wanted to prevent my participation. It hurt. I felt it was important for me to attend. There were ideas, thoughts, and new directions in study that I very much wanted to hear and share with the conference participants. I talked to a close friend who had been invited, telling her of the situation. I waited for her to say my exclusion was unjust, morally wrong. She said all that. Then I hoped against hope that she would add, "If you are not invited, I will not go. You have carried me in the past, and now I will carry you." She never said those words. If she had, together both of us would have succeeded. Indeed, another wonderful friend of mine actually did refuse to attend. Not only did his refusal begin to resolve the issue, but it was pivotal in cementing the soul print bond between us. The power of loyalty moves worlds.

Everyone has his or her own version of this story. Not always, but often, our friends go on without us. And how often do we go on without our friends?

Moses' people do not hear him. As Mordechai Lainer explains, he is left alone, lonely. An enormous hollow of loneliness is left when you've done all you can to understand another person—to fight for his cause, to wage his battle—and then to discover that when you need him he cannot hear your call, cannot understand your needs, and leaves you *levado*. It it not good to be unreceived. Moses stands solitary at the close of the Five Books, the lonely one of Exodus.

This unwillingness to receive and carry another is actually rooted deep within the soul print. We are almost always willing to carry those weaker or less distinct than ourselves to the Promised Land; that load is light enough for our arms as well as our egos. But what about the heavier loads, the struggling ones around us who challenge the very way we carry ourselves, who confront the fragile

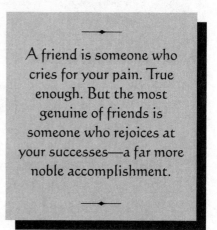

A friend is someone who cries for your pain. True enough. But the most genuine of friends is someone who rejoices at your successes—a far more noble accomplishment.

constructs of our egos? Can we carry them? Often our ability to receive gets wrapped up with our need to compete. How can we nourish another whose very greatness is a threat to ourselves, whose shadow, like a lofty oak, makes us afraid that our own light will be blocked, our own growth thwarted?

A friend is someone who cries for your pain. True enough. But the most genuine of friends is someone who rejoices at your successes—a far more noble accomplishment.

If someone undermines our sense of ourselves, then we are all too prone to secretly rejoice in that person's fall. Certainly, we can find many logical reasons why we should not carry them to the Promised Land. Rationales of this sort scatter the ground at every turn. But the root cause is virtually always the same—such people threaten our soul prints, our often weak sense of self. To receive another's soul print you must believe in your own.

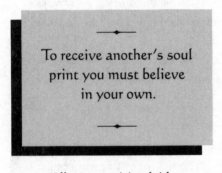

To receive another's soul print you must believe in your own.

All great spiritual ideas or moments have their own unique shadow. Soul print receiving possesses unique soul print dangers. The soul has a survival instinct, the reflex to believe there is only so much sacredness, only so much "specialness" to go around. We fear the other stars of the sky, that they may somehow, like the sun, be so brilliant that our own light is rendered invisible. We're afraid that there will not be enough room in the Promised Land for all of us.

This kind of threatened behavior is true for all of us in everyday life. But shirking the challenge of extraordinary soul print receiving is particularly true of the ostensibly pious—the teachers, gurus, and saints. Spiritual teachers often have ulterior motives well hidden from the public and sometimes even from themselves, which preclude authentic and openhearted connections with other spiritual people. As nineteenth-century spiritual psychologist Israel

Salanter is reported to have said, "There is no more ulterior motive than the ulterior motive of piety."

The problem with ulterior motives and rationales is that they do not just scatter the ground in front of your feet; they scatter the ground in front of everyone's feet. Any rationale you use not to help another into the Promised Land will eventually be used to justify not helping you. And who will carry you when your legs grow weak? Who will pray for you when the tables are turned?

Soul Print Practice

One way of soul print receiving is to pray for other people.

Even if you are unable to help them in a concrete way, you are always able to pray for them. Prayer is a powerful practice not only on a cosmic level but on a psychological level as well. On a cosmic level, we are interceding for their well-being. On a psychological level, however, prayer is effective whether or not it works in its cosmic intercession. For prayer is one of the most beautiful forms of soul print receiving. You cannot genuinely pray for a person without transforming your perception of them. Mordechai Lainer of Ishbitz interprets the verse in Leviticus that says "you shall not steal from your friend" as referring to prayer. A person who is able to pray for a friend and does not has stolen from him. I would add that those who fail to pray for a friend have stolen from themselves the pleasure of having their own soul prints received.

Has there ever been a time when you refused to enter a Promised Land without a friend?

Was there ever a time when you think you should not have entered but you did?

Think of ways you can mend that mistake.

Call that person if you can and tell her that you would have liked to have done more, to have been more.

> Next time you find yourself in a similar situation, even if it's with another person, use it as an opportunity for "a fixing."
>
> If you cannot think of any examples, try to think of a situation when you would have really wanted a friend not to enter the Promised Land without you. What would you have done if you were in that person's shoes?
>
> If it's appropriate, call your friend and talk to him about your feeling, not in the way of accusation but in the way of soul print sharing.

BELIEVING IN YOUR SOUL PRINT

Foul Whisp'rings are Abroad
—William Shakespeare, *Macbeth*

When the feeling that we haven't lived our own soul print oppresses us, it becomes very difficult for us to receive another.

Let's look for a moment at the context in the Book of Numbers, where the text affirms the uniqueness of Moses' prophecy, suggesting specifically that Moses' soul print experience is qualitatively different than any of the other prophets of the day. The context is a story of slander. Moses is slandered, gossiped about, by none other than his sister Miriam and his brother Aaron. Why would Miriam slander the brother she loved so much—Miriam, who risked her life when her brother was set adrift in a basket on the Nile? Miriam, who spent countless nights rocking her brother to sleep, wiping his tears—why would Miriam slander Moses?

The Talmudic wisdom masters suggest that the subject of the slander is Moses' relations with his wife. Something caused Moses to leave his marriage. Of course, slander usually revolves around the personal life of others. Sexual slander about the private lives of leaders has long been the way people seek to express frustration, disappointment, and even anger with them. Sex-related slander, however, is just one manifestation of a larger kind of malice. Lying, machinations, rumor-mongering, and cheating are all behaviors that we recognize more intimately than we would care to admit. Just what is the nature of the frustration or disappointment that could move decent people to these kinds of behaviors? Why would Miriam slander Moses?

Whether you are reading the biblical text as a religious or literary document is of no matter here; the point is clear. Miriam is unable to grasp the nature of Moses' experience. In some sense, Miriam is threatened by Moses' spiritual "status"; his spiritual vision is completely different from that of any other prophet in the book. Somehow, Moses' standing undermines her sense of her own spirit and prophecy. She is unable to grasp how he lives in the world, his sense of being, the places where his soul print soared. Perhaps she feels inadequate and exposed when she talks to him. Moses rankles her sense of identity. All she understands is that he has reached a place that she is unable to touch. Looking up at Moses through her own glass ceiling, she sees her sense of self-worth challenged.

Both Miriam and her brother, prophets in their own right, marry and have children. Their brother Moses, on the other hand, leaves the framework of marriage and children, called as he is to a singular and single life. The uniqueness of Moses' choices undermines their own sense of identity as prophets. They define their identity in relation to Moses. Miriam says to Aaron, "Does he think he is the only prophet?" Are we but secondary figures, minor league prophets?

Miriam does what many of us do when we want to avoid feeling threatened or inadequate. She slanders. Slander and gossip are often our last defenses against our own sense of insecurity. This is indeed what Mordechai Lainer of Ishbitz meant when he said that all gossip is ultimately rooted in our own pathology—and that only if we are willing to work through and not around our personal pathology will we be able to live with people in true love and friendship.

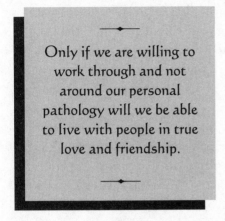

Only if we are willing to work through and not around our personal pathology will we be able to live with people in true love and friendship.

Biblical consciousness tells us that slander, which is so often the rejection of the singularity of another, is really rooted in a rejection of self. The inability to receive the soul print of another goes hand in hand with the inability to receive our own soul print. Deeper still, however, when we can't understand someone else's uniqueness of experience, somehow we feel threatened and fight to undermine another person's integrity. What better way to do it than through slandering the nature of their personal relationships, the unique decisions they had to make in the world of intimate relations, the world of marriage and divorce?

STEALING THE SOUL PRINT

A man sets out in search of truth. One night, he is walking along the moors when he sees a light ahead of him. He approaches the light and finds a small cottage that glows with what seems the light of thousands of candles, illuminating the landscape for miles around. He knocks on the door and a kindly old man lets him in.

And indeed the entire cottage is filled with tiny oil candles, their flames flickering throughout the house. The old man explains, "These are the lights of the souls of every person alive. I tend to them. I tend to life."

The visitor, entranced, approaches one candle; he notices that the oil is almost gone, and the flame is beginning to sputter. "What is happening to this person?" he asks the old man.

"He is dying," the man replies simply. "Everyone has his own amount of oil in his candle, everyone's oil burns faster or slower. And every candle burns out in the end. This is the truth of the world."

The visitor is suddenly taken with a desperate desire to see his own candle. While the old man is occupied elsewhere, the visitor searches for the candle marked with his name. Eventually he finds it, perched high on a shelf in the attic. But its oil is so low! Already the flame is beginning to waver! He is witnessing his own death.

"No!" screams the man silently. "It's too soon! I have not yet learned all I need to know. I do not yet know truth!"

He rushes wildly around the attic, scanning the shelves until he finds a candle burning brightly, filled to overflowing with thick oil. Carefully he picks up the candle and brings it over to his own ailing light, desperate for an infusion of oil. Just as he is about to pour some oil from the full candle into his own, he feels a hand grasp his wrist.

The old man is staring at him with burning eyes, gripping his wrist like a vice. "You want to know truth?" the old man hisses. "How can you know truth if you cannot bear to know yourself?"

Before the searcher can reply, he finds himself alone again, in the middle of the dark moor, with not a building in sight. After a while he begins to walk, whistling softly to himself, as he rubs the wrist grasped by the old man, who held a very powerful truth.

Sometimes, when we feel like our soul print oil is running low, we may try to steal from someone else's soul-candle. Sometimes we do this by taking somebody's oil and pouring it into our candle. At other times, the very sight of their brightly burning flame reminds us too painfully of our fainter flicker. So we seek to reduce their light lest the painful contrast between us and them be too much to bear. This is what Miriam did to Moses.

Do you remember "the fake hug," as we called it in grade school? In this pose, you wrap your arms around your chest so that, from the back, it looks like you're caught in an embrace. Amid hysterical giggles, you pretend to passionately kiss that imaginary person in your arms. Though harmless, the vision of this child's game always gave me an uncanny sense of unease, as if it revealed something very out of sorts, yet deeply rooted, about our psychic urges. Indeed, the image does strike a dissonant chord. For the fact is, you can't embrace someone else if you are holding too tightly onto yourself. It may look like a passionate pose, but in the end, such a hold is just a child's game, a fearful retreat from intimacy into self-indulgence.

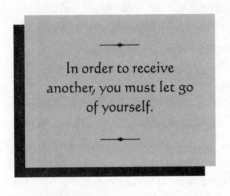

In order to receive another, you must let go of yourself.

In order to receive another, you must let go of yourself.

You are only able to let go of yourself if you are comfortable in yourself. If you're not living your own soul print, then you're unable to receive someone else's soul print. Moreover, you may often be moved to somehow negate the other, to slander, to undermine the integrity of the other and of their story. The reason, of course, is simple—when you don't live your own soul print, then your only claim to self lies in the rejection of the other. The undermining of the other's story becomes your story. Your soul print is woven from your nullification or rejection of the soul print of another. You develop, build, fashion yourself by rejecting another, because you lack a sense of your own story and your own soul print.

Another image from childhood comes to mind. Have you ever seen those psychological tests of pictures that from one perspective appear to be one thing but from another angle appear to be something else entirely? One of the examples is a drawing of twin faces, gazing at each other at close range. Of course, someone else looking at the picture may argue that it is not a picture of two faces at all—it's a picture of a goblet! When I refocus my eyes, I find that within that dark negative space between the two visages, there is indeed formed a perfect figure of a goblet. Each curve of the face creates the cut of the cup, or vice-versa.

Negative space in artistic terminology refers to the empty space that surrounds a figure. Necessarily involved in the process of creating, or defining, one figure is the creation of the space around it.

The twist in perspective that occurs in these psychological tests is that one realizes that the "negative space" itself actually becomes a figure of its own. In reference to images on paper that is fine—but when it comes to our own self-definition we need to beware of creating our image from the negative space of another. Whenever we define ourselves primarily by who or what we oppose and not by what we stand for, we risk getting caught in the negative space. A philosopher who is only a critic, a politician who only attacks his opponent's platform, and a religion that feeds primarily off its attacks on secularism are all examples of people sadly caught in negative space.

FROM KARMIC JUSTICE TO SOUL PRINT HEALING

The Miriam story moves us forward to our next discovery. The direct karmic response of the universe to her slander is to strike her immediately with a physical ailment. Its name, *Tzar'at,* which has no direct translation, is often mistranslated to English as "leprosy." Because the mind/heart and body make up a unified whole, the psychological malaise of slander and other acts of soul print malice too will often find expression in a physical ailment.

There's more to the story than that, however.

The other major reference to *Tzar'at* occurs in Leviticus (the third book of biblical myth). There, the person afflicted with *Tzar'at* is asked to leave the camp for seven days and is confined to solitary quarantine at a site apart from all human contact. Biblical myth readers, taking their cue from the Miriam story, assume that in this case as well the *Tzar'at* is a direct response to—or a kind of karmic result of—slander. But why would the punishment for slander be seven days of mandatory loneliness? One fourth-century sage, Master Joseph, suggests that slander is one of the great inducers of loneliness, isolation, and estrangement. As a result of slander, bonds of intimacy, loyalty, and friendship are destroyed. He who caused the alienation of loneliness through his slander should experience the alienation of loneliness through his isolation. The measure is a sort of sensitivity-heightening endeavor.

The Miriam story, in our reading, implicitly offers an even deeper understanding. What induces the act of slandering another? The feeling that the victim's soul print exists at the slanderer's expense. So the slanderer "cuts him down to size" through malicious and untrue rumor-mongering. The slanderer experiences a deeper malaise, she is disconnected from her soul print. The community's command to the slanderer—a week of solitude—is not meant to induce loneliness per se; instead, it invites the guilty party to wrestle with his own loneliness until it becomes a positive element of his singular soul print. Over a week of loneliness, the slanderer has the opportunity to rediscover his soul print. Once that happens, the essential motivation to slander has been removed. Would that all punishment were so enlightened.

Soul Print Practice

For parents: Think about how you impose punishment for a child's transgression. Does the punishment itself contain the power of healing and transformation?

Make a list of five punishments you remember receiving when you were a child. Write a few words about how different punishments made you feel.

Make a list of five punishments you have given your children.

Write a few words about how you could change your punishment system.

Put your writings in your Soul Print Box.

For all of us: If you find yourself denigrating or otherwise thinking less than kind thoughts about the Moses type of people in your life, try to check whether you feel undermined by them. If you do, then the following meditation may be helpful.

> *I was born where I was born.*
> *I was given the gifts I was given.*
> *I was granted the opportunities that are mine.*
> *My goal in the world is to be the best me that I can be.*
> *I have no desire to be anyone other than myself.*

HE AIN'T HEAVY, HE'S MY BROTHER

In an earlier chapter, we learned that for the Kabbalists the highest level of soul print evolution is called *yechida*. Literally translated as "singular," in the soul print consciousness of *yechida* the boundaries between the individual *one* and the *all* give way. Aloneness merges with All-Oneness. In biblical mysticism, you merge with the greater consciousness not by renouncing your individuality but by so radically accentuating it that the singular one merges with the all. It is one of the great paradoxes that the deeper you plunge into radical individuality, the more profoundly you merge with radical universality—with everyone else. The more realized your soul print, the more you realize that you are inextricably and gorgeously bound up with those of all other souls.

While this insight might seem relevant only for advanced mystics in Jerusalem and the Himalayas, it actually has enormously powerful ramifications in terms of how we all live our lives. Competition becomes irrelevant. Making it to the Promised Land all by myself becomes an absurdity. This is the enlightened knowledge of the soul print master.

To make this idea fully apparent to you, I want to share two stories of what I call soul print masters.

A few years ago, at the Seattle Special Olympics, nine contestants, all physically or mentally disabled, assembled at the starting line for the hundred-yard dash.

At the gun, they all started out, not exactly in a dash, but with a relish to run the race to the finish and win. All, that is, except one little boy who stumbled on the asphalt, tumbled over a couple of times, and began to cry.

The other eight heard the boy cry. They slowed down and looked over their shoulders. Then they all turned around and went back.

Every one of them.

One girl with Down's Syndrome bent down and kissed the fallen boy and said, "This will make it better." Then all nine linked arms and walked together to the finish line.

Everyone in the stadium stood, and the cheering went on for several minutes.

People who witnessed this event are still telling the story. Why? Because deep down we know this one thing: What matters in this life is more than winning for ourselves. What matters in this life is helping others win, even if it means slowing down and changing our course. At the end of the day, we all win the race only when each of us wins the race. Being wildly successful and wealthy in a world full of pain and poverty ultimately signals neither wealth nor success. Those Special Olympics kids are soul print masters; they know in the depths of their beings that you cannot go to the Promised Land by yourself. Those kids are my teachers.

A second teacher, whose story my grandfather used to tell at the Sabbath table, was the great master Isaac of Vorke.

Isaac, known as the Vorker Rebbe, was best friends with another well-known master, Menachem Mendel of Kutzk. They had made a sacred pact with each other that the one who died first would visit the other and share the secrets of the higher world. As it happened, Isaac of Vorke died first. Strangely, however, weeks went by and Menachem Mendel received no visitation from his departed friend. Deeply disturbed and worried for his friend, he decided to break with protocol and ascend to heaven himself to inquire after his fellow rebbe's welfare.

Arriving in heaven—through the mystical method of a soul ascension—Menachem Mendel searched for Isaac. He searched through myriad palaces of King David, Abraham and Sarah, Joseph and his brothers, Solomon and Sheba—and in all of these places they told him Isaac had been there but he left. "But where could he be?" queried Menachem Mendel, and they responded by pointing in the direction of a vast and dark forest.

Into the forest he plunged, and there he wandered for a considerable amount of time—and about what happened in the forest I cannot write in this book. After a time, he heard the rush of water—the sound of a vast sea.

Menachem Mendel followed that sound to the edge of the forest, and there he saw his friend Isaac standing—seemingly defiantly—by the sea. They met and embraced. Menachem Mendel asked his friend, "Where have you been? Why did you not come to me?"

> To be a soul print master is to be unwilling to enter heaven before the drying up of all the world's tears.

"My friend," Isaac responded, "I have been here, standing stubborn at the shores of the ocean of tears." He looked out at the vast sea and Menachem Mendel followed his gaze. "Before us are the tears of all the world throughout all the ages. I have told God that I will not leave here—not even to enter heaven—until God promises to dry up the entire ocean."

To be a soul print master is to be unwilling to enter heaven before the drying up of all the world's tears. It is to receive the soul print of humanity.

THE HERESY OF SELF-DOUBT: BELIEVE IN YOURSELF

The Miriam chapter in the Moses story initially served to deepen our understanding of why it may be difficult to receive someone else's story—because our own frail soul print tries to drain dry the soul print of another through malicious acts. We have previously discussed loneliness as being connected to our inability to find someone to receive our story, our soul print. However, there is a second reason we can be locked into loneliness. It is not related to the inability of someone else to receive our soul print. Instead, as we have seen, it is rooted in the great heresy that occurs in biblical consciousness—the inability to believe that you have a soul print. Or, as in the case of Miriam, your inability to believe that your soul print is enough.

The definition of loneliness is the inability to transmit your soul print to another, but in that transaction there are two players. The first player is the "other," the one who is unable to receive your soul print. The second player is you yourself. If you are to share your soul print with another, you need to first believe that your own soul print exists and is worthy of connection. If you do not believe that there is something about the whirls and swirls of your story that is infinitely special, that there is a snowflake uniqueness about your soul that does not melt, then you will be trapped in your loneliness.

How does knowing your uniqueness conquer your loneliness?

You will not be lonely because you will be in relationship with yourself.

We discussed this intimate relationship earlier when we talked about how you can be alone but not lonely because you have made friends with yourself. When you make friends with yourself, your painful loneliness and estrangement become precious solitude and singularity. Your soul print in all of its swirls, loops, and lines is a fascinating and beautiful world. To bear yourself in solitude is one of the highest intimacies a human being can achieve. Yet for most people, most of the time, the biblical myth proclamation holds true: [as God declared] "It is not good for the human being to be alone."

How does not knowing your uniqueness heighten your loneliness?

This question brings us to the second reason it is critical to access your soul print and live it in your life. You will be lonely because if you do not know yourself, then how can you possibly introduce yourself to other people? If you haven't heard your own story, become intimate with your own soul print, then how can you be seen or heard by another? Certainly you cannot see or hear another if you can't do so for yourself.

RECEIVING THE SOUL PRINT IN THE CROWD

In the mystical tomes, there is an obtuse textual question about how to read a particular passage in the Zohar, the book of the Kabbalah. The passage discusses what earned the biblical prophet Elijah the appellation "a man of God." According to one reading, he was primarily a man of God when he was with the people. According to the second reading of the passage, he became a man of God when he went into seclusion. This is a question we must address as well, not for Elijah (although he's included) but for ourselves. When does our divinity—in the form of our unique soul print—most shine in the world, when we are alone or in a crowd? The ultimate answer given by soul print consciousness is that it shines in both cases.

Most people correctly think that to dispel loneliness you need to be with people. And so we go to shopping malls when we have nothing to buy, attend movie theaters even though the video is available in the living room, and attend church or temple even if we don't believe in God.

A man named Finnegan meets his neighbor McDougal at the entrance to Our Lady Help of Christians. "Why do you come to church?" McDougal asks him.

"I," Finnegan says, "am a believer; I come to talk to God. Why do you come here?"

Responds McDougal without a moment's hesitation, "I come to talk to you."

McDougal was right. Community or even a crowd is a good thing even when it is just to be together in one place and appreciate each other's presence in the most general way. The caress of the crowd need not be impersonal and alienating. Moreover, sometimes we can experience the crowd even when there is no one there. Let's say I am drinking my coffee in the morning, feeling somewhat alone. My mind wanders and I start thinking about the men or women who designed the label on my coffee jar. Where do they live? Are they married or single? Do they have kids? Forget about the label—who made the coffee? Whose sun-browned hands picked the beans? Who processed and transported them? In a moment of epiphany, I realize that I am in the midst of community—at least a thousand people brought me my coffee this morning. There are the people who picked the beans in Colombia, the packers who crated them and brought them to port, the shippers, the transporters on the American side, the people who designed the label and the container, the grocery clerks who stocked the shelves of the supermarket. The list goes on. Community comes in many shapes and sizes, and you can find at least a modest soul print connection anywhere, enough to dispel a lonely dawn—if you yourself are living your own soul print.

Sometimes meditative epiphanies are insufficient, and actual people are what you need. When I need to study, I go to a restaurant called Cafit, one of the busiest places in Jerusalem. They always save me a table where I spread out my books and work, sometimes for ten to twelve hours at a stretch. Cafit is most definitely a public space and that is what I love about it. I love long-distance waving, playing peek-a-boo with babies, giving blessings, hugging and sharing the gorgeousness of being alive with everyone I meet. I love the vitality, the bustle, the people who nod hello or thanks for the television show I hosted last week, but most of all I feel embraced in the warm intimacy of the crowd.

I have my monastic mystic moments as well. I am heir to the tradition of Moses De Leon, who wrote in his *Book of the Wise Soul,* "To enter the inner sanctum one must know his soul which is modeled on the soul of his creator . . . when a person knows the secret of his soul in its ways—from that place his consciousness will expand to the secrets of the kingdom."

To learn the secrets of my soul—to believe in my soul print further—I need to leave Cafit. Like those who withdraw from the tribe to strengthen their soul prints, and in the tradition of Jesus spending forty days in the wilderness, I retreat into the silent setting of the self, to the empty middle-of-the-night Jerusalem streets, to the ancient caves that dot the city's landscape like deep pockets of a colorful skirt. In those times and places, I let myself grow quiet. I breathe, meditate, pray, and sing. No eye can see, no ear can hear, no crowd can call or comfort. Without those times of intimacy with myself—of becoming my own friend—I get lost in the loneliness. Only after receiving myself can I return to Cafit and rejoice in the kingdom, my soul print strengthened, my spirit purified of the urge for weak-souled politicking or malice, and primed for Good.

> ### Soul Print Practice
> Make a soul print date with yourself.
>
> Drive, bike, run, swim, stroll out to a secluded spot. Avoid others—just pursue yourself.
>
> Make for yourself a soul print space—a room, closet, tree house, or rooftop, some secluded space where you go to be with you. Keep it well-stocked with your favorite things, your favorite blanket, book, journal, candle, candy, music. Designate it as sacred self space for personal privacy, ritual, healing, or escape.

It is said that the lawyer and mystic of sixteenth-century Safed, in Israel, Joseph Caro, used to retreat from his heavy communal involvement at certain times, in order to study with a *maggid*. A maggid is, in simple terms, a spirit. Caro composed an entire work recording the wisdom he received from this spirit. Caro, mind you, was no charlatan or airy-headed spirit-seeker. He was probably the greatest jurist of the last thousand years and wrote monumental works of mind-boggling depth in literally every field of biblical law. Yet there were times when he needed to withdraw into seclusion, what the Kabbalists call *Hitbodedut*—radical aloneness.

There is something critical to remember about the nature of this radical aloneness: In *Hitbodedut,* you enter your loneliness, sit down in the midst of it, and do not get up, do not let go, no matter what, until you break through—until you move from loneliness to singularity and a more profound soul print awareness.

Fascinatingly, Caro's colleague and friend, Chaim Vital, living in Safed in the same period, wrote in his masterwork, *The Tree of Life,* that "a Maggid is formed from the breath of the person who studies in truth." In other words, the spirit with which Joseph Caro studied was his own guide drawn from the deepest places in his soul. We would not be wholly inaccurate if we said that a maggid is a living soul print.

The mystics call this movement between public and private space the dance of *yichud* and *yachad*. Both words sound the same and derive from the same Hebrew root. *Yichud* means "singular, special, unique." *Yachad* means "together"; it implies community, crowds, gregariousness. It is only in the dance between the two that we are received by others as well as by ourselves.

Soul Print Practice

The next time you feel lonely or are in a quandary, go to some quiet, secluded spot. Mark a circle on the ground, whether imaginary or real. Then sit down in the center of it. Tell yourself (and your maggid may be listening too) that you won't get up until you have broken through to the other side of your loneliness into your All-in-Oneness. Or to the other side of your quandary to your answer.

ONLY THE LONELY

To conclude this part of *Soul Prints,* I want to introduce you to my favorite soul print receiver, the man who taught me how to be a soul print receiver myself. His name is Mordechai, my Hebrew name as well.

If you've ever been to Jerusalem, perhaps you have seen him. If you ever come to Jerusalem, you must find him. Mordechai's garb is white, his beard is long and bleached by age, and his voice is strong as seventy men. He spends his days as a guardian of the Western Wall, trumpeting prayers onto the white stone, passing around bundles of spices and blessings, warmth and wonder, and greeting the great swarms of people and pilgrims who come there.

For a magical period in my life, I lived among the alleyways and arches of the neighborhood at the foot of the Western Wall. Mordechai's fantastic figure became a source of joy and illumination in my days. He was always surrounded by a flurry of souls seeking light, advice, blessing. He was no less than an ever-open portal into a world of peace. Ever receiving visitors, offering back to them precious glimpses of their own souls, he was a soul print receiver like I've never seen.

Late one night as I roamed the Old City's tangled streets, I glimpsed a white figure moving half-hidden among some ruins. Realizing it could only be my Mordechai, I rushed over to greet him. This time no booming voice answered me. He was quiet, subdued. This open portal of a person was suddenly closed. From behind the curtains of his closed eyes he softly sang that old Roy Orbison tune "Only the Lonely."

He quietly told me how every day he closes his great gates of communication and spends forty minutes, at least, steeped in solitude. These were his lonely moments. Hearing this, I apologized and retreated, somewhat ashamed, as if I had stepped onto hallowed ground with too-heavy boots. I slipper-stepped my way home, and each street seemed to wind me deeper into my own solitude, until I reached that cell of myself, my own hallowed ground, and carefully stepped inside.

It was a transformative experience; I had entered myself, and the next morning, I hardly knew how to exit. I spent the whole next day in the space between inner self and outside world, unable to communicate or cross the threshold of another's face in greeting.

But as I returned home from the unavoidable commerce of my day, I found Mordechai, passing out blessings on the cobblestone streets. His eyes poured forth light, his mouth abounded with song. The great gateway of his arms opened, and he welcomed in all guests. As I watched him again giving to and receiving the people around him, I realized a crucial thing. We go inside not to stay inside; we go inside to greet the outside more lovingly, more lavishly, when we come back out. I walked up to Mordechai, ready to tell him all of the enlightenment he had brought me . . . but before I could begin, he very quietly asked me for a blessing.

Giving the blessing to him, I received one in return. Just as in giving a blessing to me, he too had received.

What did we receive? The soul print of our very selves.

PART THREE

SOUL PRINT CALLS

8

◆

THE CALL OF THE SOUL

THE SOUL PRINT'S VOCATION

In the first two sections of this book, we explored how loneliness is the inability to transmit the essence of who you are to another. It is the inability to share your soul print, to have your soul print received—by friend, lover, or community. The more singular the soul print, the more complex it is to share—and the stronger the need to share it. If the purpose of biblical living, the *telos*, is to get to the good—as indicated by the divine observation at the time of creation, "God saw that it was good"—then the "not good" of loneliness remains the great challenge of every life. Overcoming loneliness and moving to connection, to loving, to union, is not merely an exercise in pop psychology fulfillment or personal gratification. It is the very goal of existence, of being and of becoming.

It is therefore no accident that the primal drive that moves us is the drive to fulfill our essential purpose in the world. In biblical consciousness, we are invited to move from loneliness to loving, from separation to union, from the pain of rupture to the rapture of connection.

Yet living our soul prints does not mean just celebrating the truth of our own individual uniqueness. Nor do we realize our soul prints only by how we give and receive our soul prints in relation to other people. For implicit within every soul print is a call to being, to self, and ultimately a call to doing. It is the clarion call that prompts us to respond to our unique mission in the world.

In this portion of *Soul Prints,* we'll explore how our soul prints call us to our vocations to be authentic selves living fully in the greater world.

THE PHYSICS OF THE SOUL

This little light of mine . . .

In the next few pages, I am going to outline the conceptual framework that underpins both this part of the book on Soul Print Calls as well the following section on Soul Print Stories. I will do so by making a simple analogy to physics. If the conceptual framework is not that critical to you, well then, skip this section and go on to explore soul print calls (page 147).

I love sappy love songs. In great poetry, classical literature, mysticism, and sappy love songs, the most often used metaphor for soul is light.

The image used most often in biblical myth to describe what I have called the soul print is also light. Your soul print is your light. When we sing, "You light up my life," or "You are my sunshine," we don't mean "You support me financially" or "You help me to advance politically." It means that your infinite specialness—your soul print—illuminates my existence.

In the language of biblical myth, the image for light is the Candle of God. And the myth masters drive our analogy home when they call out, "The Candle of God is the soul of man." Apparently the association of light and spirit is burned into the fiber of our souls.

To decipher the innate truth of the image of light as the model of the soul—besides the obvious reason that light is bright and we can see by it—we need to introduce a Kabbalistic core principle: The physical and spiritual worlds are mirrors of each other. This idea—found throughout the Kabbalah as well as comprising a basic element of Plato's thought—suggests that models in the physical world are reflected images of the spiritual and therefore often the best way to understand the spiritual world. The spiritual and physical are refractions, reflections, mirrors of each other. Given that understanding, let's explore how the nature of physical light "illuminates" the nature of the soul.

Light, modern science teaches us, has two distinct properties that describe it: the particle property and the wave property. Light is magically both particle and wave. Understood as a particle, light exists as one particular point. Understood as a wave, light possesses a flowing and more amorphous quality.

Light is understood to be a twofold phenomenon not only in modern physics but also in ancient biblical myth. Light in Hebrew is referred to as *sapir*. You may be familiar with the English word "sapphire" that is derived from the Hebrew word. A sapphire, with its incomparable blue shine, is a stone of light.

The identity of spiritual and physical light becomes clearer when we focus on two more words that spring from this luminous Hebrew root *sapir*. Those words are *mispar* and *sippur*. *Mispar* means "number." *Sippur* means "story."

Mispar, like "particle," expresses the pointlike quality of light; *sippur,* like "wave," captures light's fluid nature. They are sister terms, both born from *sapir*. Not by coincidence, these words express the unique dual nature of the spiritual light our soul prints emanate.

Now let's try to marry these concepts. *Sapir*—soul print light—like all light, has two functions: particle and wave, *mispar* and *sippur*. The physics of the soul reflects the physics of light, and vice versa.

Mispar, meaning number, corresponds to the particle nature of light. It implies a discrete unit, a place-holding point. Of course, numbering something is a way of identifying a unique and specific moment, place, thing, or person in the sea of infinity. The instant that we assign a number, we are identifying a single and singular moment. The word *mispar* in biblical-myth Hebrew also means "border." It is the discrete particle of the self. The particle function of our soul is thus our "particular" *mispar,* our singular, specified number.

Sippur, "story," corresponds to the wave quality of light, flowing and streaming, just like the tales of our lives. The wave function of our soul is thus our story, the wavelike rush of events and emotions we experience in a lifetime. We will discuss *sippur* later in the book, when we focus on the nature of our Soul Print Stories, the waves of our life-light that we are called to shine into the world. The *sippur,* or story quality, of your soul print is not your unique calling or mission but the flow of events, the unique patterns of your story line, the whorls of your soul print lines. The incidents, details, images, and apparent coincidences of your life all weave a story unlike that of any other human being on the face of the planet.

Mispar is the calling dimension of our soul prints. By "calling," I mean the human experience of being summoned to a specific mission or destiny. A number is the call of the infinite through a finite point; number is infinity limiting itself in order to be heard and seen. The person called is summoned as a one, a singular being with a discrete, defined destiny to fulfill. The soul's numbering says that you are singled out, unique, one and only, and that therefore you are called to a mission, a "point" of meaning, that you alone are charged to fulfill.

Does the prospect of being singled out sound daunting, even lonely? It is, but only at first glance. Superficially, your uniquely numbered soul does isolate you as being one and only one, alone, as opposed to being part of the All-Oneness we've discussed earlier. However, on a deeper level, only by responding to your unique call do you open up the channels in your soul print that create connection, loving, and community. Your singularity is actually the most powerful access point to the greater One. Number is the call of the One through the one.

Here in Part Three of *Soul Prints,* we will be exploring the *mispar,* the particle/number aspect of our soul print. As is true with the phenomenon of light, however, the two are not divisible. Light exists in every instant as both wave and particle. So, there will be natural overlap between the two spiritual equivalents as well. Indeed, living your Soul Print Story and responding to your soul print calling are complementary and sometimes even identical endeavors. Nonetheless, just as in physics there are different words to describe different properties of light, so too in our quest we will understand *mispar* and *sippur* as distinct qualities—and thus we will deepen our understanding of our *sapir,* our soul print light.

MISPAR—OUR CLARION CALL

Embedded in your soul print is a summons to be your truest, richest self, a vocation that sends you out into the world. That summons is a bell or a clarion that commands each of us to stand up and be counted.

A wonderful image that captures this idea is a third-century biblical myth text that describes how, twelve hundred years before, the census of children of Israel was taken in the desert. "Moses entered the tent of the person being counted in the Census . . . at the moment of the counting, the Cloud of glory"—the presence of God—"left the Tent of Meeting" (the mini-temple of the desert) "and dwelled lovingly atop the tent of the person." The numbering of each individual person was an affirmation of the unique dignity, absolute adequacy, and value of that person. In every way, each person "counted." That dignity and inherent value is a function of—and is expressed by—the call we hear that makes each of us special.

Of course, when we reduce "counting" to the census—a gathering of technical data—and forget that number is the window to unique calling, then we make room for a dark shadow. Every great idea has its own unique and dangerous shadow side. The shadow side of numbering is the reduction of a person to an "it," an entity numbered like cattle merely for reasons of bookkeeping. This phenomenon occurs in the biblical text, when the divine presence that rests upon the counting in the desert becomes corrupted. Centuries later, the biblical monarch, David, takes a census of the people to affirm his power and control. In the tradition of biblical myth, which never hesitates to expose the flaws of its heroes, David is severely criticized for the hubris of his counting. In the soul print counting in the desert, the final number was irrelevant; the whole point was to affirm that each person counted. In David's counting, the only number that mattered was the final number, the bottom line. Bad fortune befell him when he counted—so much so that there grew a mystical tradition never to enumerate people aloud, as when one might count the number of people around a table.

The full shadow of the idea of a personal number became horrifically apparent in Hitler's Germany. In a demonic attempt to undermine the beauty of the number's personal call, the Nazis tattooed every person in the concentration camps with a number. Rather than evoking uniqueness, calling, dignity, or value, the intent of the Nazis' reckoning was to identify each person so that his or her execution, by gas, torture, or starvation, could be duly recorded. This image of the arm branded with a number haunts humanity's imagination, the numerical tattoo becoming a symbol for the most grotesque debasements of humanity's soul print.

Hitler's explicitly stated goal was to destroy the core ideas that biblical myth gave to the world and replace them with Teutonic myths of blood barbarism and what Hitler saw as Aryan grandeur. "I stand against the Bible and its life-denying ten commandments," his advisor Herman Raucshning remembers him saying in his memoir, called *Voices of Destruction*. For Hitler, the Jew, or what he called the "Jewish Spirit," infected all people who had absorbed the biblical ethos. "I am freeing men from . . . the demands of . . . freedom and personal independence," Hitler said to Raucshning. "Two worlds face one another. I set the Aryan and the Jew over against each other and if I call one of them a human being I must call the other something else. The two are as widely separated as man and beast." Since most of my family was killed by this very Teutonic myth, I count the fact that I am traveling all over the world helping reweave the biblical myth fabric of our civilization as no small victory over darkness. Every person who embraces the singular gorgeousness of his or her soul print is one more proof that the light of *mispar*—of a person called—will triumph over the darkness of the reduction of human beings to statistics to be filed or exterminated.

THE DRAMATIC FACT OF THE CALL

The third biblical book opens with the words *"Vayikra el Moshe."* Literally translated from the Hebrew, this phrase means, "God called to Moses." Moses is "the called one." To the Kabbalistic readers of biblical myth, we are all called. As it was for Moses, so is life for each of us either an adventure in which we answer the call, or nothing. Living means being called—and responding.

Sometimes an idea becomes clear only when we consider its alternative. In this sense, it is helpful to compare the biblical myth with Jean Paul Sartre and his school of existentialism, which has shaped much of the modern sensibility. In an important work aptly titled *Nausea,* Sartre writes:

> Man can will nothing unless he has first understood that he must count on no one but himself; that he is alone, abandoned on earth in the midst of his infinite responsibilities, without help, with no other aim than the one he sets himself, with no other destiny than the one he forges for himself on this earth.

Sartre understands that an unfriendly universe that issues no call of destiny to the individual is a place of nausea. For those engaged with biblical myth consciousness, there exists an essential energy, a force, if you will, that courses though the universe, knows your name, and calls you. To live, for biblical man and woman, is to be addressed. To be addressed is to be called by a personal destiny that is important to the world and can be fulfilled by you alone.

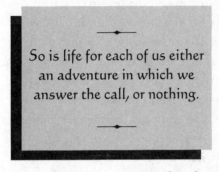

So is life for each of us either an adventure in which we answer the call, or nothing.

Psychology in some of its classical forms seeks to undermine our sense of calling. It pathologizes our urge to find our vocation, assigning it diagnoses like character disorder, neurosis, manic depression, and grandiosity. So much of classical psychology seems to dismiss our authentic and urgent human ambitions. One wonders, along with therapist Otto Rank, whether psychology's denial of human grandeur was itself responsible for the symptoms and complexes it then so delightfully labels. All of the psychoanalysis in the world will not allow you to find out who you are, why you are here on earth, why you have to die, or how you can make your life a triumph. When psychology tries to offer itself as a full explanation of human motivation, it becomes a fraud. It makes the human situation a morass from which we cannot escape.

"Through my flesh I vision God," Job tells us. The Kabbalists imply that human psychology must take the human experience seriously. If a billion human beings feel called to spiritual missions, then they probably are. If we feel that our lives must matter, that we must be called to some great adventure—then we probably are. In the feeling of being called lies the first echo of the call itself.

The American Puritans are stunning examples of individuals captivated by their calling. Their entire identity was animated by their belief that they were "being called" to God. Their calling brought them across the ocean to seed a new frontier. They envisioned themselves latter-day Hebrews summoned to an exodus. Biblical texts were their maps to a new land of promise, which they named the New Jerusalem. Thus were biblical myth's concepts of calling planted into the New England soil, sprouting into much of the mythology that has propelled America forward into its own destiny. For nations, too, have their calling in the world.

Just as Job visioned God through the flesh, the Puritans heard their calling echo in the physical world, in every hymn they sang, every house they built, every cow they milked. For the word *calling* includes a summons to divine service as well as worldly vocation. The Puritans took this wordplay seriously. The dual meaning of calling united the spiritual and the physical strivings of each individual in one sacred destiny. For Puritans and for the rest of us as well, to be called is to integrate a spiritual move toward the divine with a physical move toward the world—to straddle the two, feet firmly planted in both fields.

PRINT HINTS

How do calls make themselves heard, especially if you're not the kind of person who ordinarily hears voices talking from burning bushes or car radios? For those of you who missed the car radio allusion, I am referring to *Oh God,* a seventies movie starring George Burns and John Denver. God (played by George Burns) speaks to Denver by talking to him through his radio. Of course, everyone thinks Denver's character is crazy, and so begins the movie.

With all due respect to George Burns, the universe is usually more veiled and sophisticated in its calling mechanisms than AM/FM car radios. The cosmos employs a gorgeous and complex system of what we will call "soul print hints."

Soul print hints can be sudden and cataclysmic or slow and subtle. Slow and subtle soul print hints are life events, places, or images that happen over and over. They are patterns of life that point you in a particular direction. For example, if you always seem to find yourself running into the same person, then that person is in some way—major or minor—important to your soul print fulfillment. Alternatively, if you always find yourself in the same dynamic at work or in a relationship, then the truth of your soul print might be telling you to pay close attention. Perhaps learning to deal within this dynamic is part of your soul print call. Dreams that recur can hint at the soul print secrets your subconscious needs to share with you. A movie, play, or song lyrics that keep replaying in your head, or a book, tape, talk, or overheard conversation that seems to be speaking directly to you, all might be the teachers of your soul. They may guide you in a decision you need to make, an insight you need to gain. Places you find yourself returning to over time, longings that persist over the years, or symptoms of illnesses that recur over extended periods, may have underlying themes, coded messages, or may even be thinly veiled warnings or guideposts along your path.

Soul Print Practice

Soul print calls come to us in many different ways and speak in many different voices. Can you ascertain what calls you may have received, and how?

Keeping in mind all the examples we listed above, and adding your own intuitions—try to list what calls you might have received.

In the first column, list the call itself (for example, a song that you can't get out of your mind, or an event, experience, perhaps a place that moved you deeply).

In the second column, list where, when, or how such a call came to you.

Then in the third column, without thinking, purely from the gut, write down in a few words what you were called to.

Call	When/Where did it happen	A call to what?

THE CATACLYSMIC CALL

My own life has been shaped by a dramatic version of the sudden sort of call—the kind that emerges from a cataclysmic shift of events.

When I was thirteen, I went away to boarding school. There I met an angel. His name was Pinkie Bak. He was twenty-nine years old, a wise and kind man, a brilliant teacher, and principal of the school. Since the school had no dormitory, I lived in his house. Until I reached high school, my life was difficult on many fronts; like many kids, I landed in my teens with little sense of worth, adequacy, or dignity. Pinkie taught me that I was valuable, that I mattered, and that I was loved by one of God's angels himself. Moreover, he implicitly conveyed to me that to share the truth of human specialness was the most important thing in the world. All of the education I absorbed in high school was secondary to what I learned from my school principal; Pinkie had given me the gift of self, the knowledge that I counted.

As was his custom, in the middle of a rollicking religious holiday school party, Pinky was dancing like a wild man—ecstatic, alive, on fire, his energy contagious. At some point the music died down and the students began their yearly satiric play, which poked fun—sometimes gently and other times sharply—at the staff of the school. Pinky was standing next to me, laughing uproariously.

Suddenly in the midst of his laughter, he fell down. He looked up at me and said, "Don't worry I'll be okay, go on . . . ," and then he simply died. We found out later he had suffered a brain aneurysm. I accompanied his body to the hospital and sat with him, stunned, until the morning.

Representing the student body, I spoke at Pinky's memorial service. I don't know what possessed me as I stood before the grieving crowd. I do know that in those moments I was granted the gift of speech. My words felt like wings; they soared through me effortlessly, lifting and falling, carrying the crowd. Before a packed auditorium, I promised to pick up the baton that Pinky had dropped—to become a teacher of wisdom in the world.

I did not know before Pinky died that this would be my path. Ever since that speech, however, it has been clear to me that I was called and I have never wavered from the path. Even when I have tried to veer from it, I somehow always have wound up walking it again.

My response to Pinky's death is an example of an unexpected call, one that arises from sudden rupture in the way life was. Such calls happen differently for everyone. Below, I've listed some examples of dramatic moments that can result in cataclysmic calls we need to heed. Read them over, and add the circumstances that may have abruptly forced you, at some point, to reevaluate your own mission and destiny:

An ultimatum from your partner.

An unexpected job offer or contract that seemed too good to turn down—particularly if it was something you'd always dreamed of.

Getting fired or having to run away.

Strange coincidences that suggested a calling.

A movie, book, or experience that changed your life.

A death, an accident, or a divorce.

A new love affair.

A birth.

Did you respond to these uproars in your life that may have signaled your calling? Why? Why not?

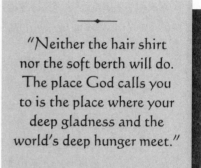

"Neither the hair shirt nor the soft berth will do. The place God calls you to is the place where your deep gladness and the world's deep hunger meet."

WHAT CALLS YOU?

Protestant theologian Frederick Buechner defines vocation this way: "Neither the hair shirt nor the soft berth will do. The place God calls you to is the place where your deep gladness and the world's deep hunger meet."

Following the Soul Print Practice below, you can examine the instances, activities, and interests that shape the contours of your own soul print calling.

Soul Print Practice

Ask yourself three questions:

> What am I good at?
> What do I enjoy doing?
> What is most needed in the world?

For each of the three make a list of at least five activities.

Then rate each item on the three lists from one to five.

Five is reserved for the things that you are fabulous at, that you absolutely love doing, and that the world desperately needs.

After going through the whole exercise, see how the three lists relate to each other.

For example, if that which is most needed is that which you enjoy doing most and that which you are best at, then you really have very little question about your calling. I have found that this turns out to be the case for a remarkably large number of people.

If there is something that is very much needed and you are fairly good at it and enjoy it a fair amount, then you have to decide whether to let need override absolute enjoyment.

Conversely, there may be something that gives you radical pleasure but is only moderately needed in the world. You then have to decide whether to let pleasure override a measure of need.

One of the important variables in the chart will be how you determine need. Are you talking about personal need, family need, or the need of your community? A healthy chart should probably make room for all three.

9

———◆———

CHARACTERISTICS OF CALLING

THE FIVE TRUTHS OF VOCATION

My vocation is not my job, it's my calling. Vocation comes from the latin word *vocare,* meaning "voice." My vocation is my calling—the place I found my voice. As we continue exploration into the nature of soul print calls, my goals are to remind you that the call is the primary reality of life, to help you recognize a call when you hear one, and to provide you with the tools necessary to align your life with your call.

Our method will be to unpack what we might call the five truths of vocation.

The question we need to answer is, What does a call look like? What are its demarcating characteristics? How does it behave in the world? Does biblical myth have any particular understandings about calling that may be different from the understandings in other wisdom systems? We need to think, however, not only about the "characteristics" of the call but also about the "character" of the person being called.

What are the inner spiritual tools we need to develop our characters as we explore our calls? What kind of character muscles must you exercise to make you strong enough to be one who answers the call?

THE FIRST TRUTH: THE UNIQUE CALL

The best image for understanding the idea of uniqueness—not always easy in our world that vaunts egalitarianism—is the symphony. In the orchestra, there are many instruments, all of them necessary for making music. Each instrument is distinct and special without being "better" than any other. A symphony is the opposite of hierarchy. To participate in the symphony, you need to be familiar with all the instruments, yet in order to make music each member of the symphony needs to be particularly responsive to the unique call of her own instrument. While you may be a dabbler at many instruments, you must be a master of your own. Every calling is great only when greatly pursued. If everyone played the same instrument, the music would just be loud and boring—there would be no texture, no harmony. Music emerges from the diversity of pluralism but never at the expense of radical individualism.

A calling is not a job or an occupation—it is a vocation. It is not what you do for a living—it is your very life. Vocation literally means "calling"—the word is derived from the Latin *vocare,* to call. Our vocal expression in the world is melodious if we sing in response to *vocare,* the call of our vocation. Calling is an issue of voice. You must sense the voice of the caller, then find your own voice, and realize that the two are the same. When you find your own radical uniqueness, your voice, then you find God.

Often we try to escape from the singularity of our call. The clarion call can be so loud that we go deaf from its decibels. Its voice can shout so directly to our soul prints that it is exhilarating and affirming, yet frightening. The first response of the Hebrews to the calling voice at Sinai—and according to many Kabbalists it was an inner voice—was to be absolutely overwhelmed and run. In an earlier story, Moses himself hides his face so as not to be overpowered by the voice calling him from the Burning Bush. When the prophet Jonah hears an inner voice calling him to teach in the Assyrian city of Nineveh, he books immediate passage on a boat—going in the other direction. It is only when going in the opposite direction wreaks havoc with his life and he finds himself trapped in the belly of a whale that he sets course for Nineveh.

The prime cause of our desire to run is the fear that we are not up to the job. So we ignore our unique calling. We try to join the magnificent symphony of being without learning our particular instrument. But that strategy never works, for everyone knows that you're not invited to join a symphony without having mastered your particular instrument.

Ever present in us is the temptation to take the Eden express back to the idyllic oneness of the Garden, at that time before the human being was called to action. The tree of life must be the tree of *your* life, your instrument, your soul print. The seer named Chabakuk, teaching several hundred years before Jesus, exclaimed, "The Righteous live by their faith." Contemporary mystic Abraham Kuk rereads Chabakuk emphasizing the phrase as "*their* faith"—that is, their particular faith, their soul print.

We are all heading in the same direction, toward the vocation that comes from the authentic realization of our soul prints. Yet we can only reach our destination by taking our different paths. All-Oneness is achievable only through aloneness and singularity. Beyond our important ties with a particular spiritual community, we must all create our own religion. It is the faith of our unique life-calling like that of no other. You are called to be the priest in the temple of yourself.

To understand the uniqueness of our singular soul print call, we return to the Baal Shem Tov, the soul print master and founder of Hasidism whom we met earlier in our journey.

It was the practice of the Baal Shem Tov to go out into the forest alone. What he did there was a mystery that greatly intrigued his disciples. So one morning, when the Baal Shem asked three of his Hasidim if they would like to accompany him into the forest, they readily agreed to go. These three were Sendril, Yehiel, and Gershon. Do not be deceived by their simple names; each one was a master in the making.

Everyone climbed onto the wagon, and this time the Baal Shem himself served as the driver. Although he did not crack the whip, the horses raced forward. It seemed to the Hasidim that the horses' hooves and the wagon's wheels never once touched the ground. Soon they arrived at the entrance to a forest so pristine they were reluctant to venture in, for fear of breaking a branch or breathing on a flower.

Without saying a word, the Baal Shem dismounted, unhitched the horses from the wagon, and motioned the others to follow. Never had the Hasidim seen a forest like this. The trees were so ancient that each sat as wide as a house and stretched as high as heaven's halo. Yehiel tried to peer into the top branches of one especially tall and magnificent tree. There he glimpsed a high nest where there roosted a golden-winged bird. Yehiel remained rooted in that place, drinking in the gold light of its wings. The others continued into the forest, leaving their awestruck companion behind.

A little further on, they came to a beautiful pond. When the Hasidim saw the Baal Shem lean over and peer into the waters, they followed his lead. But this was no common pond, for the image they saw there was not their ordinary visages, but rather the face of an angelic presence gazing back at them from the crystal waters. Now the Hasidim greatly wondered over this and raised their eyes to ask the Baal Shem of its mysteries, but when they did, they saw that he had already moved beyond the angelic pond. Sendril hurried off to catch up with him. However, Gershon remained staring at that angel, transfixed, for he understood that this was his own guardian angel that he beheld, and he could not tear himself away from the sight.

Further in the forest the two remaining Hasidim came to trees that shimmered as if aflame. They emitted no heat and they were not consumed. Sendril wanted to stop to explore the strange sight, but the Baal

Shem barely paused to glance as he continued on his way. Sendril, remembering well the vision of Moses and the Burning Bush, remained behind, trying to discern the mystery of the fire in the trees, and hardly noticed that the Baal Shem had left him to go on ahead.

The Baal Shem reached the tree of life alone.

The tree of life in mystical thought is said to be a "glimmering of *yechida,*" the highest of the five soul levels. If you recall, *yechida* has connotations of the singular, the special, and the alone. We sometimes shirk the call of soul print by trying to bring others on the journey. For most of the way, we do need partners to accompany us. Yet, there is one stretch of the journey, the final steps up to your tree of life, which can only be trekked alone. There is a part of the call that is addressed exclusively to you, to your sole soul print.

The Baal Shem wanted so much to have company on his path. He wanted as well to share his wisdom with his disciples, and he was sure that he could lead them to their tree of life. The master learns in this story that his tree of life may well not be theirs. He can bring them in his coach to the edge of the forest; they can even walk together into the trees. But each one will be called to a different destination.

After reaching the tree of life, the Baal Shem Tov returned to his community with renewed energy, commitment, and joy. We too need to return to our involvement in family and community. However, we can never skip that stretch of the path, which must be walked alone.

A MISSPELLING OF MY SOLE

Chaim Vital, a sixteenth-century Kabbalist who lived in Galilee, expressed this idea by saying that every person has his or her own specific letter of the Bible. My letter is not yours and yours is not mine; our sacred text is created when all the unique letters form sentences, paragraphs, chapters, and ultimately an entire narrative. The paradox of singularity as the result of the distinction is not separation but merging, not division but harmony, not conflict but relationship. You only become your letter in the Bible by reaching down to your deepest level of singularity. It is in the cauldron of authenticity that your letter of the Bible is forged. Your false self, no matter how colorful, idiosyncratic, or ostensibly distinct, can never become a letter in the Bible. It is a misspelling of your soul.

Master Jose, son of Hanina, a third-century biblical myth master, told of the great miracle of revelation in the Sinai desert thousands of years ago. When we think of revelation at Sinai, we usually imagine a majestic voice proclaiming a decalogue of order for all mankind. Jose adds an extra dimension to that image: "When revelation took place, and finite consciousness opened up to the infinite, each individual standing at the foot of Mount Sinai heard God's words as a personal and unique address to each one alone."

Embedded within the public revelation was also an intimate, private call to every individual. To respond to the divine, in Jose's view, does not exhaust itself in ethical or spiritual practice. The address of the divine commands each of us to realize our highest unique self.

UNIQUENESS AND THE MESSAGE

To be called is to have a message to deliver, a song to sing, an instrument to play. I once asked a class I was teaching, "How many people here consider themselves messengers of God?" They looked at me as if to say, "He has finally lost it." Wouldn't we be excited waking up in the morning knowing we hold vital information in our hands that the world cannot spin without?

I remember in college anxiously awaiting a return call from a woman named Amy. I had met her at a philosophy lecture. When that astounding comment about Michel Foucault came out of her beautiful and eloquent lips, I—along with the rest of the class— was instantly smitten. I mustered up all of my courage to introduce myself. Asking for her number took Herculean strength, and the fact that I actually called her and left a message was a small miracle. If that wasn't torture enough, I then had to wait for her to call me back. Every day I waited. She never called.

For two weeks, I was devastated by the apparent rejection. One night as I was borrowing a piece of paper from my roommate's notebook, I noticed the name Amy and a number scribbled on the back of the notebook. I couldn't believe it—my roommate, my friend, with Amy. I confronted him. "Amy," he said, squinting, confused. "Who is that? Oh yeah, a girl named Amy called for you a couple of weeks ago. Forgot to give you the message. Sorry, buddy." And he was off and I was left speechless. Indeed, in the words of A. J. Heschel, one of the great readers of biblical myth: "We are messengers that have forgotten our message."

The Zohar, the magnum opus of biblical mysticism, goes one dramatic step further. We are not only all the messengers, it says: We are the message. Each of us has a different piece of the message. In Kabbalistic terms, each individual personifies a unique idea, or character trait or experience, or perspective or talent. That is your *message* to the world. This uniqueness is reflected in the fact that everyone smiles slightly differently. Every person through his or her singularity adds something to the divine smile that is the world. Several decades ago, the famed communications guru Marshal McLuhan reminded us of the Zohar's teaching when he declared that the medium is the message—and we are the medium.

The message is encrypted into our individual psyches. The code is accessed through the call to destiny received by every individual human being. To break the soul's unique code, each of us needs to listen deeply to hear when our number is called. To put it in terms of the metaphor of music, only then can we pluck out the tune on our instrument, play the unique part of the symphony that is ours alone.

We are the message. We are the scroll. The Bible, the Koran, the sutras are us and we are them. It is heresy to ignore the call of your message or to confuse it with a message not your own. For we all have a different piece of the message, one that we need and that our community needs as well.

Your unique contribution to the message is your knowledge of your call. To deny its uniqueness is to deny your ability to contribute to the community. Genuine community can only emerge from genuine communication. Real communication is when a soul print exchange takes place in which we share with each other our unique letters and piece together another word and another sentence and ultimately another world.

Soul Print Practice

What is your message to the world?

If you are having a hard time connecting to your message, then visualize this scene: You are given three minutes of prime time television to say to the nation—to the world—whatever you want. Write your script.

Make a sticker of it, hand it out to friends, stick it on walls!

SURVIVAL OF THE SPECIAL

My third grade teacher told me that the animal that survives is the one who is best able to blend in with his environment. This was so much a fact of nature that certain animals, like the Arctic hare, actually turn different colors to blend in with the changing seasons. "What a wonderful gift," she exclaimed.

Indeed for the hare it is a wonderful gift, but for human beings it can be deadly. Beware of those among us who are copycats and parrots! Or mockingbirds, for that matter. The mockingbird is so designated because unlike every other bird, which has its own song, the mockingbird imitates the song of all the other birds. It has no singular song. Thus it is a mocking bird. To mock is to make light of that which deserves gravitas. It is to treat lightly the weighty issues of the soul. To merely imitate is to suffer what novelist Milan Kundera has called "the unbearable lightness of being." Personal gravitas comes from being connected to your soul print.

Sometimes though, as we all know, a comic treatment can be the most serious. Woody Allen's funniest and perhaps most tragic movie is the film *Zelig*. Zelig is a man whose identity and personality change radically throughout his life. Each time he changes into an imitation of his environment. The end of the movie is a tragedy. Zelig is a chameleon, a human version of the lizard that survives by masterfully blending in with his environment. But what happens when, as with Zelig, his masterful blending backfires?

If you don't believe in synchronicity, listen to this: On the very day that I wrote the lines above, I received an e-mail from a student. David is his name—we affectionately call him Dovidel. The week before, he had been at a class I taught about the mystical underpinnings of the soul print idea. His e-mail was in response to the class:

It rained Friday, perhaps for the last time of the season. Though the midday sun was shining brightly, Saturday was not hot at all. The scent of eucalyptus and honeysuckle permeated throughout the wadis of the north, but forsaking scent for sight, I took the highway and surrounded myself with graves of old mystics, prophets, and fools, and fields of wildflowers in full bloom everywhere.

The words of your teaching last week dance in my mind. I know that you always say that one hears only the teaching that his soul needs to hear . . . and sees only the sights he needs to see. So here is what I saw.

Leaping into my consciousness, at first sight it appeared an iridescent green grasshopper, the likes of which I had never seen outside of Vermont in high summer. In fact this creature was a lizard, a chameleon. I paused, utterly transfixed, as the reptile transformed its color to blend into the black asphalt road it intended to cross with alacrity. I thought to aid this creature in its journey, but owing to the heaviness of traffic, stood behind to watch.

Bedecked in flags, the white Fiat was third in a line of vehicles heading eastbound. Its left wheels passed over the lizard, which flipped over and lay on its back.

The following day, I visited the grave, a black splotch on the road.

All its evolutionary history had taught this reptile that in order to survive it needed to blend into its environment. Feeling a kinship, as if we had both gone to the same school, I pondered the revelation it revealed. Was it mere foolishness and chaos or a prophecy of changed times?

The point of the lecture Dovidel had attended was that human beings have an evolutionary mechanism of survival not shared by any known species in the animal kingdom. It is the mechanism of uniqueness. Our only path to survival is the path of the unique self. Attempting to blend in or shed our distinctive character is a move against our survival; it is a fatal bid to blend into a black asphalt highway. This, however, is what our grade school teachers forgot to teach us.

The primary responsibility of a teacher is to communicate to the student two elemental truths:

1) You are special. There is no one else like
   you in the whole world.
2) Your friend sitting next to you is no less
   special. There is no one else like her in
   the entire world.

THE CALL TO BE A KING

Reb Zushya of Anipol, mystical master, was found crying on his deathbed.

"Why are you crying?" his students asked. "You who were so pious—what do you have to regret or fear?"

Reb Zushya of Anipol responded, "If they ask me in the world to

come why I was not a teacher like Moses, I will have an answer. If
they ask me why I was not devout like Elijah, I will have an answer.
But if they ask me why I was not Zushya, to this I will have no
answer."

And finally the poet Emily Dickinson:

> We never know how high we are
> Till we are called to rise;
> And then, if we are true to plan,
> Our statures touch the skies.
> The heroism we recite
> Would be a daily thing,
> Did not ourselves the cubits warp
> For fear to be a king

There are only two great fears that should exist in a person's life,
the fear of deceiving oneself and the fear of imitating someone else.
Both of these prevent us from being ourselves, from being kings.

THE SECOND TRUTH: THE GRAND
CALL OF THE ORDINARY

The soul print call belongs to all of us. It is not limited to people
whom history has deemed great or has granted celebrity.

Celebrity is a relatively modern invention. Fame can actually be
a kind of drug needed by a person who is disconnected from his
soul print and alienated from his call. Fame allows someone to
silence the gnawing doubt of self-valuation. When heeding the
siren's call to fame is the goal instead of the ancillary result of the
soul print call, then we are sure to be dashed against the rocks.
Fame is a result of something else and not the thing itself. In short,
fame is not a calling. Indeed, it is often used to hide the lack of true
vocation.

ACADEMY AWARDS FOR THE ANONYMOUS

My grandfather was a huge movie fan. He used to say to me, in his thick European accent, "Marc, did you ever watch the Oscars, the Academy Awards?"

"Sure," I would reply.

"The Oscars," he would say, "are your greatest spiritual teacher."

"Why?"

He would invariably answer, "You win an award for playing your part like a pro, the absolute best that you have been given. It doesn't matter whether your destiny is to be the rich man, the poor man, or the thief. Play your part in the story to the hilt, and for that, God, the world, the universe, gives you your award."

My brother-in-law Brad, one of the loveliest human beings you will run into on the planet, shared with me a similar Taoist idea. The Taoists teach that whatever we are doing we should play that role to the hilt—when someone asks you what you do, you should respond, "I am playing being an author," or "playing a pediatrician," or "a plumber." By acting our part, no matter how ordinary it seems, we realize that it is not about what role we receive but it is all about how well we play the part we were scripted for. Hmmm. I wonder if the Taoists knew my grandfather.

William Safire of *The New York Times* fame put out a wonderful book called *Lend Me Your Ears—Great Speeches in History*. The only problem with the book is the second phrase of the title. The contents in the book are not the great speeches in history. They are rather, and the difference is critical, the great speeches in recorded history, the words uttered by famous and memorable people. I would wager that the truly great speeches of all time were made by everyday people in kitchens while washing dishes or gathered around the dinner table, between lovers on country lanes, or even soliloquies by farmers harvesting their fields.

The Kabbalistic tradition of the "Thirty-Six Just Men" makes precisely this point. According to the Kabbalah, there are thirty-six men, and I would add women, who have fully realized their soul prints. These people have heard the music of their unique sirens calling them to live fully their own depth. And they have responded. They are the people of voice and the people of face. What is so wonderful, however, about the Kabbalistic tradition is that all of the members of the Kabbalistic society of thirty-six just men are anonymous.

Soul Print Practice

Name the five wealthiest people in the world.

Name the last five winners of the Miss America contest.

Name the last five people who have won the Nobel or Pulitzer Prize.

Name the last half dozen Academy Award winners for best actor and actress.

Name the last decade's worth of World Series winners.

How did you do?

I know I did horrendously. The point is this: We forget yesterday's headliners. These people are the best in their fields. But the applause dies. Trophies tarnish. Achievements are forgotten. Accolades and awards are buried with their owners.

Here's another quiz. See how you do on this one.

List a few teachers who aided your journey through school.

Name three friends who have helped you through a difficult time.

Name five people who have taught you something worthwhile.

Think of a few people who have made you feel appreciated and special.

Name half a dozen heroes whose stories have inspired you.

THE UNSEEN—A STORY

The Baal Shem Tov and his Hasidim found themselves lost in a forest one Friday afternoon. Beyond the thick trees, they saw that the sun was soon to set and the Sabbath would soon begin. Luckily, they stumbled upon a cottage at the edge of the wood. They knocked on the door and asked if they could stay for the twenty-four hours of the Sabbath, for at that time the pious do not travel.

The woman who opened the door was the ugliest person they had ever seen, exceeded only perhaps by her husband behind her. "You can stay," she answered reluctantly, with not a little annoyance, "but only on one condition. You say not one word the entire Sabbath. You sing not one song, or clap one hand. We do not want to hear you. We do not want to see you. You can stay in the barn, but you must stay in silence."

Having little choice in the matter, the Baal Shem and his followers agreed. Accustomed as they were to joyous conversation and sacred dancing throughout the Sabbath, they passed together a most painful twenty-four hours. As soon as the sun set, they hurried to their wagon to escape the accursed place.

But before they could go, the door of the cottage opened once again. This time though, light shone forth from what seemed to be a palace, and the woman and her husband emerged to greet them. But now she appeared to be the most beautiful woman in the world and her husband no less beautiful than herself.

She spoke gently, as if in song, to the Baal Shem. "Master," she asked, "don't you recognize me?"

The Baal Shem looked deep into her eyes until finally recognition dawned across his face. "Why, of course. You are Sarah, the orphan girl who worked in our kitchen so very, very long ago."

"Yes, it is true," she said, as a smile spread across her delicate features. The master waited for her explanation.

"When I worked in your kitchen, I was destitute. The older girls would comb my hair daily to get the lice out. They combed so hard that it hurt. I cried out, but you never noticed. You never recognized me.

"So I left your home and wandered until I met my holy husband. My husband, I must tell you, is the head of the hidden society of the Thirty-Six Just Men. When we married, we completed each other's cycles through this world. We perfected each other's souls. That is, except for the one thing that kept my cycle from being complete. And that was this truth: Because of me, because he ignored me as a servant girl, the Baal Shem Tov lost his share in the world to come. He who does not recognize the soul of another cannot be recognized by God.

" 'So what are we to do?' I asked my husband. He said, 'The fixing can only happen if the Baal Shem himself spends a Sabbath at our house, unseen and unheard. A full Sabbath without voice and without face will atone for his having not heard your voice and seen your face. But that is not yet enough,' my holy husband said to me. 'At the end of the Sabbath, for the fixing to be complete he must recognize you.' "

By the time she had finished talking, tears were streaming down the Baal Shem's face. Silently, they embraced, her cycle perfected, his share in the world to come received.

We have forgotten that the servant girl has a calling no less than does the lady of the house. We have forgotten the people who change the linens in our hotel rooms. And if we do remember them then it is as objects of our largesse rather than as human beings called to destiny. The overpowering message of biblical myth is that every human being is called. For we are all the servant girls, the changers of linens in hotel rooms.

SEEING THE BIG PICTURE

We have lost a sense of our grandeur. Not just because of the soul-denigration of psychology, but because we Westerners have so vaunted the rugged American individualist who does it all himself—pulling himself up by his bootstraps to achieve fame and fortune—that we have largely devalued everyone else. While rugged individualism is one expression of the soul print, it is certainly not the only expression and not even the best expression. Our soul prints reveal themselves best not in our independence, but in our interdependence. Everyone needs help—no one has ever succeeded purely on his own. The luckiest people are the people who know they need people. For some, soul print destiny is in the public eye, while for others it is behind the scenes. We need to learn to value and vaunt not only the one who scores the goal but just as much, and sometimes more, the one who executes the assist.

Callings are not limited to seemingly self-made men and women. Every person on the team is called. Biblical myth—particularly the story of Moses—underscores this idea when it teaches that the spoils of battle are split equally between the heroic warrior and the lowest person working the supply train. In a way different from the Greek model, in which only the prowess of the hero is sung and considered to be of the gods, biblical myth affirms that callings come in all shapes and sizes, to people of all shapes and sizes, who have tasks of all shapes and sizes.

My wife, Cary, loves to tell the story of a trip she made to Italy. Coming across a church under construction, she stopped, as is her way, to talk with some of the workers on the site. "What are you doing here?" she asked the first worker.

"I weld," he said, showing her proudly the tools of his trade.

"And you, sir, what do you do here?" she asked a second man.

"I am the stone mason," he said, explaining to her just what stone masons do.

Finally, she asked a third person, a young man who looked not a day past his eighteenth birthday, "And what are you doing here?"

To which he answered without a moment's hesitation, "Why, I am here building a church to the glory of God."

My wife is a poet who very much believes in poetic license, so I am not sure whether the story actually happened, but the point strikes me anew every time she tells the tale. The decision about how to view the vocation of your soul print is yours alone. To be connected to your calling is to feel as if you are part of building that church. To be disconnected means that you are never part of anything. You may be a stone mason, but if your craft is disassociated from the dreams and visions that underpin the buildings you build, that is the beginning of your soul print distortion. After denying your work its meaning, it is a surprisingly short step to building roads for a regime that tortures and abuses its citizens, or becoming an arms merchant who sells chemical weapons to the highest bidder. Such people do not look like monsters and may well be good fathers and considerate husbands, but they have lost touch with their role in the larger scheme of things, and tragically so.

Soul print distortion always leads to moral aberrations. Part of recovering your soul print is to begin to reconceive your place in the larger scheme of things.

THE HOLY HUNCHBACK

I first heard the story of the holy hunchback on a radio show that I hosted in Jerusalem. Two wonderful women, Elana and Dari, who over time came to be my closest sisters, were my permanent guests on the show. Dari told this story about her father, a beautiful spiritual folksinger and luminescent teacher named Shlomo Carlebach. To honor her and him, I will tell the story as he told it to her.

One of the greatest masters of modern times was Kalonimus Kalman, the Master of Piacezna, who perished in the Warsaw ghetto. He would say that children at five years old already need a master: They need somebody to connect their souls to heaven. So he gathered around him a kingdom of children. He had a school with thousands of kids, and he was their father, their mother, their best friend. He was moved by the Nazis to the Warsaw ghetto in 1940. There he wrote a most precious book called The Holy Fire, *which recounted the teachings he gave in the dark of the ghetto. He was killed in the death camp Treblinka.*

When his book came out after the war was over, I couldn't believe its beauty, it so pierced my heart. I asked everyone, "Where are those kids? The precious children who heard these teachings every week? I'd love to speak to them." And I was told there was nobody left, nobody.

But one day, a few years ago, I was walking down Yarcon, a street near the beach of Tel Aviv. And here I saw a hunchback. So broken. So broken. His face was beautiful, so handsome, but his whole body was misshapen. He was sweeping the streets. I had a feeling this person was special and so I said, "Shalom, peace unto you."

He replied to me in the heaviest Polish. I asked if he was from Poland. And he says, "Yes, I'm from Piacezna." And I couldn't believe it—Piacezna! I asked if he had ever seen the holiest Kalonimus Kalman, Piacezna's master. He said to me, "What do you mean, have I seen him? I was a student in his school from the age of five until I was eleven. When I was eleven, I went to Auschwitz. I was so strong they thought I was seventeen. I was whipped and hit and kicked and never healed—that's why I look the way I do now. I have nobody in the world. I'm all alone." And he kept on sweeping the ground.

I said, "My sweetest friend, do you know, my whole life I've been waiting to see you, a person who saw the Master of Piacezna, a person who was one of his children. Please, give me one of his teachings."

The hunchback glared at me. "Do you think you can be in Auschwitz five years and still remember teachings?"

"Yes, I'm sure of it," I said. "The Master's teachings—how could you forget them?"

And so he said, "Okay, wait." He went to the water fountain to wash his hands. He fixed his tie, put on his jacket, and then said to me one more time, "Do you really want to hear it?"

"I swear to you, I'll tell your teaching all over the world."

So he began. "I want you to know that there never was such a Sabbath as this one. We danced, hundreds and maybe thousands of children, and the master was singing a song to greet the holy angels, and at the meal he would teach between every course. And after every teaching this is what the master would say, 'Children, Kinderlach, der goyseh zach in de velt iz tuen emetzen a'tovah—*the greatest thing in the world is to do somebody else a favor. The greatest thing in the world is to do somebody else a favor.'"*

The hunchback sighed. "You know, my parents are gone, my whole family, no one exists anymore. And so I was in Auschwitz and alone and I wanted to commit suicide. And the last moment I could hear my master say, "Kinderlin, children . . . do somebody else a favor. Do somebody a favor.'"

He looked me directly in the eye. "Do you know how many favors you can do in Auschwitz at night? People are lying on the floor crying, and nobody even has any strength to listen to their stories anymore. I would walk from one person to the other and ask, 'Why are you crying?' and they would tell me about their children, their wives, people they'd never see in this life again. I would hold their hands and cry with them. Then I would walk to the next person. And it would give me strength for another day.

"When I was at the end again . . . I'd hear my Rebbe's voice. I want you to know I'm here in Tel Aviv and I have no one in the world. And I take off my shoes, go down to the beach, I go up to my nose in the ocean, ready to sink, and I can't help but hear my Rebbe's voice saying, 'The greatest thing in the world is to do somebody else a favor. Remember, my precious children, the greatest thing in the world is to do somebody else a favor.' "

He stared at me again for a long time and said, "You know how many favors you can do on the streets of the world?"

And he kept on sweeping the street.

It was the end of summer and I had to go back to the States for the fall. But when I returned to Tel Aviv, I went searching Yarcon, looking for my holy hunchback. I couldn't find him. I asked some people who told me, "Don't you know? He left the world early this fall."

I said to Dari that day on the radio after she told her dad's story, "The holy hunchback cleans the streets of the world by telling everyone, 'Do someone else a favor.' " That was his vocation; that was his call. But aren't we all in some sense holy hunchbacks? We have all been beaten up a little bit, sometimes a lot, by the world. We all sometimes ask ourselves late at night, "What is it really about anyway? What are we doing here?" The answer is that each one of us has a calling, a special job only he or she can do in sweeping the streets of the world. No one can tell us what that job is. No one but no one can take it away from us. It is to do that job that we get up in the morning. That is our soul print calling."

Soul Print Practice

Try to view every telephone call as a calling.

You receive a telephone call. The caller says something to spark your anger. Could you view it as a call to work on anger?

If the person seems to be rambling, could that be your call to work on patience? Or alternatively, a call to work on boundaries?

You can be called to work on a specific area in your personal growth. We are so used to thinking of calling as a public affair that we forget that our own growth, our own learning, and the healing of our particular soul may well be our purpose in the world. Every soul has its own lessons to learn, its own healing to undergo and its own wisdom to share. To identify your special place of healing and learning may be the most important part of hearing your call.

10

———◆———

COUNTERFEIT CALLS
Choosing the Right Trumpeter

THE THIRD TRUTH

One of the overwhelming reasons that responding to a call is such a high-stakes proposition is that you cannot respond to every call you hear. William James wrote that he would like to be "a great athlete, and make a million a year, be a wit, a bon vivant, and a lady-killer, as well as a philosopher; a philanthropist, statesman, warrior, and African explorer, as well as a 'tone poet' and saint. But the thing is simply impossible. . . . Such different characters may conceivably at the outset of life be alike possible to a man. But to make any one of them actual, the rest must more or less be suppressed. So the seeker of his truest, strongest, deepest self must review the list carefully, and pick out the one on which to stake his salvation. All other selves thereupon become unreal. . . ."

We cannot respond fully to more than one call, for fulfilling our One will complete our All-Oneness.

David from Liluv cherished his yearly pilgrimage to pray in the court of his master for the high holy days. He journeyed a great distance and the pilgrimage was arduous, sometimes dangerous, but he always came. One particular year, his wagon broke down not once but twice and heavy rains slowed the way. Obstacle after obstacle kept him lagging, until the final day was on the verge of falling into the sacredness of the holiday night.

Finally, David could see the miniscule silhouette of his master's shtetl in the distance. Yet on the horizon he also saw a figure on the road, running toward him. The man reached him, calling out with heaving breath, "Thank God you are here! I knew someone would come. Sir, please stop, I have a dire request of you. We have only nine men in our town and as you know, we require ten people to form a quorum that will allow us to recite the public prayer, to read from the Torah, and to say the Kaddish on this holiday. With less than ten, sir, as you know, we will be unable to do any of these things. The tenth person in our town just this morning passed away." The man gasped with urgency. "We have only nine people! Please, sir, won't you please stay with us this holiday and be the tenth?"

Although David was moved by the request, he replied, "I'm sorry, but you will have to pray privately this holiday. You see, I have traveled very far to come to my master for the holiday prayers. I have waited all year to see him, and our meeting is a great spiritual moment. I cannot miss it."

David of Liluv went on, forgetting the brief encounter with the man in the road, until he arrived at his master's house just in time for the evening prayers. But strangely enough, his master refused to greet him. All through the holiday, his master averted his gaze from David, speaking not a word to him.

David of Liluv was devastated. What had he done to deserve this treatment from his master? He could not imagine. At the end of the holiday, his master called him for a private audience. "What did I do?" David asked him. "What sin could I have committed to possibly earn such displeasure from my master?"

His teacher looked at him, pale with disappointment, and said sadly, "David, my sweet David, what a mistake you have made. Your soul came to this world in order for you to be the tenth person to pray in that little town along the road. Only you could have been that tenth person. And you, so intent on your own spiritual goals, failed to respond to your soul's calling."

We can only be in one place at a time. There is always a false dream to give up in order to grasp the dream that is ours. I always tell my male students, "There are two women in every man's life—the woman he marries and the woman he doesn't." Only when we are willing to give up the image of the woman we don't marry can we say "I do." (I would imagine the same is true for a woman.) Such is the nature of all life's offerings. There is always a sacrificial moment that of necessity precedes the moment of fulfillment.

False calls, like false messiahs, always come well disguised—as fear, public opinion, parental expectations, communal pressure, religious teachings, or scientific dogma. Often we're sure that our call is here when really it's way over there. Often we're sure that we need to respond to one calling, when really that calling is not the calling of our soul, but the calling of our culture, of our parents, of our fears. We miss the true clarion. We choose to hear the wrong trumpeter.

THE FOURTH TRUTH: CALLS IN DISGUISE

As we discern our mission in life, we must watch out carefully for two pitfalls: calls that are disguised, and personal baggage rearing its head, disguised as a call.

First, let's explore calls in disguise. We would like our calls to be neat and elegant spiritual affairs, appearing with incense burning, chiming bells, and meditative music. For whatever reason, it just doesn't work that way. Not even the progenitor of us all, the great father, Abraham himself, was that lucky. The classic biblical myth story of the call is the *Lech Lecha* story of Abraham. It sounds pretty straightforward: "God spoke to Abraham saying, *Lech Lecha*, Go to yourself." It would seem to be the classic story of the call come down from heaven—clear as day—addressed directly, and exclusively, to Abraham.

Lest we get too comfortable with the concept of the clear call, the Zohar, the foundational work of biblical mysticism, steps in and revisions the whole tale. In the Zohar's picture of the world, God says to every human being—every day!—"Go to your self. Begin the journey that only you can make." What then was special about Abraham and his journey that it should occupy such a prominent place in biblical myth? The answer? He was the only one who heard the call. Indeed, the divine call went out to everyone, echoing throughout the inner corridors of the human spirit. Yet Abraham was the only one who responded. The Zohar implies it's not that God chose Abraham. It is that Abraham chose God!

And if that's not enough, a later mystic, following the interpretive tradition of the Zohar, further undermines our usual understanding of the neatly ordered call. As the Master of Berdichev points out emphatically, Abraham was *lech-lecha*-ing because he was in trouble with the law. The government of Charan, not to mention his own father, had just tried to kill him for challenging the religious establishment of his day. Abraham's life was a mess. In this reading, what moved Abraham to journey to Canaan was not a call from God at all. He was running away! Given his predicament, that must have seemed like a fine idea.

So why, the reader may ask, does the text declare this story to be about a call from God? The answer is that the text speaks from the vantage of Abraham remembering his life. After he ran away— years later, looking back—he realized that his escape was the beginning of his spiritual journey. Only in retrospect did he realize that it was a call.

Callings, we must always remember, often come in the most clever disguises.

FALSE CALLS

At the same time, we need to always be on the lookout for unresolved personal issues or agendas that disguise themselves as calls.

Let's look for a second at a later Abraham story, what is referred to in biblical myth as the binding of Isaac. It is a difficult, complex, and disturbing story. Abraham heard a call telling him to sacrifice his son. Abraham responded to the call, taking his son Isaac to Mount Moriah—apparently in order to sacrifice him. Then, with knife poised above his son, Abraham heard a second call, this one telling him not to sacrifice his son but to sacrifice a ram in his stead.

I want to offer a radical reading of the story that I believe is implicit in one possible understanding from the Zohar. The Zohar says that the voice Abraham heard calling him to sacrifice his son was an *"aspaklarya delo nahara,"* a clouded mirror. Abraham actually wasn't sure about the call he heard. He gazed into that blurry mirror and thought he discerned a call to sacrifice his son.

Of course, we readers of biblical myth know some interesting things about Abraham's psychological profile. Remember the reference we made earlier to Abraham's rather troublesome past? The recorded story tells us that he had very narrowly escaped his own father's attempt to throw him into a furnace of fire. His death was to be a sacrifice to appease Charan's supposedly godlike and immortal king, Nimrod.

You don't have to know a lot about psychology to understand the idea of repetition compulsion. We are driven by the deepest of forces to do to our children what our parents did to us. I would suggest (together with my friend Michael Lerner) that Abraham was merely doing to his son what his father did to him. This is indeed the way I have read the Zohar. The first voice that Abraham heard was unclear. Based on his personal history, he misunderstood this to be a call to sacrifice his son. In reality, it was nothing of the kind. Rather, it was the voice of his inner psychological needs. (It's not God being nasty and capricious, demanding Abraham offer blind loyalty to his commands, giving him a test of absolute loyalty to the Ultimate Dad.)

Abraham became a hero in the story because he heard a second calling, this time telling him it is immoral to sacrifice your son. Abraham was able to break the powerful pull of childhood; he was able to break the pattern set by his father. He learned to distinguish between a true call and an old psychological wound disguised as a call.

To be free means to be free to hear and respond to a call. When your frequencies are jammed by unresolved issues, you cannot pick up on your true call. Even more dangerous, you are prone to hear calls where it is only unresolved trauma and pain. Trauma speaks in many tongues. Beware of the venom in its counterfeit call.

Soul Print Practice

Here is the final, all-stops-out, get-your-attention soul print call set of questions. The insights provoked by these questions will never fail to provide you with vital soul print hints.

1) If you knew that you had exactly one year to live, how would you spend it?

2) If you did not have to work for a living, what would you do?

3) You are walking with your thirteen-year-old son or daughter. Your child turns to you and asks, "What are the things you are most proud of in your life?" How do you answer your child?

Employing a powerful biblical myth custom, write an ethical will to your children. An ethical will contains the beliefs, practices, and wisdom you have gathered in your life that you want to leave to the next generation. If you don't have children, either imagine children, or write an ethical will to your friends.

Your answers to these questions should set you well on the path to finding your soul print calling.

THE SPIRITUAL TOOLBOX

In the first four truths we explored the major elements of the calls we need to be listening for. Now, we can look at the primary personal characteristic required for you to respond to your call.

This truth will identify the contents of your spiritual toolbox as you develop the innate skills you have as part of your soul print.

THE FIFTH TRUTH: RISK-TAKING

Every call involves an element of risk for the simple reason that in answering the call we are almost inevitably asked to give something up. Most frequently, we are asked to give up conceptions we have clung to that are no longer useful in our growth. You can respond to your call if your soul is willing to take the risk.

One of the most seductive and subtle comfort zones is what psychological literature sometimes calls "old maps." Old maps are the views of reality that guided us, perhaps even successfully, for a period in our lives but that have become outdated. Reality is always changing. Growth means always being willing to look at reality honestly and, if need be, to draw new maps that can lead to a greater awareness of the missions we are called to in the world.

Psychologists once performed an experiment with a monkey where the creature was taught to take food and hold it wrapped in his fist. Then the same food was placed in a cage within the monkey's reach. The monkey, as expected, reached his hand into the cage to take the food. However, with his fist clenched around the food, he was unable to remove his hand from the cage. The monkey—guided by the old map for getting food—guarded his claim with a clenched fist, simply refusing to open his hand. Without outside intervention, the monkey would have died of starvation. And at least on this score Darwin was right—human beings and monkeys are remarkably alike. It is enormously difficult for us to give up the old maps that guided us and made us feel safe for a time—sometimes even when it costs us our life.

A party of theologians was climbing in the Alps. After several hours, they became hopelessly lost. One of them studied the map for some time, turning it up and down, sighting on distant landmarks, consulting his compass and the sun. Finally, he said, "Okay, see that big mountain over there?"

"Yes?" asked the others eagerly.

"Well, according to this map, we are standing on top of it."

It's hard to surrender our maps even when they are obviously wrong. For example, sometimes it is important for you to believe that people are not trustworthy. It can even be your only hope for psychological survival, especially if people close to you, like your parents while you were growing up, actually were untrustworthy. As a child, you probably found it easier to believe that people in general cannot be trusted than to believe that your parents were the ones who were deceitful. The hurt of trust shattered could be too painful to bear—and too dangerous. At such a time the key to your map might read, "People are untrustworthy—navigate accordingly." Later in life, you might encounter a new reality—in marriage, in a business partnership—where trust is absolutely essential to the success of your venture. In order to trust, you need to redraw your reality map. You need to chart a course with the new premise that some people are untrustworthy, while other people are completely reliable and faithful.

This evolution can be enormously painful, for in acknowledging trust as a possibility, you explode the myth you lived by, that "people can't be trusted." Instead, you revise that myth into a more complex truth, as you realize that it was "only certain people"—perhaps your parents, a lover, a friend—who could not be trusted. The full implication of the betrayal you experienced then becomes clear and is often too painful to confront. One way we avoid that pain is to clutch desperately at the old reality map. The problem is that the old map is incapable of helping navigate your new circumstances and can potentially lead into dangerous and destructive waters and keep you from the call that is your soul print's declared destination.

PAINTER OR POLICEMAN

Many years ago, a man came to see me who was a policeman in the town where I served my first congregation. He was a lovely man, responsible, courageous, a good father and husband, and yet he suffered from mild depressions. I'm not a therapist, and I counsel in no formal professional sense, and yet when I pass on a client to a professional, I am usually intuitively able to convey some sense of what's wrong. In the case of the policeman, I had no clue. The man was in therapy for almost a year with little effect. After a year, he came back to me in quite a bad state; his depression was getting worse and he didn't understand why.

It so happened on the day the policeman came to see me again that I needed to go down to Miami for the opening of an art gallery owned by a close friend. I suggested we drive down together and talk on the way. I wanted to leave the gallery not that long after we had arrived. Although I love art, I must admit that it doesn't hold me for an enormously long time. When I went to find my friend the policeman, I saw him wandering in what seemed to be near rapture through the gallery. All of a sudden, the potential source of the man's problem occurred to me.

On the drive back I asked him nonchalantly, "Do you paint?"

"Yeah," he said, "I paint, but it's not really that good. My older brother, though—he's the painter in the family."

"Really," I said. "Would you mind showing me something that you've painted?"

"Well, I don't really have anything," he said in a low voice.

"You must have something."

Indeed, he did have a few pieces, he said, and though there wasn't "really any point in it," he would bring them to me. A week later, I saw them—and they were magnificent. I asked him why he didn't paint more often. He said that he wanted to, but his responsibilities lay elsewhere. Anyway, he said, his brother was really the painter in the family.

Over another six months of deep conversation, we tried to understand why he became a policeman when it was so clear that he was a painter. The answer turned out to be straightforward. His brother was the painter in the family; that dogma was vital, for myriad reasons, to the myths that his family was built on. As you can already imagine, not all of those myths were healthy and still fewer were rooted in reality.

My friend the policeman/painter went through a long but relatively gentle process of giving up old maps in order to open him up to the map of his future—the soul print call to paint. Giving up old maps involved great emotional risks for him. He needed to reevaluate the family support structure he had taken for granted for so long before he could take the risk he was called upon to make. Today he is a noted painter in the southern United States.

PUTTING THE BABY CARRIAGE BEFORE THE BABY

Here is a story the mystics like to tell:

Every year at the time of the harvest festival, two brothers would travel to visit their teacher. Being wise men themselves, they were heedful of the advice of the sages who taught that one should always sleep at the same inn each year. One year as they greeted their now long-time friend the innkeeper, they noticed that he was more downcast and listless than they had ever seen him before. "What is wrong?" they inquired.

After some prodding, the innkeeper answered them. "It is my wife. Time beckons her to have children, and she so much wants to be a mother, but we have not been able to. I know your teacher is a worker of wonders whose prayer is powerful. Tell me, do you think he could pray for us?"

The brothers assured him that they would ask their master to include them in his prayers.

The next morning as they set out on the day's journey, they encountered the strangest sight. The wife of the innkeeper was out walking
around the village with a brand-new baby carriage! Baby carriages
were luxurious items and cost a great deal of money—more than the
innkeeper probably had. "Congratulations!" people called out to her,
thinking she must surely be with child.

"Oh no," she replied, "I am not with child yet."

The villagers then exchanged pitying glances, thinking that her
yearning for a child must have driven her mad.

The brothers themselves were concerned as well. Here their friend
the innkeeper's wife had spent much of their savings and it was not at all
guaranteed that the teacher's prayer would be answered. They were
pious men but not fools. There being little to do, however, they went on
their way.

At the next harvest, the two brothers again set out to travel to visit
their teacher. They wished to stay at the same inn but were afraid to. If
no child had been born, then they would certainly not be welcome
guests. They decided to listen at the door. If they heard the sound of a
baby crying, they would enter. If not, they would find another place to
lodge.

They arrived to find the inn was full of festivities. Sure enough, it
was the day of the birth party. There was great rejoicing in the house
and the brothers were made the godfathers of the newborn child.

One of the brothers, though happy for the couple, hid a deep sadness
underneath his smile. When they arrived at the home of their teacher,
this brother requested an urgent audience with the master. Since he was
a wise and loyal student, his wish was granted. The brother sat down,
and with tears streaming down his face he asked the master, "I don't
understand. Was I not important to you? My wife wanted a child as
well. She too is called to motherhood. Every year for twenty years I have
asked you to pray for my wife. You have agreed, and yet we are still
childless. This innkeeper who you do not know, who is not your student,
who bears you no love or loyalty, asks you to pray, and within a year his
wife has a child!"

The master looked at his student ever so gently. "Tell me, my dear student and friend," he asked. "Did your wife ever go out and buy a baby carriage?"

When we respond to a call, there is always a moment when we need to buy a baby carriage. We have to choose to leap, believing that the net will appear, to risk the uncertainty and take action. For—to return to our original metaphor—that is the only way new babies are born.

LEAP AND THE NET WILL APPEAR

In this story, the master teaches his student an elemental truth— that to respond genuinely to your call, you must show yourself that you are prepared to take the risk. The woman in the tale risked her savings and bought a baby carriage on the belief that she would become a mother. "Leap and the net will appear" would be a good way to sum up the philosophy of the called. You first need to leap— risking a fall—before the net is ready to make its appearance.

The closer the issue is to your soul print calling, the more you must be willing to risk. There is a general rule in biblical thought that you never take ultimate risks. Other than in very limited cases, when there is risk to life or limb, in biblical myth generally, it is better to be careful and live even if just to fight another day. The master Mordechai Lainer of Ishbitz, however, suggests a major exception to this rule. Every person has a unique calling in some area of his or her life. No two people have precisely the same call. In the area of your calling you must be willing, in his words, to "risk you soul."

"Risk your soul"—that's an extreme statement, but quite sensible after all. For your unique calling is a part of your soul print. If you lose that calling and become just another statistic, then you have lost your soul anyway. The best example is the painter/policeman we met previously. He had a stable income and secure position on the police force. Further, he was making a substantive contribution to society by being a policeman. No small accomplishment. To

risk that for anything less than a family member or a soul print calling would have been foolhardy. Taking a calculated risk to pursue
his soul print calling was courageous. When it comes to soul print
issues—those decisions and challenges that are bound up with your
personal call—you must go for broke.

The process of self-knowing, which Mordechai Lainer calls *bir-
rur*—best translated as "psycho-spiritual clarification"—is focused
on knowing yourself well enough to know in what areas you need
to take your major risks. But knowing yourself that well takes discipline, spiritual rigor, and insight.

RISK AND RESISTANCE

Because of the risk inherent in responding to a call, we sometimes
hear an authentic call clearly but simply do not want to respond.
There can be so many reasons why. Two are predominant. The first
is laziness and the second is fear.

By laziness, I don't mean the too-difficult-to-get-out-of-bed
kind of laziness. The difficulty of getting out of bed is not to be
underestimated, but I refer rather to all the effort and energy that is
always needed to respond to a true call. Like a drug, we are all
under the influence of heavy inertia. It is always easier and more
comfortable to stay where you are. A call always involves some
degree of movement—of action, as we saw in the last chapter.

The second reason for resistance is fear—the fear that the call
will conflict with your agenda. This fear is the demon dancing
between the lines of the Jonah myth. Jonah is the biblical prophet
called to the task of reforming the great city of Nineveh. The complexity of Jonah's story lies in the fact that Nineveh was the capital
of Assyria—Israel's archenemy. As no less than the leader of Israel,
the last thing Jonah wanted to do was to go teach wisdom to the citizens of Nineveh. He had a competing agenda. The result? He
ignored the call. He pretended, to everyone, himself included, that
he hadn't heard a thing.

Jonah promptly slipped out of the city, reached seaside, bought a ticket, and boarded a ship to set off as far as possible from his impossible call. But his calling pursued him, pouring down storms on his stiff neck and hard head. The waters raged—as they are wont to do when we ignore our calls. The whole ship was endangered—for unanswered calls can be treacherous to ourselves as well as those closest to us. Jonah asked to be thrown overboard, preferably to his death, but he fell right into the mouth of a whale. There in its cavernous belly his call finally caught up with him.

Perhaps it happened there because of the awful stench and the fact that he had no place else to run; or perhaps because the whale's belly was a chamber of meditation where Jonah met himself. However it came about, eventually Jonah was deposited upon dry land and pointed in the direction of his destiny: Nineveh. Soggy but reconciled, he set off for the great city. His is a passionate story whose point, of course, is that the call can't be calmed, can't be conquered, ignored, or escaped. Whatever we do, the call comes back.

We all have some degree of what human potential psychologist Abraham Maslow called a Jonah Complex. We all try to some extent to divert our attention, to look the other way, and to cotton our ears to the call.

In the cycle of the biblical-myth year, the Jonah story is read on the holiday of forgiveness. Why on this day? Jonah teaches us that the greatest sin that we must account for is when we allow our fear of risk to blind us to our calling. A missed call is more than opportunity lost; it is trouble gained. If we neglect the garden of our calling, then it will sprout thorns. The forgiveness festival is somewhat like the belly of the whale, the meditation chamber, where we are given the space within the stormy sea to sit and decipher the sounds of our call. The time of forgiveness reminds us that it is never too late; the invitation to meet our destiny awaits. If you listen closely on that day you can hear the spirits whispering, "It's never too late. It's never too late."

Soul Print Practice

Here I want to be careful. It is irresponsible to tell someone I don't know personally how and what to risk, but let me take a little bit of a risk and make some risky suggestions for you.

Ask a person out, in an act of potential romance or friendship, whom you have been afraid to approach.

Take sensual risks. Be creative with your senses, in how or what you eat, or make love, or in your adventures.

Name something you have always wanted to do and never had the guts to—and do it (providing it is ethical and does not put you or anyone else in genuine danger).

11

THE JOY OF THE CALL

HAPPINESS: A BY-PRODUCT YOU CAN'T BUY

A child found an egg. Not knowing that it was an eagle egg, he placed it in the warm nest of a backyard hen. The eggs hatched, and out came an eaglet among the chicks. Knowing of no other way to be, the eagle grew up like a chicken, scratching and pecking, clucking and cackling, flapping clumsy wings.

One day he heard the majestic call of an eagle, soaring high overhead. He gazed up at the magnificent bird, gliding, glorious atop the winds.

"Who's that?" he asked a neighboring chick.

"That's the eagle, king of birds. He belongs to the sky. We belong to the earth. We're chickens."

Circling in the air, the soaring eagle let out a last long call.

But the eaglet had gone back to clucking and pecking at the dusty ground.

He lived and died a chicken. He never responded to the eagle's call. He never stretched out his wings in flight.

This is an ugly duckling tale where the misfit never is transformed into the swan. The fledgling eagle never responds to the call of his high, true self. He believes he is just like everyone else, earthbound—and so earthbound he is. He never stretches out to his full wingspan, never rises to who he could have been.

An odd duck in his own time, the poet William Blake wrote, "No bird soars too high, if he soars with his own wings." Indeed, if we do not respond to the call of our destiny—to the *mispar* of our soul's light—if we do not soar as high as we can soar, then we will endanger our fundamental happiness. And happiness is a pretty big deal.

In light of our unpacking of the *mispar* moment—destiny's unique call to us—I want to return to the ever-important topic of happiness.

In the beginning of our discussion of "mere joy," we uncovered the biblical myth idea that happiness cannot be pursued. Quite the opposite, we said; happiness is only achievable as a by-product of the pursuit of important goals—goals other than happiness itself. What, however, are those important goals? What pursuits yield happiness? You could suggest—and indeed, some very good thinkers have—that those goals would be something general and admirable, like goodness, depth, values, and meaning. By actively pursuing one or some combination of these four, we may indeed achieve as a by-product some measure of happiness.

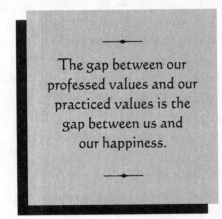

The gap between our professed values and our practiced values is the gap between us and our happiness.

Yet will following those abstract goals truly make us happy? To make this question even clearer, let's take one of those four goals and see how it plays out. Values, for example. We all have sets of values that govern and guard our lives. However, at best we are only partially successful in living by those values; for all of us, there is a gap between the values we profess and the values we practice. By actively pursing our values, we narrow that yawning gap. The gap between our professed values and our practiced values is the gap between us and our happiness. Thus the more we pursue our values, the happier we can be—or so it seems.

Clearly, there is some truth to this line of thought. However, the argument falls apart once we realize the distinction between happiness-potential and happiness itself. Without values, goodness, meaning, and depth, our happiness-potential goes down to zero.

However, if we pursue these things only in a general sort of way, though it's a lovely thing to do, we will not find happiness. We may well receive a degree of satisfaction, self-esteem, and peace of mind. Yet while all those are important ingredients in the happiness formula, the ingredients do not happiness make.

> Happiness is only a by-product of living your soul print. You can only be happy if you are fulfilling your call and living your story

You can be good, deep, possess impeccable values, and live a meaningful life and still be miserable. For there is still one essential element you are lacking. That is a profound connection with your soul print.

As we have said, happiness is only a by-product of living your soul print. You can only be happy if you are fulfilling your call and living your story. *Happiness is a natural result of the way your values help weave the singular tapestry of your life, lived in response to your call. Happiness derives from the pursuit of the meaning of your life, the plumbing of your unique depth, and enacting the good that you are uniquely capable of doing in the world.*

It's very simple. You can buy the best clothes in the world made from the finest fabrics by the most elegant of tailors. If the clothes don't quite fit—and even if you are the only one who notices—they will not give you that joyous feeling that comes from putting on great clothes that fall perfectly on your body. So too regarding what the Kabbalah calls "the garments of the soul." These are garments made of goodness, meaning, depth, and values. It is not enough that they be woven from the finest fabric. You need to have had a private fitting with the tailor. The clothes must be made with you and no one else in mind. Garments of that nature are transformative and joy-inducing. Happy is the person who wears them.

FROM DAIMON COMES EUIDAIMONIA

The novelist Honoré de Balzac wrote, "Vocations which we wanted to pursue, but didn't, bleed, like colors, on the whole of our existence." This quote provokes for me an image of a painter who does not paint; all of his unused colors come spilling after him, staining his life until he takes them upon his brush. If we do not pursue our particular call, then the ghost of that call will pursue us, like a haunting that stains our days.

For when you respond to cues that are not yours, when you're a policeman instead of a painter, ultimately you can't be happy. Happiness comes from being yourself in the most profound way possible. The ancient Greeks referred to happiness as *euidaimonia*. *Daimon* is the word for calling. You are happy only when you are responding to your *daimon*. Your *daimon* calls you to realize your soul print. Your happiness lies in your hands, if you would but take it.

To be happy, then, is to be responsive to the call of your deepest self. To be happy is to wake up in the morning and feel that you have a mission in the world that no one else can perform. To be happy is to know that among the billions of people on this planet, you are irreplaceable. This is true for every human being on the face of the globe, for what we share in common is our uniqueness.

The Western notion of the sacredness of every human life bursts from the same bedrock of the biblical myths that brought forth the idea of the soul print. The prospect of happiness exists for us only because the call of soul print animates the universe.

A PARADIGM SHIFT IN UNDERSTANDING JOY

Despite disagreements over nuance and intonation, biblical myth mystics share two ideas about joy. Both are different from our modern notion of happiness.

Joy, teach the Kabbalists, is both a source and a conduit of energy. The word most often associated in Kabbalah with joy is *chiyut,* roughly translated as "life energy," somewhat like the Chinese notion of *chi.* To be happy is to be plugged into the *chiyut* of the universe. The portal to that energy is the self, the vital soul print. At the same time, once you are plugged in, the joy itself is not only an energy source but also serves as a medium to channel ever more divine energy.

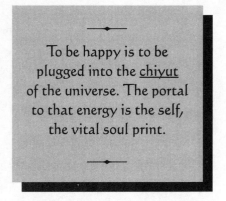

To be happy is to be plugged into the <u>chiyut</u> of the universe. The portal to that energy is the self, the vital soul print.

The idea of joy as divine energy is expressed by the Kabbalists in many different codes. Let me share one of them with you. A favorite epigram of the Kabbalists is *Simcha Poretz Geder:* "Joy breaks through fences." Joy is more than an attitude; it is a potent and powerful source of energy. One Kabbalist, the master Simcha Bunim (whose first name actually means "happiness"), used this epigram to give a novel explanation of a famous mystical passage, "All the gates are locked, the gates of tears are never locked." Traditionally, this verse has been taken to extol the power of a broken heart to break through all barriers when all other avenues have proven ineffective. When nothing else works, tears can still open all the gates.

In a subtle twist, Simcha Bunim turns the passage on its head:

If you are sad, he says, then you can only enter if the gate is
unlocked, already wide open. Thus God has no choice but to
leave the gates of tears unlocked. If you are joyous, however, then
even the gates that are locked you can still get through. After all,
Simcha poretz geder, Joy breaks through all fences. That being the
case, God sees no reason not to lock the gates. For they can
always be opened with joy. And indeed that is precisely what
God wants.

Soul Print Practice

Joy is always present. It's just a question of plugging in.

Every time you think of something you lack, recall something you have.

Make a list of the thirty things most important to you in your
life.

See how many of them you have.

For example, seeing, hearing, intelligence, talent, family, feeling, health, your son, your daughter . . .

Now think of that which is now making you unhappy.
Where is that lacking thing listed on this list?

More often than not, that thing that is causing you grief lies
toward the bottom of the list, and sometimes it's not even part of
the list at all.

THE HAPPINESS LOOP

Consider this cycle: The portal to joy is the soul print. Once we
access joy, it becomes contagious, self-generating, itself a channel
for more and more joy energy.

This simple set of observations is remarkable in that we so often
ignore it. We forget what joy really is. Too often, we automatically
associate happiness and success, although in our heart we know this
association to be false. Success, after all, has little to do with the soul

print. One teacher on happiness suggests a simple exercise. Ask people what it would take to make them happy. A better job, bigger salary, different spouse? Write it down. Then come back in five years and see if the people whose wish lists were fulfilled are any happier. If you are the impatient type, go to the people you know who have those very things—hot job, swollen salary,

The portal to joy is the soul print.

and trophy spouse—and see if they are happy. Chances are that the answer is no—or if they are happy, their happiness is probably unrelated to their accoutrements of success.

CHOOSING JOY

In their second core teaching, the Kabbalists instruct us that happiness is a decision. In the original mystical language, this idea is expressed in the maxim, "The source of joy is *binah*—understanding." One interpretation of that sentence tells us that happiness is accessed through contemplation, which is twofold. The first axis lies in the contemplation of the nature of the world. One reflects on life and death, sickness and health; what is permanent and real and what is fleeting and illusory. An entire biblical myth book—Ecclesiastes, in Hebrew *Kohelet*—is devoted to this meditation. "Illusion of Illusion, All is Illusion," says the king named Kohelet, as he begins his Buddha-like quest for meaning. His expedition, in all its byways and adventures, is a topic for a separate book. However, in the end, he reaches understanding as he finds the world to be a place of joy.

The second focus of Kabbalist contemplation—and here again biblical myth parts ways with Buddhism—is the contemplation of what we are calling the soul print. In this contemplation, you let your mind dwell on the singular signature of your soul as you ask yourself, "What is the unique story that I am supposed to be living in the world?"

Finally, to conclude our meditation on the nature of soul print joy, I offer a second interpretation of the Kabbalistic epigram, "The source of joy is understanding." If joy is a product of understanding, then it is no longer an option or an event or a feeling we await. Joy is a decision. It is a conscious choice we make. It's even an obligation.

Soul Print Practice

A friend, author Dennis Prager, talks about the missing tile syndrome.

Look at a ceiling that has every tile except one. What does your eye always focus on?

The missing tile, of course. That's what we do in life. We can have so much and still focus all of our energy on what we don't have.

NO FAR-FLUNG LOCALE

We sometimes think that we need to cross worlds to find our calling. Sometimes we do. However, usually our destiny is within easy reach. Sometimes it is right under our nose, when we're out searching in all the wrong places. The nature of a Universe of Love, teaches the Safed Kabbalist Isaac Luria, is that all that you need to answer your call and realize your soul print is part of your life right now. It's all rattling around in the toolbox we carry within.

The story is told of Sali, a tailor in seventeenth-century Cracow, who felt deeply lonely even as he was married to a lovely wife and had five beautiful children. Nightly, Sali was plagued by a dream—that beneath a bridge in Prague there lay a buried treasure. When the tailor told his wife his dream, she scoffed at it. When he told his friends, they mocked it. Still, Sali felt he needed to respond to the call of the dream, and so he set off to Prague.

The tailor arrived in the great city and soon enough he saw precisely the bridge he had beheld in his dreams. Unfortunately for Sali, however, the bridge led to the castle of the prince of the province.

Sali spent some hours studying the bridge, trying to figure out how he could get to the moat underneath it without the guards noticing him. Of course, when he ventured toward the bridge, the guards did notice him and, suspecting him of foul intentions, arrested him. They took him to the guardhouse for questioning, and Sali resolved not to tell his true name or village for fear of harm that might come to his family.

That night he was interrogated by one of the guards. "I had a dream," Sali explained to the guard. "I had a dream, and in the dream I saw that there was a treasure under this bridge."

"That's ridiculous," the guard said. "You came all the way from your town because you had a dream there was a treasure under the bridge? Let me tell you—I also have dreams. I dreamt that there's a person named Sali who lives in a faraway hamlet and there's a treasure under his stove. Do you see me traveling all the way to that hamlet to look for the treasure under his stove?"

All of a sudden Sali realized the truth of his situation.

When he was finally released, he hurried home in great joy. Arriving at his cottage, he immediately looked under his stove. And miracle of miracles, there lay an immense treasure.

After this great discovery, Sali's loneliness started to lift. He was happy, not just because of his new wealth, but because he had followed the path of his soul and found the treasure that can be discovered at home.

As was true with Joseph's famous biblical sleep-visions, dreams are the archetypal symbol of calling. Even when you travel far-flung distances in search of yourself, those distant sites can do no more than direct you back home. It is only when you have returned home that you can create the relationships that redeem you from loneliness. Realizing that the treasure of your soul print lies under your very own hearth and calls you home to yourself, you find happiness.

PART FOUR

YOUR SOUL PRINT STORY

12

LIVE YOUR STORY

Whether I shall turn out to be the hero of my
own life, or whether that station will be held
by anybody else, these pages must show.

—Charles Dickens, *David Copperfield*

Truth set out upon the town, naked as the day he was born. Being naked, no one would invite him in for talk and tea. All the people who saw him turned on their heels and ran. He was quite lonely and felt terribly unappreciated.

One day he came across Story, surrounded by an eager and admiring crowd. Story was dressed splendidly with fine cloth and colors, telling an elaborate tale. Truth walked up and the people ran, leaving Story and Truth alone in the middle of the square. Truth started to wail, "How is it that everyone gathers around you to listen to your tales? What I have to say is at least as important as what you say, but people treat me like the plague!"

Story replied, "For someone so smart, you sure are stupid. Look at you, naked as the day you were born! Of course no one wants to see you! You need to spruce yourself up. Here, take some of my clothes. Once people see you dressed up with Story, you will be the talk of the town."

Truth took the advice and put on the Story's splendid clothes. From that time on, Truth and Story went hand in hand.

And so to this day—to find your truth you must tell your story.

From the *sapir*—the light of the soul—springs forth both a number and a story line, both a particular particle and a flowing wave. Remember how, in the magical dance of biblical Hebrew, the word for number, *mispar,* and the word for story, *sippur,* are born from a single root? That root, *sapir,* means "light." Just as light has two properties, particle and wave, so too the light of our soul is expressed in two ways—as *mispar* and *sippur,* number and story. Until now in this book, we have talked about soul print as a *mispar*—a specific number. You are singular, unique, a one and only. You respond only when your number is called.

Your soul print, however, is much more than a number or even a specific mission. It is also your story, a wave of emotions, actions, and interactions. There exists a *sippur* to each of our souls, the story of our light. To realize your soul print you need to follow the outline of your own story. For it is your own story, your unique story, that calls you. *Mispar* and *sippur,* the wave and the particle, merge into one.

We now turn our attention to story, to the wave function of our light. Our Soul Print Story. This term refers not to one specific mission or moment—it is, rather, the uninterrupted flow of your entire life story. The Soul Print Story is made up of the common moments that we all share—eating, sleeping, loving, arguing, studying, taking care of the details, and all the rest. The wonderful poet Charles Reznikoff writes:

Not for victory
But for the day's work done

As well as I was able
Not for a seat upon the dais
But at the common table

Reznikoff's "common table" speaks of that which is normal, routine, unextraordinary—life's daily fare of food. But "common" also means "communal," that which we all share, there where we all sit. Your story is in large part how you live uniquely at the common table. Each of us sleeps, eats, loves, rages, works, and speaks. Not one of us, however, does those things in quite the same way. Living your story is about expressing the originality of your commonness. It is about making the ordinary extraordinary. You can make your common, true-life story into something novel.

Of course, that is not all. Your story is also the revealer of your unique destiny. Unlike a call, which is focused and specific, your story is the unique weave, the blending and the melding of all the moments and encounters of a lifetime. All of these are bound together into the book of your life.

In the final (and my favorite) stage of our soul print journey, we will explore the *sippur,* the story quality of soul print light.

SIGNING THE BOOK OF LIFE

In biblical myth ritual, there is a special prayer in which we ask to be written into the Book of Life. Really though, explains the Kabbalistic Master of Slonim, it is not us asking God to be inscribed, but God asking us. "Please, this year, write yourself in the book of life!" God entreats us. Now what could God, the force, cosmos, possibly mean by such a plea? A beautiful explanation is hidden in the mysteries of ancient Hebrew. Remember that our core soul print word is *sapir,* light. The word for book, as in the book of life, is *sefer*—deriving from the identical three-letter root as *sapir* and its derivatives *mispar,* and *sippur. Sefer,* your book of life, is made up of the chapters of your *sippur,* your story. "Write yourself in the book of *your* life," God says, as he turns to every human being and says, this year, "Live your story!"

God has placed a pen in our hands, inviting, some would even say commanding, us *to become both the authors and the heroes of our own tale.* Every incident, relationship, residence, and experience is part of the plot. The essential question of living is whether you will be the hero of your story—or tragically, a minor character in your own drama. The greatness of a piece of literature is not determined by whether or not its protagonist has succeeded or failed. The main concern is rather, has the writer succeeded or failed? Has she deeply expressed the passion of the story? Has she deepened her hero? Does she have full command over all the plots and subplots? Is she comprehending and guiding the course of action from some deep intuitive place, or does she aimlessly write, spurting and stopping, hoping that it will somehow become a flow?

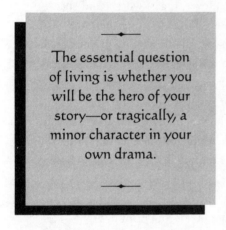

The essential question of living is whether you will be the hero of your story—or tragically, a minor character in your own drama.

It is the expression of our unique and personal passion play that signs us in the book of life. Remember the powerful teaching of Chaim Vital—that each of us has our own letter in the Bible. Only through our unique story do we realize our biblical letter and become part of the cosmic scroll.

Biblical myth's radical affirmation of the value of your distinct and singular life story is a fundamentally different outlook than that of many popular spiritual understandings. To cite but one early yet surprisingly persuasive example, the great lover Don Juan in *Journey to Ixtalan* writes, "I had a terribly strong attachment to my personal history . . . I honestly felt that without [my personal history] my life had not continuity or purpose. . . . I don't have personal history anymore . . . I dropped it one day when I felt it was no longer necessary."

This notion of moving beyond personal history is particularly strong in Buddhism. Buddhism is one of the most powerful systems of consciousness ever known, and in fact, one of my most exciting writing projects has been an analysis of the meeting points between biblical myth/Kabbalah and the Buddhist sutras. For meditative practices the Zen master is my model no less than the biblical myth master is. Yet, my respect and love for a sister system in no way implies agreement with it. Quite the opposite. One of the reasons that I am a biblical myth mystic and not a Buddhist is because my whole being rejects the Buddhist idea of moving beyond our personal story as the path to Nirvana.

Let me try to state the Buddhist position clearly. And for those readers more familiar with Eastern spiritual systems, what I am about to say accurately reflects both early Buddhism (Theravada, the small vehicle) and later Buddhism (Mahayana, the great vehicle). For Buddhists, the goal is to move beyond *samsara,* "the vicious circle of the world of existences," which is fueled by ignorance. This world is a realm of suffering and confusion. The major source of suffering is ignorance and the major expression of ignorance is the belief in a Self. French scholar Alfred Foucher was not all wrong when he suggested that for biblical myth the goal is immortality while for Buddhism the goal is to disappear. At least one school of Buddhists (the Middle School) would explain that to disappear means to merge with the infinite goodness and wisdom that is the force of the universe. Yet, even with this moderate formulation of the idea of disappearance, we biblical myth mystics take strong issue with our Buddhist brothers and sisters. Yes, the goal is to be one with goodness and wisdom. However, it must be accomplished with-

"God loves stories."

out losing your unique place in the universe, your sense of self within the One.

For me, the cycle of my life, or the cycle of my successive lives—in Buddhist terms, my karma—is something I want to fix, but not escape. There is a *tikkun*—a fixing, in Kabbalistic language—that I believe is the plotline of my story, and of every story. Our goal is never to escape our stories but to make our stories sacred. That is why the core book of biblical myth, called the Torah, is written neither as a series of Zen koans nor as a sutra, nor even as a Western philosophical essay. The Torah is, pure and simple, a story. Because as the masters said, "God loves stories."

Our story is our essence. To move beyond it would be to lose ourselves. That may be success for the Buddhist, but it is failure for the biblical mystic.

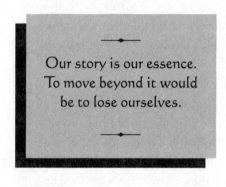

Our story is our essence. To move beyond it would be to lose ourselves.

THE ENDURING INDIVIDUAL

The self and the sanctity of an individual's Soul Print Story is challenged by another source besides Buddhism: postmodernism, or what is known as deconstructionist or poststructuralist ideas of the self. For this source, I admittedly have far less sympathy then I do for the sutras or Don Juan, for the simple reason that sutras and Don Juan reach toward meaning while this third source seeks to deconstruct and undermine all meaning. I am aware that in writing this bluntly I leave myself open to the heinous charge of cultural "unsophistication." Heaven forbid that we not be sophisticated. Yet a careful perusal of the postmodern philosophical literature has led me to this understanding. If my reading is wrong, I look forward to being corrected. And so I take the risk with a light heart.

Postmodernists, led in part by two French thinkers, Jacques Derrida and Michel Foucault, seem to have reinvented relativism. Relativism means there exists neither any objective values to guide us, nor any individuals to be held accountable. For Foucault, we are all social constructions—that is to say, puppets of our sociocultural conditioning. Foucault is, of course, correct in pointing out that much of what we experience as individual choice is indeed really the product of the invisible power webs that ensnare us, whether social, economic, or religious. However, to vault from there to the dismissal of the individual is a leap that he and his colleagues take as a matter of faith. Like all dogmatists, they never bother to prove the point other than to ridicule the notion that it could be otherwise.

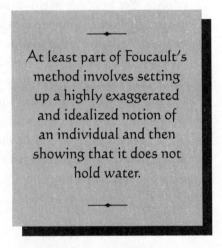

At least part of Foucault's method involves setting up a highly exaggerated and idealized notion of an individual and then showing that it does not hold water.

At least part of Foucault's method involves setting up a highly exaggerated and idealized notion of an individual and then showing that it does not hold water. Postmodernists point out, for example, that we are all influenced by advertisers telling each of us to "Be Yourself" by buying a particular product, car, cosmetic, and the like. We think we are being ourselves when in fact we are responding to purely external conditioning. Therefore, conclude Foucault and his postmodernist colleagues, we are not individuals. After all, an individual is one who is not directed by such obviously conditioned reflexes.

Of course, I have caricatured Foucault to some extent. Yet I believe that this is indeed the crux of his method, as do many academic Foucault readers. By setting impossible standards—positing a straw-man definition of individuality—he dismisses the notion of a self. However, this conception of the ideal, independent self, absolutely uninfluenced by outside forces, is nowhere put forth by biblical myth. (In effect the postmodernists have merely resurrected in new guise the age-old controversy between free will and determinism. Yet Foucault gets lost in the absurd and fundamentalist demagoguery of claiming to have solved the issue in favor of determinism.) An individual is someone who is part of a community and nurtured by society, but who still has the ability to act against conditioning, particularly in response to the call of her Soul Print Story. For biblical myth, what makes an individual special and grand is precisely that his direction is affected by the music of all sorts of societal pressures—and yet an inner core of freedom and choice allows him ultimately to transcend those pressures and march to the beat of his soul drummer.

DON JUAN MEETS DOVID OF LILOV

Don Juan, the sutras, and Foucault can be most starkly contrasted with a biblical myth mystic whom we encountered earlier, Dovid of Lilov. We met him at the cusp of a high holy day, when his headlong rush toward spiritual fulfillment—represented by his urgent need to pray with his master during the holiday—deafened him to the unique call of his daimon. When we meet again later in life, however, he has deepened and grown.

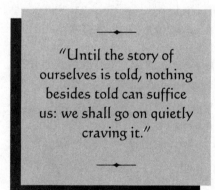

"Until the story of ourselves is told, nothing besides told can suffice us: we shall go on quietly craving it."

Dovid of Lilov was asked by his students, "What section of the Talmud will you study in heaven?" The Talmud is divided into twenty volumes, each with its own subdivisions; each section, or "Tractate," deals with a particular section of law and philosophy.

Much to the surprise of the students, Dovid of Lilov did not respond with any of the known Tractates. Rather, he said, "In heaven, I will spend all my time studying Tractate Dovid Lilov."

Dovid of Lilov did not fall into obsessive narcissim late in his life. Instead, he realized that his life was sacred ground. Laura Riding, one of the most exciting yet unsung American poets of the twentieth century, captured Dovid of Lilov's idea in one elegant sentence: "Until the story of ourselves is told, nothing besides told can suffice us: we shall go on quietly craving it."

FOLKTALE THERAPY: STORIES TO SAVE THE SOUL

In telling our stories, we realize the soul print upon which our lives depend. This was literally the case for Scheherazade, the queen who is narrator of the stories that make up the *Arabian Nights*. The Sultan of Persia had issued a decree that the women he married should be executed the morning after the wedding. Nonetheless, this heroine agreed to step into the lion's den and voluntarily marry this murderous monarch.

On their wedding night, Scheherazade began telling the Sultan a story of great enchantment—and great length. When it came time for her execution, the Sultan, thoroughly seduced by her tale, agreed to stay the execution in order to hear to the story's end. When Scheherazade finished the story, she started another one before the Sultan could object, a story that of course she did not quite manage to finish before execution time. Again her execution was stayed; she finished the story and started another—and so it went for one thousand and one nights and one thousand and one stories. By this time, the Sultan, transformed by the stories and smitten with his wife, agreed to nullify his barbaric edict. Scheherazade did not save only her own life and the lives of the sultan's brides who would come after her. Through her stories, she saved the life of the Sultan too. She saved him from himself.

Scheherazade in her wisdom is the prototype fairy-tale therapist.

Recent years have witnessed a wonderful explosion of storytelling classes, seminars, and workshops on folktales. The stuff of childhood imagination, a topic unheralded if not ignored for centuries, now piques great intellectual, spiritual, and even therapeutic interest. People have started using the mythic story as a path back to their past, as a key to their present, and a map to their inner territories. As Swiss folktale therapist Verena Kast wrote, "Parents, sibling, friends, lovers, and children are not the only ones who play their parts in our biographies; so do stories . . . folktales accompany us through life."

We are starting to learn what Scheherazade knew—that the telling of a tale can heal and transform. She ventured into the cage of a destructive despot, armed only with the strength of story, and tamed the beast. She succeeded not only because of her tales' instructive morals, but because of their seductive and transformative power. Unlike a law, the story does not externally impose its power on the listener. Rather its message is planted like a seed. The seed sprouts in the soil of the listener's soul, if the listener allows it.

I use folktale therapy with many of the people I counsel and teach, encouraging them to summon up their own versions of soul-print-sustaining stories from their memories and the tales they recall from childhood. I encourage you to read over and try the Soul Print Practice outlined below, and then explore the soul print folktales that two of my soul print seekers created.

Soul Print Practice

How can we use fairy tales as therapy? How can we (like Scheherazade) transform the tyrannical king who too often rules our lives, making him into a loving partner?

Think back to your far past to the folktales that most captured your imagination. Maybe it was a story that delighted you or maybe a tale that terrified you. What caught your heart. Why?

Either with a group, a partner, or alone, close your eyes and let your mind wander into the world of your youth. Imagine that the ground is scattered with bits and pieces of stories you have heard or read. Pick up these pieces of memory and inspect each one of them.

Write down all you can remember. Let the words stream out of you.

Are there characters you identify with, figures that scare you, adventures you long for? These bits of images have not lodged themselves in your memory for no reason. They are characters and symbols that reflect your soul print. Take the associations seriously. Either write out or discuss the associations, seeing how they speak to your present.

Here's an example of the exercise as written by Todd, a marketing director:

There was a little boy on this big blank page. And he had in his hand a big fat crayon. And he started simply drawing lines—these wonderfully thick lines upon the wide white page. And eventually he drew a door, and stepped into it. And he drew a house . . . walking through it, kind of creating each room as he went. That's all I really remember of it . . . but the memory is so distinct, of those big fat lines, that it's even pleasurable to picture them. When I am able to recall the vision of those lines and his plump little crayon, I feel great joy, like it's such a precious memory.

Todd discussed the associations summoned up by this tale. His greatest strength had always been creative thinking. He was considered "talented" by most who knew him. He had no problem being creative, but he did have a problem being organized and responsible. It was so easy for him to always just create his own reality that oftentimes he didn't fully deal with the world's reality. Whenever he wanted, he could just pull out his crayon and draw a door of escape into his own world. He definitely felt a fraternity with the boy in the story. But all of that unfocused creative power and play was undermining his responsibilities to the greater world. The memory of the story confirmed the fact that he indeed was creative, but how could the story help solve his problems?

Todd decided to apply his creative skills to time management. On a sheet of paper, he drew up a daily planner, like a building of blocks of time. His time management device became his creation, a part of his world, not something simply imposed by outside forces. Like the boy in the story, his crayon was his greatest gift. Todd realized that the last thing he should do is give up his creativity. Rather, the first thing he should do was to apply his creativity to his responsibilities.

Another student, Sandra, summoned this tale from her memories and experiences:

One of my favorite books . . . I would read it again and again . . . was about a most adorable dog. A clumsy and lovable old dog. And he was owned by a little boy and they were the best of friends. Until one day the little boy got an egg . . . and this egg hatched into a very annoyingly adorable little chick, all fuzzy gold and chirpy. And so the old dog went down to the riverside all depressed because his boy no longer wanted to play with him. And there at the riverside he told his friend the beaver of his problem. And they cooked up a plan to get the boy's attention.

They decided to construct an egg around him . . . [the dog]. The dog sat there all mopey as the beaver built this elaborate egg around him. I mostly remember the bright colors he painted on the egg. And then that night he rolled this huge, wild-looking Easter egg up to the boy's house. Come morning, when the boy came out to play, the egg started to crack. Astonished, the boy watched as the egg fell apart, revealing his old dog, sitting there with the sweetest sheepish look in the world. The book ended all hugs and kisses . . . the boy remembering how much he loved his dog.

Sandra discussed the associations that the story invoked in

her—the fear that she was being replaced by new-fangled toys; her anxiety that her husband might be interested in other, perhaps younger, women; how she was dressing up in painted shells that were not her authentic self in order to get the attention she needed. Or perhaps the egg was symbolic of her own birth; she no longer had to be the old dog but could be a newborn, fresh and just as fluffy as any chick. After pondering her tale, Sandra recognized that her relationship with her husband was indeed deep and strong, but that they needed to work to keep it fresh. She didn't need to be anything except herself.

THE LOST THREAD

What if we can't remember the stories of our past or make sense of the stories of our present?

Remember the Greek myth of Theseus and the Minotaur? Our hero, Theseus, travels through the underground labyrinth to slay the Minotaur. His challenge, however, is more than to slay the beast; he must also find his way back out of the maze after his success. Often we get lost in our own accomplishments. We slay the beast, but stay stuck in the maze. Ariadne, the king's daughter, symbol of the feminine energy, has given Theseus a length of thread to help him retrace his steps. The thread in our personal myth is what keeps us connected to the light as we wander in the labyrinths of darkness. The thread is the thread of the story. When we lose that thread (no matter how many beasts we slay), we are lost.

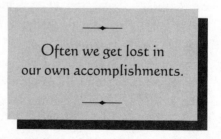

Often we get lost in our own accomplishments.

This is precisely what Franz Kafka had in mind in his masterpiece, *The Trial*. The plot of the novel is intentionally an impossible path. The thread of meaning frays, and at points when the story line seems in reach, it slips out of grasp again, like a lure drawing the reader along. Frustration, anger, and a radical hopelessness gradually build in the reader as Kafka subjects us to the very feelings that his protagonist K. undergoes as he is arrested, for what and by whom he doesn't know. Every time he detects a glimmer of sense in the proceedings, it vanishes into nonsense. K. is overwhelmed, incapable of making sense of or telling his story, tortured by a nonsensical system of bureaucracy and human inanity. In an all too apt passage, Kafka captures how we all feel on occasion about our lives: "He was too tired to survey all the conclusions arising from the story. . . . The simple story had lost its clear outline, he wanted to put it out of his mind."

> The unique torture of modernity is the sense of being disassociated, de-storied, displaced.

What Kafka is describing is the unique torture of modernity, the sense of being disassociated, de-storied, displaced. K. is just an initial; he is essentially nameless, devoid of context, history, or soul print. Through pain, the torturer aims to force the victim to betray and abandon his story.

There is a straight line from *The Trial* to George Orwell's *Nineteen-Eighty-Four,* the quintessential modern torture novel. A diabolical anti-self social system featuring the omnipresent Big Brother turns individuals into veritable slaves of the system. Winston Smith, the protagonist, attempts to rebel against Big Brother's ever-watchful eye. His growing rebelliousness culminates in an epic love affair. When the lovers are inevitably caught and tortured, they betray each other, their selfhood crushed. In literature and movies—and sometimes, tragically, in life—we have seen how torture can push people beyond the bounds of their story.

To lose hope in life is to lose the thread of your story. To recover hope is to reweave the fabric of your story. A single thread can be enough to lead us back to reweave the full tapestry of our tale. Nobel Laureate for Literature, S. Y. Agnon, who drew much of his inspiration from biblical myth and the Kabbalah, loved to tell the following anecdote:

When the Baal Shem was faced with a particularly difficult challenge, he would go to a certain place in the woods, light a sacred fire, meditate in prayer, and the challenge would be met.

When his successor, the Master from Mezerich, was faced with a similar challenge, he would go to the same place in the forest. There he would say, "We no longer know how to light the fire, but we have the prayer and that will be enough." And the challenge would be met.

When his successor, the Master from Sassov, was faced with a similar situation, he would say, "We no longer know how to light the fire, and we have forgotten the prayer, but we know the place in the woods." He would go to the sacred spot and the challenge would be met.

Finally, however, in the fourth generation, a great challenge arose, and the Master from Rishin, successor of the earlier generations, was called to action. "We do not know how to light the fire," he said. "We have forgotten the prayer. We do not remember the place in the forest. What shall we do?"

He put his head down in defeat, only to lift it a moment later. "We shall tell the story of what they did!" he exclaimed.

So he sat in his chair and told this story. And the challenge was met.

A story can have the strength of a thousand incantations, the incense of the most sacred of spaces, the heat and light of the most brilliant of flames. Never lose your story, for the lines of your soul print are the lines of your story. Live it; tell it loud.

13

---◆---

TELL YOUR STORY

STANDING ON SACRED GROUND

When Moses hears the voice from the Burning Bush, the first words of the call are, "Take off your shoes, for the earth on which you walk is holy ground." This charge is not some audio command that blares, "Shoes Prohibited!" Rather, these instructions imply the essence of Moses' call: "The ground on which your feet are walking—the path of your life, your story—is sacred ground."

"Shoe" in biblical Hebrew is a *na'al,* literally translated as "closed" or "locked." We are so often closed off from—locked out of—ourselves. Shoes are at once a sign of culture and a symbol of our alienation from our own footprints. The foot print, like the fingerprint and palm print, is a physical expression of the soul print. Reflexologists and foot doctors will tell you that no foot is the same. In fact, the sole of the foot, like the palm, even has its own set of lines, swirls, and unique curves.

In the great 1960s attempt to free the individual from the stranglehold of establishment culture, going barefoot was a prime symbol of the awakening. The image is powerful and obvious. First, the sensual feeling of lush grass beneath your feet is an unparalleled pleasure, offering the freedom you feel walking unshod on easy pathways, down pleasant roads. Moreover, have you ever pondered the difference between the print you leave when you're wearing a shoe and the print you leave with a bare foot? The print left by your Nike is the same print left by every Nike, but the print left by your foot is unique to you. That unfettered foot was important a generation ago as a symbol, as it should be also in our post-flower-child world. In this chapter, as we explore ways in which you can tell your story to the world, remember the print of your foot and consider your story as holy ground. Unloose the locks on your sole! Touching the holy ground of your story demands that you shed your outer shell, the carapace of social conditioning and conformity, and let your singular soul print speak.

Emerging out of soul print consciousness, we will explore a path grounded in a specific biblical myth ritual that guides us in actually becoming the tellers of our story and the heroes of our lives.

STEPS IN THE SAND

An old wisdom tale has grown so popular it has lost its original soul print intention. Here is a version that retains its holy footprint:

A man was walking on the beach. Whenever he looked behind him, he saw his footprints, accompanied by a second set alongside his own. He was comforted, for he knew God was walking with him.

Along the way, he fell into misfortune. He looked behind and was greatly troubled, for he saw only one set of footprints.

He called out to God, "How could you abandon me in my time of trouble?"

He heard a voice respond, "I have not abandoned you—I am carrying you."

This is not just a nice story about God's support in time of trouble. Let's read the images more carefully. When the man got into trouble and saw only one set of footprints, he recognized them as his own. He felt abandoned. The resolution of his crisis came via a voice he heard—an inner voice, a higher voice—that said, I am carrying you. If your footprint is not just the coincidental contours of your feet but a reflection of your soul print, your divinity, then when your footprints merge with God's you are truly living your story. You are being carried by your own divinity.

The Zen master Basho said, "Do not follow in the footsteps of the wise. Seek what they sought." Basho's point is that the wise created their own footprints. To follow another's footsteps is an impossible and profitless task. Their footsteps are theirs alone; you cannot do what they did, or walk as they walked. But you can seek what they sought. As you set out on your journey, you can seek to leave your own footprint.

Soul Print Practice

Next time you get the chance, take off your shoes! Whether on a blanket of grass, puddle of mud, or sun-warm concrete, walk barefoot. Feel the sensuality of it. Unloose the locks on your sole.

Learn the unique print of your foot.

Remember that the ground of your path is sacred ground.

ALONE AGAIN—*LEVADO* REVISITED

"Take off your shoes, for the earth on which you walk is holy ground." It is only after Moses internalizes this sole revelation that he can hear the second part of his vocation, the call to fulfill a destiny that is his alone. He grows from connecting with the ground of his own story to accepting his call.

The Zohar declares that we are all Moses. Like the Master from Rishin who sought to tell the story of the ones before him—and through the telling *became* them—so can we retell the tale of Moses and make his story ours. We too—from our armchairs—retell the story and rise to the challenge before us.

We have become well acquainted with the *levado* stories of the biblical myth heroes Moses and Jacob. Their stories helped us establish the nature of the soul print, and, in the tale of Moses, aided us in focusing on the particle or *mispar* aspect of soul print light, the dimension of calling. As we return to other plots and subplots in the stories of these mythic men, we will seek to understand how realizing your soul print comes not only from your calling but also from telling your story. Like the wave and particle functions of light, although we talk about them separately, they are inseparable. You reclaim your story by finding your voice, and you find your voice by telling your story.

The lives of the *levado* characters Moses and Jacob are the narratives that form the core of the dramatic biblical myth ritual we are about to explore. The ritual is in its essence the telling of a story. The story is no less than the central chapter in the life of Moses, the Exodus of the Israelites from Egyptian slavery.

THE POSSIBILITY OF POSSIBILITY

Moses is a redeemer, the archetype and inspiration for every Spartacus who will follow him in history. Activists, revolutionaries, visionaries, and all who believe that human initiative can create

Telling the story of our journey—is the journey itself.

a better world take as their model the man who threw off the shackles of Egyptian bondage and led the slaves to freedom. In this activist understanding, redemption is something that can be achieved if we change the conditions of the outside world.

Certainly, the hopeful belief in our ability to reshape external social reality—the possibility of possibility—is essential to biblical myth. Yet the Kabbalists call us to read this story with eyes turned inward. Redemption, they say, should not be dependent on something happening to us on the outside. Real redemption is a shift in consciousness. To be redeemed is to be free. True freedom cannot be dependent on external circumstance. This is the profound intuition of singer Bob Marley's legendary song of freedom: "Emancipate yourselves from mental slavery. None but ourselves can free our minds." The Kabbalists tell the Moses story not merely to recount the historical story of the Exodus but to understand the Exodus as a personal inner journey from mental slavery to freedom. Telling the story of our journey—is the journey itself.

A modern expression of the freedoms we seek in the story ritual are expressed well by family therapist Virginia Satir. She points out that a highly functional individual is one who has all her inner freedoms intact and in action. Satir lists the five freedoms we have to:

1) See and hear what we see and hear, rather than what we are told to see and hear.

2) Think what we think, rather than what we are supposed to think.

3) Feel what we feel, rather than what we are supposed to feel.

4) Want what we want, rather than what we are supposed to want.

5) Imagine what we imagine rather than what we are supposed to imagine.

Soul Print Practice

Are there ways that you feel free inside that have nothing to do with your external circumstances?

List them.

Here are two examples from the Zen of Driving: When I am "caught" in traffic, instead of feeling like a prisoner caught in the cell of my car, I use the time to let my mind freely wander or I listen to classical music—both activities that I do not always have enough time to do. . . . We have all experienced that guy who drives around in a very foul mood, yelling at other drivers for *their* bad driving. Next time you meet him on the road, try not to let him draw you into his foul mood. By maintaining your equilibrium in the face of his harangue, you are refusing to let him and his ill temper be your slave master. . . . One of my favorite ways to hold my center is by imagining our driver friend wholeheartedly laughing.

If no personal examples of inner freedoms come to mind, think of ways in which you would like to be free. List them. Saying them aloud is the first step to freeing yourself.

FREE TO WALK IN THE WIDE PLACES

To be free is a goal not reachable solely by political revolutions. Emancipation is not a political goal to be realized in the distant future; it is an accessible psycho-spiritual reality that comes when you live your authentic Soul Print Story. "I call out from the narrow places—answer me please with the expanses," said King David. The Hebrew word for Egypt is *Mitzrayim*—which, the Kabbalists note, literally translated means "the Narrow Places." The philosopher and early psychologist William James—speaking soul print language without using the term—told us we need to expand into our "wider selves." For us today, the Exodus is an intimate spiritual journey in which we depart the narrow, constricted straits in our lives and seek wider vistas.

In the Kabbalistic version of the Exodus from Egypt that we have explored, Moses is not only a revolutionary but also a spiritual master. His journey from Egypt to the Promised Land is also a spiritual journey home to an expanded self. Every human being is invited to embark.

It is the second century BCE, in Israel. The disciples approach their master and say, "There is a man blowing the ram's horn in Galilee, claiming to be Messiah. Master, is it true?"

The teacher opens the window and reaches out his hand to feel the wind. After a moment's concentration, he says, "No, it is not true."

Most of the students are appropriately impressed at their master's ability to sense the spiritual reality by the wind. However, one novice, a slightly impudent disciple, is troubled. "If you are so spiritually intuitive," he asks the master, "then why did you need to put your hand out the window? Why couldn't you sense the air in the room to see if Redemption had arrived?"

The master responds ever so softly, "Because in my room, the Messiah has already come."

The master in the story was a mystic, one of the precursors of the Kabbalists who would later manifest themselves in thirteenth-century Spain. Starting with this ancient Israeli master, the essence of Kabbalistic teaching has been the possibility of immediate redemption by moving from constricted to expanded consciousness, by claiming your room—a room of your own as it were—the great dimensions of your story.

RECOLLECTED PIECES: THE STORYTELLING RITUAL

How do we do it? How do we pass over from the narrow to the wide? The answer comes through a drama. Biblical myth lays out a specific plan, a psycho-spiritual process, a ritual under the full moon of early spring. It takes place as part of the biblical myth freedom holiday that occurs at the spring seed-planting time. It is no coincidence that this is the dramatic ritual that Jesus and the disciples were enacting at the Last Supper. Each year the process invites us to act out and actualize our exodus. In Hebrew the ritual is called "Pe-Sach," which the Kabbalists interpret to mean "the Mouth That Speaks"—which is, as we will see, a profoundly appropriate name. The formal name of the dramatic ritual—quite a mouthful in every way—is "Telling the Story of the Exodus from Egypt." The key word here is *sippur*—story—deriving from *sapir* or soul print light. The *sippur*—telling the story of the Exodus from Egypt—is the path to *sapir*. Kabbalistic sources understood this appellation to mean, "to tell the story of your life, and through the telling to leave your Egypt, your narrow straits."

Henceforth we will refer to it as the Storytelling Ritual, the tale of the Exodus from slavery into freedom. It is a ritual that all human beings can make part of their lives. Retelling the myth of emancipation from slavery impels you to reclaim the story of your wider self.

"In every generation there is a new understanding of leaving Egypt," said Master Isaac of Gur. "Egypt is inside us. We all have our own Pharaohs. Indeed, not only in every generation, but also in every person there is a point of freedom—to touch that point is to take leave of an inner Egypt. That point is known only by the person himself."

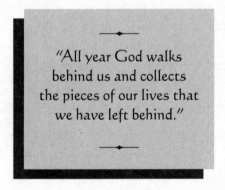

"All year God walks behind us and collects the pieces of our lives that we have left behind."

The Exodus myth enjoins us once a year to re-narrate our personal tale. In the graphic imagery of one mystic, "All year God walks behind us and collects the pieces of our lives that we have left behind." For example, we might relinquish the memory of a relationship that hurt us deeply. We forget all about that job that didn't pan out. Conversely, we repress moments of success and achievement, either because they're too good to be believed or give us vertigo, inviting us to heights that frighten us. Once a year God gives us back the lost pieces of our lives by charging us to tell our stories. Those pieces are rewoven into the tapestry of our tale.

"Won't you help me sing these songs of Freedom, they're all I've ever had," asks Bob Marley on behalf of all of us. The Divine answers, "Yes, I will help you sing your song of freedom. Here are the pieces of your story—re-sing it and be Redeemed!" For to redeem is to deem again, and to deem is to reckon to be worthy of attention. Redemption itself is therefore inherent in re-collection, the attention we pay to old details that we re-claim with renewed appreciation.

At a recent confirmation service for Jason, the son of a friend of mine, we heard an amusing case of the recollection of objects lost. Jason has a sense of humor wide as a football field; he even dressed up like Mr. Rogers during his speech to the congregation. He is known for his good humor, his good grades, and his immense forgetfulness. In the middle of the usual speech by Jason's good friend, the priest, telling us how wonderful Jason is, he reached behind the pulpit to reveal an overflowing box. The box contained all the things Jason had lost over the years, things the priest had retrieved from outings, summer camp, and classes. He presented his young friend with the gift of years' worth of baseball caps, books, balls, and T-shirts. As much as the gesture teased the boy, it was a testimony to the depth of their relationship. That the priest would have gone to the trouble to gather everything together, to notice what belonged to Jason and what didn't, meant that he really did care. By deeming the boy's lost items important, he redeemed Jason, item by forgotten item.

So too can we redeem ourselves by repossessing our pasts and including them in the drama of our continuing Soul Print Stories.

Soul Print Practice

Close your eyes and try to collect the piece of your story that you have lost over the years.

Have you ever reclaimed a part of your story—an event, an unresolved encounter?

Has anyone else ever reclaimed it and returned it?

Do you have any "unredeemed" pieces of other people's lives that you could return? This could range from that jacket left at your house, to a book you "borrowed" a long time ago, to a memory of when your friend was particularly helpful to you or a time when he or she shone? Return those items to your friends.

THE TALKING CURE

The night of the Storytelling Ritual is called *Leil Shimurim*—A Night of Guarding/Watching. Instead of being the audience of the spectacle of history and humanity, we turn into the actors of the drama; it is God who turns into the watcher, the wide-eyed, hand-clapping audience to our recollections. The divine promise is to remain silent but present during the drama.

One of the inheritors of biblical myth consciousness was Josef Breuer in Vienna, who collaborated with a man named Sigmund Freud in developing what they called "the talking cure." Or as the contemporary writer Eric Hodgins wrote, "Talk: The four-letter word for psychotherapy." At the core of the process sits the client, who retells her story to the silent listener. In the telling, the forgotten or repressed tatters of the story are reclaimed and integrated into the whole self. At the time of *Leil Shimurim,* it is as if God sits in the therapist's chair, silent but listening, healing us with a cosmic hearing.

A more mystical approach to this interaction happens among the initiates of Hasidism who make pilgrimages to pray at the graves of the Righteous Ones. They do more than pray there. As the tradition goes, they narrate their entire life stories before the resting place of the Righteous. The promise of the process is that the devotee, through this telling, will be "returned" to a state of wholeness. The Righteous Ones, resting in their graves, are understood to be the silent but present witnesses of the tale.

My wife, Cary, set out to create a version of this pilgrimage for herself. After we married, she made the trek to the Ukraine to visit the grave of the soul print master featured the most in these pages—the Baal Shem Tov. For three days, meditating at his gravesite, she engaged in this process of telling her story, pulling up details from her past long forgotten. She compared the process to a "dusting off," as if picking up objects from an old dusty shelf, inspecting them, and cleaning them to a shine. Indeed, she came back from the journey with a certain shine—bearing the gift of a new perspective on her past, as well as her future.

In the Storytelling Ritual, we reclaim both our greatness, which frightens us, and our failures, which embarrass us. There is a Hebrew word—*shalem*—that denotes what is holistic, complete, inspiring equilibrium and integrity. Only when our story is complete do we have the inner equilibrium and integrity necessary for healing and growth. When we leave behind sections of our story, we can never realize our soul print.

Soul Print Practice

Make a map of your soul-scape: Base it on the lines of your palm. The palm features three main lines—the life line, the love line, and the head line.

One way to map your soul-scape is to make a time line of your lifeline. Mark landmark events, first and favorite moments—for example, the first time you wrote your name, your favorite piano recital, the time you ran your fastest track race, the day you graduated college, and the day you married.

If you choose, you could also follow your love line: your first love, your first broken heart, and the time your heart was mended. And you can trace your head line as well: the book you read that you loved the most, your first paying job, the time you won an award.

See the line as the trajectory of your soul print.

SUBLIME STORIES

Every age contributes a more advanced chapter to the spirit's quest for freedom. Only recently has our consciousness evolved to a place where we grasp that the greatest story in the universe is our own. Yet when we leave an earlier epoch behind, we don't trash their truths—rather, we refract their light through the prism of our more evolved understandings. To understand where we are in the evolutionary scale of the spirit, we need to trace the history of the spirit's stories. We will follow the spirit's evolution from the telling of Sublime Stories, to Saint Stories, to Soul Print Stories.

Early biblical mysticism centered on what I call sublime story-telling—elaborate recounting of the divine realm. The central text of this lofty tradition is called *Ma'aseh Merkavah,* the "story of the Chariot"—and emerges from Ezekiel's ecstatic vision.

The entire first chapter of Ezekiel is a soul-stunning recording of the prophet's vision of the divine chariot, replete with emerald wheels, four-faced angels, a throne of sapphire, and radiating rainbows. Each elaborate detail was taken by the mystics to symbolize a different dimension of higher spiritual reality. The vision was a blueprint of the divine, as the soul in its yearning for meaning, reached for the heights and told stories of the divine realm.

SAINT STORIES

Later mysticism shifted the locus of significance from heaven to earth, grounding and transforming the sublime story into what I will call the saint story. Isaac "the Lion" Luria and his students in the Renaissance years, as well as succeeding generations, said that the chariot is actually incarnate in the great masters. "The Masters are the Chariot!" cry out the mystics. The search for meaning has shifted. The Chariot has landed in the souls of the saints.

In this understanding, Ezekiel's chariot represents an intricate depth-psychology charting of the souls of the spiritually developed.

In the souls of these spiritually masterful teachers we find the divine vehicle as well as the divine road. God's presence is experienced in the world in the person of the spiritually evolved, the yogis, masters, bohdisattvas, and saints. This is the mystery of incarnation—that infinite beauty and spirit resides in finite, imperfect, and frail human beings. The *Ma'aseh Merkavah* is translated into the story of the Masters. This idea is actually the spiritual antecedent of our modern idea of biography. From uniquely lived lives, we can derive important information and insight.

Thus, there developed a new mystical genre, *sippuri tzadikim,* in English called Saint Stories, the stories of the mystical masters of the ages. Every detail of a master's life dripped divine import; each event was a new chapter of spiritual significance. The master's childhood adventures, his first teaching jobs, friendships, and failures—all these were the design and detail of Ezekiel's chariot. Each detail of dress and behavior was a beacon of illumination. Even the unique pathology of a saint became a lesson, with stories ranging from manic depressive bouts, or cutting humor, to irrepressible sexuality and conflicts with other masters. These were people parables. While this stage of evolution offered important stories to further the path of the spirit, the saints so transcended our reality that while we might be awed and occasionally even inspired by them, we viewed their behavior as totally beyond our grasp and therefore not worth the reach. These were not *our* stories. Yet, is it not wonderful to allow ourselves to be awed?

Soul Print Practice

Tell someone the story of a master or a saint you have met or heard of. If you can't think of such a person, make up your own.

What makes this person a master?

How did the master get to be so masterful?

How is this master different from other people?

How is the master different from you?

Could you do what the master did?

Finally, do you have any saint stories that feature you as a saint? Are there things you have done that are particularly masterly or saintly? Keep this question in mind as you read the next section.

SACRED AUTOBIOGRAPHY

The next critical stage in the spirit's evolution is occurring here and now, as we tell our own stories, our Soul Print Stories.

We all have sacred stories of the great mysteries within us. We are the masters; we are Moses, we are Buddha. You are the Chariot. The saint story you must tell is the story of yourself, your Sacred Autobiography. The Mysteries are within you.

Creating Sacred Autobiography is the spiritual imperative of our generation. We need to know that in the details of our lives dangle the keys to heaven. No corner of our story is created in vain; we have never been down any dead-end street, never met an unnecessary face, never heard a senseless song. Every nuance, event, image, and incident of our lives is a source of vital psychological and spiritual information. Telling our autobiographies, we forge a coherent narrative out of our life stories, shedding light on the meaning of our lives.

One of the saddest lines I have read in psychological literature appears in *Solitude,* an otherwise learned work by British psychoanalyst Anthony Storr. Storr develops his arguments using anecdotes about various famous people. In a chapter paradoxically titled "The Significance of the Individual," he makes the following observation: "The literary genre of autobiography is now so popular that men and women of little interest and no distinction feel impelled to record their life stories." What a tragic and misguided sentence! There are simply no men and women of little interest and no distinction existing in the world. Indeed, it is far from certain that the anecdotes of the famous on which Storr builds his work have the most to teach us. In fact, it is certain that they do not.

On Friday nights, my wife and I often host large meals full of singing, feasting, and stories. We try to make a point of engaging everyone at the table, allowing each to shine in her own particular way, whether it's through telling a story, reading a poem, giving a teaching, leading a meditation, or just engaging in casual conversation. One Friday night at an open-door meal, one of our guests was a middle-aged woman named Miri. Possessed of a kind smile, she seemed sweet, helpful, and shy, and otherwise remarkably unexceptional. That is, until we went

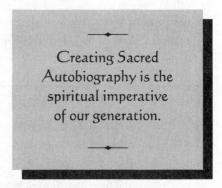

Creating Sacred Autobiography is the spiritual imperative of our generation.

around the table and asked each person to share with us one thing he or she would like to accomplish in the next five years. Miri surprised us by saying she was planning to paint her life story, in a series of a hundred canvases. Everyone seemed a bit startled by her comment; she'd been so quiet all night we'd almost forgotten she had a story at all. But of course she did! My curiosity piqued, I walked her halfway home after the meal and after asking a few simple questions, I could glimpse the gorgeous mural of her life. In her lifetime, Miri had stirred revolutions in college, written books on healing, built houses in Maine, pioneered self-expression workshops, embarked on Alaskan adventures, loved and been loved. Through the journey of her life she had flowered. I was reminded again that soul print adventures are the birthright of us all and often find their most glorious expression in those who on the surface seem most ordinary.

It may appear easy for the seasoned artist to see her life as a work of art, producing canvases and manuscripts infused with the meaning and metaphor of self-discovery, but what about the nonartists of the world—the plumbers, the accountants, the rest of us in general? We too can be creative, innovative, exaggerated! Plumber, perhaps you have a heaven-sent knack for nudging, for pushing an issue until it gives, until the plugged-up pipes of life flow as flutes of song. Or perhaps you are in need of "decongesting" yourself, and you are drawn to your work to effect your own inner fixing. And you the Accountant, what is your role of keeping order in the world? Do you have a soul gift of balance and stability to be shared? What would your Account of the Chariot look like?

Soul Print Practice

A necessary ingredient of the film or novel is the symbol. A symbol is like salt, for it preserves meaning, conveys the taste of the character, flavors the facts with a little imagination. What might the seemingly insignificant details of your life symbolize? Remember that scene in the movie *American Beauty* where Ricky the boyfriend shows his video clip of a plastic bag being cast about by the wind? The scene moves us because we see how precious this image of the bag has been to him. That symbol represented a truth to him. What is your wind-tossed bag? What recurring themes have captured meaning in your life? List some of the symbols that have spoken to you.

A butterfly, a rock smoothed by water, or an exploding soda bottle . . . List as many symbols of yourself, images of meaning, as you can.

READING REALITY

We all have storybook lives. We just need to transcribe them into soul print narratives. Practice reading your life. Reformat it into an illustrated deluxe edition, a classic where you trust that the author has imagined the tale with artistry, intention, and genius—every image and incident purposeful.

Each detail in the pageantry of our lives provides the ideal conditions for realizing our soul print. "In all your ways know God," writes King Solomon in the Book of Proverbs. For the Kabbalists, this means in *all the ways* and byways of your story. *"In all your ways" means "know God in all the unique and special manifestations that define your individuality; with all the quirks, strengths, idiosyncrasies and pathologies that are yours. They are your way to God." In mysticism, there is no contradiction between the individualism inherent in "know thyself," and the spiritual imperative to "know God."* The latter is unattainable without the former. As we've seen earlier in this book, to "know" in biblical myth is to know someone intimately, to have carnal knowledge. Each of us is invited to intimacy with the textured surfaces and complex patterns of our story. So often, our lives appear as a series of disconnected and disjointed dots and lines, pocked with rupture and dislocation. In retelling your story, you connect the dots of your life. Patterns begin to emerge, images crystallize, and some of the haze of unconscious living is dispelled.

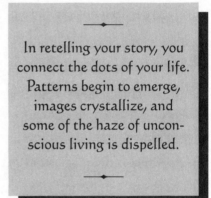

In retelling your story, you connect the dots of your life. Patterns begin to emerge, images crystallize, and some of the haze of unconscious living is dispelled.

Carl Jung wrote, "In the last analysis the essential thing is the life of the individual. This alone makes history. Here alone do the great transformations take place . . . the whole future, the whole history of the world, ultimately spring as a gigantic summation from these hidden sources in individuals. In our most private and subjective lives, we are not only the passive witnesses of our age and its sufferers, but also its makers. We make our own epic." What Jung suggests is that only by living your epic—that is, your story—can you participate in the drama of your civilization. This notion is echoed by the playwright Christopher Fry: "We must each find our separate meaning in the persuasion of our days until we meet in the meaning of the world." Our personal stories, when fulfilled, can fit seamlessly together into the larger tapestry of life's tale.

IT'S NOT THE MOUNTAIN, IT'S THE CLIMB

A true-life epic does not exhaust itself in grand finales or in what psychologist Abraham Maslow called peak experiences. It arises from the details of daily living. Most of life, after all, is a plateau and not a peak. We are taught not to explore plateaus but to scale mountains, aiming only for the top. We become so focused on the summit that we no longer experience the echo of each footstep along the way. We laud this type of living, calling it strategic, effective, and goal-oriented. We ignore the precious and profound pleasure of the climb.

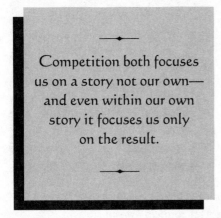

Competition both focuses us on a story not our own—and even within our own story it focuses us only on the result.

To make matters worse, we focus not on reaching the top of our own private mountain—everyone can and should have a personal Sinai—but on reaching the top of *the* mountain. When the urge to compete motivates your climb, then your story by definition is determined only in relationship to somebody else's story. It is the word *only* that makes that situation so problematic. Who remembers the runner-up for the Oscar, the underbidder on the contract, the loser in the congressional campaign? Competition both focuses us on a story not our own—and even within our own story it focuses us only on the result. Process becomes a necessary evil, a means that has no value toward an end that has supreme meaning.

Do we really communicate to our kids the belief "It's not whether you win, it is how you play the game"? Or do our kids know in their heart of hearts that we would rather they won than played fair? Over twenty years of teaching, I have asked scores of my students, "If by cheating you could get accepted to Harvard Business School, would your parents want you to do it?" I have asked parents, "Would you want your son or daughter to cheat to get admitted?" Sadly, overwhelming numbers answered yes to both questions. Most of the students, quite interestingly, said that their parents would never admit their wishes openly and probably would not want to know their kids had cheated, but their joy at their children's competitive success would, in the minds of many of the students, far outweigh their censure.

When we tell our children's stories, we tell of their successes and first-place finishes. We rarely acknowledge their near misses and certainly try to exorcise their failures and defeats. There is a horrible practice at many synagogues and churches of announcing children's achievements. What makes this custom so pernicious is that children's academic and competitive public achievements are all that are celebrated. When was the last time you heard someone say, "My child had a bad fall off his bike. He's had to do therapy for the last six months and he has done a wonderful job"? Yet falls and recovery are what life is all about.

> ### Soul Print Practice
> Recall a story of your own fall and recovery.
> Or acknowledge a heroic recovery tale of your child. Give that child, or yourself, a special ritual to celebrate that recovery.

RATS AND RICH MEN

Every parent owes his or her child the gift of one great quote and one great story. So for my children and yours, here goes.

The quote is from actress Lily Tomlin: "Even if you're ahead in the rat race, you're still a rat."

And this is the story:

The tale is told about the nineteenth-century mystical master whom we have had occasion to meet before in these pages. Zusia of Onipol was the poorest of masters for many years. Before he revealed himself as a master, he wandered, Buddhist style, from city to city disguised as a beggar. In one city, he would often seek the assistance of a particular wealthy patron, but to no avail. The patron had little time for the likes of him. Later in Zusia's life, he was revealed as a master and came not only to fame but also to fortune. As it happened, he had reason to pass through the town of this wealthy patron again and was of course invited to sup at the patron's table. Zusia accepted.

However, a very strange scene ensued. Zusia would take the fine food from the patron's plate and instead of putting it in his mouth, he would ever so delicately dump it on his clothes.

The patron was aghast. He tried to restrain himself, but as the master kept dumping food onto his garments, he could hold back no longer. "What are you doing?" he cried out.

"Why, it is very simple," Zusia responded calmly. "When I was poor you never invited me. The only thing that has changed since then is my clothes. Therefore, I assumed you must have invited my clothes to dine with you. So I was feeding them."

Imagine the message absorbed by his children every time the wealthy patron sent the ragged and poor master away. While he may have preached piety, the patron's values became clear to his children by whom he deigned to honor. When they saw the needy ignored and the renowned and powerful being catered to, the children understood that fame and power were the values their father truly prized.

A FALL, A JOURNEY, AND A DESTINATION

If I had to describe in one sentence the core narrative of biblical myth, I would say it is the story of a fall and the process of a recovery. The Bible begins with a fall—the fall out of the Garden of Eden—which results in alienation, loneliness, and exile. In the rest of the five books of biblical myth, the people attempt to rise and recover from their fall. The epic of biblical myth ends after much tragedy, triumph, betrayal, and nobility, with the people finally getting there . . . almost. The story ends just outside of the Promised Land, on the other side of the Jordan, on the brink of culmination.

Perhaps the greatest modern echo of the sacred journey notion of biblical myth resonated in a speech by the Rev. Martin Luther King, Jr., given literally on the eve of his assassination, April 3, 1968. In this speech, he talked about traveling to Memphis and hearing of threats against his life. He wasn't afraid of these threats, though, or of dying early. He had, he said, already seen the promised land and knew that one day all his people would, too. He had caught a glimpse of heaven and was happy.

Most of us are not the targets of hate's bullets, but all of us die before crossing into our Promised Land. We can take comfort and gain power from knowing that what is true for Moses or Martin Luther King is true for each of us: The journey itself is our story. The story itself is our destination. On the way, we will stumble, fall, and pick ourselves up, just as Moses did, just as Martin Luther King did. As good a teacher as we'll ever have, Dr. King was a great, good, beautiful man—and yet a flawed man, who, like all of us, rose and fell and rose again.

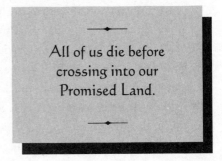

All of us die before crossing into our Promised Land.

The question we must ask about our journey is this: Are we headed in the right direction? Are our sights toward Canaan? Will we at least see a Mt. Pisgah view of the Promised Land?

THE RACE TO MEDITATE

Remember Dovid of Lilov, whom we have already met twice in these pages?

As he was in an earlier story, Dovid was traveling on the eve of the holiday to be with his master, the Seer of Lublin. This time he traveled with a group of the seer's most senior disciples. Encountering trouble with the wagon, they were again very late to arrive, entering Lublin only minutes before the evening meditation was to begin.

As soon as they reached the livery, all the disciples jumped out of the wagon and raced to synagogue so as not to miss a word uttered by the master. However, the Seer of Lublin was unable to begin the meditation. Although the room was jammed with people, he sensed that Dovid, his beloved disciple and friend, was not present. "Where is my Dovid?" he cried.

The seer's assistants searched the entire town, but Dovid was nowhere to be found. "Tell me where you saw him last?" the seer implored them.

"Why, in the livery with the horses."

The assistants rushed into the livery and found him, sitting quietly in the hay, feeding the horses.

Even in spirituality, we can become so goal-oriented that we race to our destination, even if that destination be study, meditation, or prayer. We do not allow the time to feed the horses that got us here. A few years ago, a popular story told of a college student who, tired of all the competition and superficiality of the academy, decided to go to India. He wrote his parents back home, praising the holiness and tranquility of the ashram. In a P.S., he added, "I am doing really well here, learning *zazen,* and by June I should be number two in the ashram."

Spiritual seekers can get just as fanatic about success as a Wall

Street trader in a bull market. We just shift our ego drives and obsessions from one set of goals to another. We become stockbrokers of the soul, buying, merging, selling short, and selling out. Only by letting go of our obsession with competition, goals, and results can we begin to gather in the lost pieces of our Soul Print Stories.

THE HUG FORMULA

Living in the journey, honoring the process, and recollecting the details, are all essential strategies for telling our story. But what happens when we are on the wrong road altogether? Honoring the way will not help us because we are lost, having taken a wrong turn awhile back.

Often we get lost very early. As children, most of us do not receive the full "hug quotient" we need to feel safe and loved in the world. Need being the grandmother of invention, you come up with a formula that will get you the hugs and attention you need. Soon you stumble on a strategy: One day you do something that, to your surprise, gets you a higher hug dose than usual. You say something funny and everyone laughs. You pray with extra fervor at church and Mom lovingly strokes your hair. You dress up extra fancy and everyone says how pretty you are.

The little scientist in you tries to repeat the results; you try your hug activity several times to see if it consistently elicits a similar reaction. From this data, you extrapolate what I call the Hug Formula. Every one of us has our own ingredients. Some people may be more sexual than they care to be. Others may write more books than their soul wants to offer up, or tell more jokes than would come naturally. Others may always be calm and smiling, smiling until quite unconsciously their smiling faces become masks.

The Hug Formula takes you into your drama and away from your story. Your drama is the way you "act" in order to achieve your hug quotient. It is fueled by your need for the superficial approval of others, whereas your story earns the genuine approval of your self.

Sometimes, through inner work, therapy, guided meditation, and the like, we can come up with almost the precise time in our lives when the Hug Formula kicked in and we began acting in our drama instead of living our story. Finding that moment can be a turning point in your quest to realize your soul print. Telling your story, and thereby distinguishing it from the drama of syndromes like the Hug Formula, helps you reconnect with the person behind the mask.

However, that does not mean, as popular psychology would have us believe, that the Hug Formula is bad. After all, the Hug Formula only activates a part of us that already exists; it highlights a particular line of your soul print. Your drama is your drama and the central prop of drama is a mask. We all wear masks and that is the way it should be. A good mask hugs the contours of your face. Your mask is *your* mask. It fits your face.

> Your drama is the way you "act" in order to achieve your hug quotient. It is fueled by your need for the superficial approval of others, whereas your story earns the genuine approval of your self.

Fascinatingly, "mask" is the biblical myth word for idolatry. "You shall not make for yourselves Gods of Masks," says the biblical myth text. It's not that masks are bad. You just cannot make the mask your god. Although it is a reflection of who you are, it is still not your deepest self. You can't let the mask get stuck to your face. When the mask becomes that sort of idol, it means your hug-earning ambition has become so important to you that you feel as if you would die if it disappeared. This may severely warp your judgment. If your need to be a great dancer, singer, teacher, or fireman becomes pathological, then you will dance until you drop, sing until you lose your voice, teach until your class goes deaf, and enter fires that are unsafe—or maybe even set them so you can put them out. Eventually you'll get burned.

To get to your deepest self, you need to apportion time when you are consciously unmasked—when you let the Hug Formula fall away and seek to touch the deeper you that was present before the Hug Formula kicked in.

One of the most familiar hug-seekers among us is the comedian, his mask the joker's needy grin. So it is with every persona; it becomes so important to us that we become dependent upon it. We all need to create contexts where we can take off our masks. The funny guy needs to set aside meditative time where he does not entertain. He must have friends who don't expect him to constantly make them laugh.

A man made an appointment with a psychologist. He arrived at the office and said to the doctor, "Doctor, I am so incredibly sad. No matter what I do, I can't get out of it. How can I get rid of this depression?"

The psychologist looked at him sympathetically and said, "Come with me to the window."

The man followed. The psychologist pointed outside and said, "See that tent over there in the distance? The circus is in town, and what a circus it is! There is a certain clown there named Rosario. He is your answer. One look at him and your depression will be gone!"

The man looked at the doctor sadly and said, "Thank you for trying to help me." He got up to go, handing the doctor his card on the way out. The doctor looked at the card. It read: Rosario the Clown.

> Soul Print Practice
> What was—or still is—your Hug Formula?

FORGERS AND EDITORS

When we sanitize our life stories, telling only the tale of our triumph as judged by the external standards of success and failure, we risk turning our beautiful lives into failures. Since no one wants to be a failure, we begin to edit, forget, plagiarize, or just excise out whole sections of our story. We become forgers of our own signature.

We admire celebrities and idolize those who triumph in the world's arenas. We even have a term for such people—"success stories." As anyone who has ever participated in a competition knows, a significant and totally unpredictable x-factor often produces unanticipated winners and surprised losers. Although our effort is certainly a significant variable in any endeavor, it is very far from the determinant. Still, rather than include the parts of our lives that have not been graced with success according to the artificial standards we have set for ourselves, we delete them from our résumés. I recently encountered a high school friend who became very involved in spiritual practice about five years ago. I offhandedly asked him how old he was. Without a moment of hesitation, he responded, "I just had my fifth birthday." It took me a second to realize that he meant that it had been five years since his "enlightenment." He was implicitly declaring that his life before enlightenment was valueless. He had ripped out those pages from his book of life. I told him sadly that I did not believe he was five; we cannot tear out pages from our book of life without paying a very heavy price.

MASTERS OF RETURN

One of the paths of inner work in biblical myth is called *teshuva*. A hard word to translate, its closest equivalent might be "return."

To return is one of the prime goals in biblical myth. The most profound return is the return from the exile of the self. *Teshuva* is an act of spiritual excavation, digging beyond the buildup of dust to the authenticity that has always rested deep within. One of the great gifts as well as dangers of spiritual movements of return, whether it be the Great Awakening Revivals of 1800s America or the waves of New Age religiosity presently washing up in the world, is that when hearts are stirred, they are stirred en masse. Though the call may be addressed to the individual person, all too often the call of the community triumphs over the quiet call of the individual's own heart.

Does a spiritual community facilitate a return to *your* soul print? If it does not, then you can be sure that it is missing the true ingredients of the spirit.

> ### Soul Print Practice
> When has your heart called you to do something different from the normal calls of the community around you?
> How did you respond to the call?

To return is to go back to the place and time where you went into hiding, so you can tell yourself that it is okay to come out now. My own attempt led me to a game of hide-and-seek I played at around age six. I was hiding in a closet under a huge pile of winter clothes. Everyone had gotten back to base and was called free. I didn't want to come out. The world I'd experienced outside seemed an arbitrary and dangerous place and the winter clothes were warm and protective. I must have stayed in there for over an hour, wishing I could stay forever. In the end, I came out for dinner. I didn't really come out until twenty-five years later, after a painful divorce. Only then did I return to reclaim my story. Only then did I paste back in all the pages that I had ripped out of my book of life to make it prettier and less painful.

Telling our stories means coming out of hiding and returning to our sources. That is the only way we can really find freedom.

	Soul Print Practice	
What have you hidden from?	Where did you hide?	When did you come out?
Example:		
Lightning	Under the covers	Morning light
Responsibility	Drinking	When I stumbled down the stairs and broke my collarbone
My own gifts (be more specific)	Bouts of anger	I began to come out of it when I wrote my first article

TO SEARCH OUT THE BROKEN

As we seek to return, reclaim, recollect, and retell our stories, we return to the Storytelling Ritual on the biblical myth-freedom day. That is, the feast of Pe-Sach, the ritual we referred to at the beginning of this chapter by its formal name "Telling the Story of the Exodus from Egypt." For all of us, no matter our faith, this Storytelling Ritual simulates and celebrates our movement from exile to redemption, from slavery to freedom. It is a time when we free ourselves from the internal editors who, though wanting to help us, have falsified the stories of our lives.

At the opening of the Storytelling Ritual, a round matzah cracker is broken in half (this cracker being the source of the wafer used during the Christian communion service). As if the breaking of the cracker were a starting gun, the evening takes off along the track from slavery to freedom. Each person relives leaving Egypt. Each one invites, invents, and enacts his or her personal return from the dark and narrow to the wide and bright. The storytelling builds until the journey culminates with the famed *afikoman* hunt. What is an *afikoman*? Remember that matzah cracker broken at the beginning of the meal? Well, somewhere along the way to freedom someone has very surreptitiously hidden half of that broken cracker—the *afikoman*.

Late in the night, after we have each told and been told, given and received the stories of emancipation, we send the children to find the hidden *afikoman*. In a symbolic sense, the children we send are none other than ourselves, returning to that moment when the world seemed so broken that we began to hide.

The children go searching throughout the house, and having exultantly found the flat broken bread of slavery, they come running to return it to the adults. This is the child in us bringing our broken piece back to the adult in us. The process of healing has begun. The Storytelling Ritual is complete. Perhaps most important, the child who finds the broken treasure gets a prize.

14

---◆---

RECLAIM YOUR STORY

Biblical myth rituals revolve around stories. In our Storytelling Ritual focusing on the Pe-Sach return to freedom, we retold the historical and symbolic tale of the Israelites' journey from the slave houses of Egypt toward the Promised Land. Included in that ritual is a second story as well, about a familiar figure from an earlier time—one of the central characters in the book of Genesis. It is none other than Jacob, the protagonist in our other *levado* soul print tale. For Jacob in the biblical tale is the penultimate spiritual traveler. The ritual recounting of the Jacob myth provokes us to recount our own tales. The mythic hero is both a historical figure, and a projection of our very own soul. His story is our story.

First, let us set the stage for this night's drama in the Storytelling Ritual. For days, in a preparatory rite, the entire house has been meticulously cleaned and polished. On the day of the ritual, the crystal arrayed around the table glistens like gems in the candle-light, and all present are gowned in their finest whites. It is a regal celebration of freedom. Behind each person's back a lavish pillow rests, in each mouth is a song of freedom, in each hand a storybook, and in each storybook the text of the myth that will be retold this night.

As the ritual begins, those gathered begin a wordless, mantra-like tune that resounds through the halls of the house. As it hums to a close, a hush falls as the master of ceremonies begins to read a passage from the biblical myth. The room concentrates on the first words of the story—and of their journey.

"My father is a lost deceiver."

Confused heads cock, jeweled ears strain to make sure they heard right: We were expecting an ecstatic introduction, a prologue dripping with poetry that befits this auspicious occasion. Here was an opportunity for the Bible to present the quintessential tale of the glorified ancestor, the saga of Jacob, father of the house of Israel. His name has sat on the tongue of storytellers for millennia. His descendants produced what may well be the single most important foundational document of civilization, the Bible. Yet instead of starting an epic with a promise of adventure, drama, and glory, we begin with our hero deceiving someone and getting lost!

LIFE'S LOST AND FOUND

O human race! Born to ascend on wings,
why do ye fall at such a little wind?

—Dante, *The Divine Comedy*

As we saw earlier, Jacob's story is a tale of fall and flight. Jacob got lost because he ran away. If you recall, after deceiving his father and stealing the blessing intended for his brother, Esav, Jacob fled to the house of his Uncle Laban. These were the events immediately preceding the prologue line of our story ritual, "My father is a lost deceiver."

Spiritual journeys begin with a fall because recovery, the question of how you get up from the fall—how you reclaim your Soul

Print Story—is the essential art of living. Plato and the Talmud both teach that we receive all the knowledge of the world while still in the womb—knowledge, that is, not wisdom—yet we forget everything upon entering the world. Our lives are a process of recovery and remembering. We are all characterized by some degree of *Zerrissenheit,* what William James translated as "torn-to-pieces-hood." Like Humpty Dumpty, we have all gotten cracked, double-crossed, tossed, or tumbled from our walls. We need to put the pieces together again. We need to reclaim ourselves.

In Kabbalistic nomenclature, the fall-off-the-wall is called "the shattering of the vessels." The Lurianic creation myth begins with light streaming into vessels. The vessels, however, are flawed and unable to hold the too intense concentration of light. The vessels shatter. The work of humanity is to reconstruct the vessels in a way that they are able to hold the light. The literary matrix cited for this idea by the Kabbalists is none other than the Jacob story, the subject of our myth-telling ritual.

Jacob has great light, but he lacks his own solid soul print vessel to hold it. We too are unable to hold our own brilliant light, so our vessels shatter. The great endeavor of life is to reconnect the shards that form the vessels of our lives. We are not Humpty Dumpty. We are not ridiculous, pathetic, or incompetent. When we put the pieces back together, our new vessel is infinitely more beautiful, grand, and magnificent than the vessel that shattered.

COLLAGE: CUTTING AND RECREATING

My friend Myrna, an artist renowned for her magnificent collage pieces, creates what she calls "shattered landscapes." She uses as her media the tattered, torn, and broken things of her personal world—cloth from old clothes that no longer fit the fashion or her form, photos of long-dead relatives, letters from long-doused old flames. She fashions stunning landscapes by intricate arrangements and rearrangements of her life, epics that journey across the canvas.

I once asked her how she found her style. She answered me with a story:

A few years ago I was going through an old photo album and I started noticing that certain pictures had been awkwardly cut in half, or were missing altogether. I kind of wondered about it, but didn't think too much of it. That is, until one day I noticed that in my closet, one of my favorite old flower-print skirts was bundled up on the floor. I shook it out and saw that at the hem there had been a long lengthwise cut and the bottom several inches of the skirt was gaping, gone. I hadn't worn the thing for years. How did it get ripped like this?

Rather disturbed, I started searching around the house for signs of explanation—coming across other strangely cropped articles, papers, pictures, knickknacks, along the way.

Finally, I found myself in my daughter Andi's closet, surrounded by small piles of slivers. Slivers of pictures, cloth napkins, report cards, even coupons. My immediate reaction, I must admit, was horror. Horror at the destruction, fear that my little girl (and Andi was only nine at the time) may have some destructive tendencies, pent-up anger—who knows what! That is, until I noticed a flash of yellow to the side of the piles. It was that missing strip of my skirt! It was centered upon Andi's blue baby blanket. Placed carefully upon the skirt was a photograph. It was a picture taken years ago of me, sitting Indian-style on the grass in the park, wearing my favorite yellow flower skirt, and there cradled in the skirt's yellow folds and a sky-blue baby blanket, was my Andi as a newborn nestled in my lap.

Overcome with emotion, I sank to the floor and sobbed into the blanket. I was so moved, by the colors, the symbolism, the care of the placement, and so overcome with love for my daughter and this life and its precious peculiarities and its pleasures and its pains. For I did feel pain, the pain of someday losing that little baby in my lap, the pain of severing ties, the pain of cutting up old pictures and passions and garments that I will never wear again. The pain of shattering. And the pleasure of putting back together, recreating.

Andi had made art, art that touched me at the deepest direst fiber. So you ask when I found my style of shattering? I stole it from my nine-year-old. Each time I create, I try to reach that emotionally wrenching place that Andi brought me to. My latest creation was cutting my college diploma into bits and gluing it back together in a different scramble. Collage-making takes me through the pain and pleasure of tearing down and putting back together again . . . and again and again.

Myrna's story reminds us that we can make our fall into our finest art, reclaim our shatterings and transform them into our Sacred Autobiography.

Soul Print Practice

Make your own collage of the tattered and shattered things retrieved from your personal world. You can use old clothes, photos, letters, any objects you want. Is there something you want to tear apart or transform into something new?

Try to experience the pain and pleasure of tearing down and putting back together again.

Frame your collage. Turn your fall into your fine art.

LOST AND WHITEWASHED

His past in tatters, Jacob found refuge from his angry brother in the house of his Uncle Laban. He had run away, left the land, and thus abandoned his family and destiny—for, in biblical myth, destiny is bound up with land and family.

As we begin this ritual, we ask, Why did Jacob get lost? Every story in the Bible is understood through the story that precedes it. Context and text must be coupled to birth full meaning. So let us look for a moment at the deeper meaning behind Jacob's theft of his father's blessing, the act that necessitated he flee the country, his first step on a long path of lostness.

In order to steal the blessing, Jacob dressed in his brother's clothes. He was urged to dress this part by the voice of his mother,

Rebecca. She believed that in order for him to be successful, he had to imitate big brother Esav. She made her son into a deceiver. He played a role that was not his to play. After all, what does it really mean to steal blessings intended for another? It means to live in someone else's story.

"The breath of our nostrils is the Messiah of God," proclaims biblical myth master Solomon. Simply read, this verse merely says that the Messiah is of vital concern to us, right down to the passionate basics of our breath. Mystic philosopher Abraham Kuk audaciously interprets the verse to mean that the breath of *our* nostrils *is* the Messiah of God. Only through believing in our own divinity, and hence our infinite potential to repair the world, can we usher in a messianic age in our lives. Our very breath can bring redemption. But only if it is *our* breath. You may remember that the Hebrew word *neshama* means both "breath" and "soul." Breath in biblical myth is a soul print metaphor. No two people breathe in quite the same way.

Jacob's mother loved him the best way she could, but she did not fully believe in the strength of her second son's story. She dismissed his own psychic wardrobe as inadequate to the call of his destiny. She believed Jacob's inner messiah would only come if he masqueraded as Esav. When his blind father, Isaac, asked the disguised Jacob his name, Jacob's response was "Esav." He refused his own name.

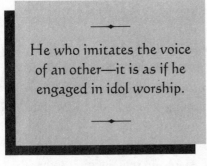

He who imitates the voice of an other—it is as if he engaged in idol worship.

Jacob was trying to counterfeit his soul print, replacing it with that of his brother.

Jacob understood the danger in this imitation. He said to his mother's voice, "If I pretend to be what I am not I will become a *metatea*." The myth masters, seeking the meaning of this strange biblical word, offer an epigram: He who imitates the voice of an other—it is as if he engaged in idol worship. *Metatea* connotes idol worship. "Idol worship," however, is a mistranslation of the Hebrew idiom *avodah zarah,* which literally means "strange worship."

Strange worship, explains the master Mendel of Nemirov, is to live through the stranger in yourself. In a related context, *metatea* is translated as "mocking"—for to live the life of the stranger is to take yourself lightly, to mock the gravitas of your soul print. To be a lightweight is not, as is usually understood, to lack power or influence; it is to ignore your own depth. When we meet a person and say she has gravitas, we don't mean to say that she is wealthy or influential. We are referring to a person of depth, a person who is one with her story. Yet in the biblical myth of Jacob, the mother-voice overpowered Jacob's soul print voice. Jacob, trifling with his depth, stole the blessing intended for his brother. Jacob had become a mockery even if he did not yet see it; he was engaged in strange worship.

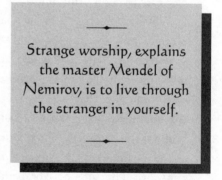

Strange worship, explains the master Mendel of Nemirov, is to live through the stranger in yourself.

In biblical myth, losing yourself is always expressed in the same way—exile, being thrust out from the Land. Estranged from his own authenticity, Jacob was exiled from his physical place. He went to the home of his uncle.

His uncle's name, Laban the Aramean, is rich with meaning. *Laban* means "white" and *Aramean* derives from the Hebrew root word for "deception." Laban was a whitewasher, a deceiver; he didn't tell the story like it is. Whenever we run away, we wind up in places and situations that mirror our soul print crisis. Jacob became a deceiver—one who distorts and whitewashes his story.

Jacob had also become a slave. Textual and thematic parallels abound between Jacob's stay in the house of Laban and his descendants' sojourn in Egypt. The Storytelling Ritual we explored in the previous chapter celebrates the movement from slavery to freedom, and according to the Kabbalists, the Jacob story is chosen as the introduction to the Storytelling Ritual because it illustrates most dramatically that slavery is not just about the sociopolitical subjugation of a people. It is ultimately about consciousness. Jacob, who had lost his story and become a slave, had lost consciousness.

For Jacob to be freed, he must first recover his story.

EAST OF EDEN

Biblical myth readers notice a soul print danger signal embedded in a textual pattern, which reveals the great spiritual threat posed to Jacob by the house of Laban. Patterns in a text—whether that text is biblical myth or our own Sacred Autobiography—always provide vital soul print hints.

When Jacob left his father's house he is described as traveling *"kedma,"* eastward, to the house of Laban. Jacob was not the first person in the book of Genesis to travel eastward. There are six other incidents before Jacob in which biblical characters journey east. Going in that direction invariably signals a spiritual fall. Adam and Eve were exiled east of Eden. Cain, after murdering his brother, was sent east. The builders of the Tower of Babel are the people of the east. Lot, upon separating from Abraham, traveled eastward. The sons of Abraham's concubines, who were not to inherit with Isaac, were sent by Abraham to a land east of his own. And of course the name of one of Ishmael's sons is Kedma, meaning eastward. The pattern is clear.

Thus, when Jacob traveled eastward to his uncle in the story it signals two things to the reader. First, Jacob had fallen, having just deceived his father and taken the blessing due his brother. Second, Jacob was in enormous spiritual danger of being read out of the story. No one else in the book of Genesis had ever returned from eastern exile. To be east is to be east of Eden—that is, estranged from the natural habitat of your Sacred Autobiography. Would Jacob be able to break the *kedma* pattern and return to the Land, the Genesis symbol of his spiritual story? If he succeeded, he would be the hero of the book and a people would emerge from him. If he failed, he would disappear from the story. The essential question is, can Jacob become the hero of his own life?

For twenty years at Laban's house, Jacob worked as a shepherd for his cheating uncle, avoided his wider responsibilities, and ignored his dreams of angel-laden ladders touching the heavens. The word used repeatedly in the text by both Laban and Jacob to describe their relationship is *eved,* the Hebrew root for slave. This is a more subtle form of slavery than that conjured up by images of the Hebrew slaves building pyramids beneath a taskmaster's whip. Yet slavery it was, and no less insidious for its subtlety. So deadening were its effects that the entire biblical story could have ended then and there.

After marrying one of Laban's daughters and fathering children, Jacob had an opportunity to return to the land and to the house of his father and felt the first stirring of his long-dormant soul print. Laban, however, offered him a business proposition that could make him a wealthy man. Laban's world operated on mercantile, "I-it" principles, contravening everything biblical myth stands for. He said to Jacob, "Name your price for giving up your dream of Canaan and I will pay it. I need you to run my business." Laban had no notion of family beyond business and power relations. His daughters were pawns in his transactions with Jacob. Jacob, his close kin, had no place in his home unless Laban could gain measurably from his presence. Bereft of his own truth, oppressed by values contradictory to his own, exiled from his own authenticity, Jacob was trapped in the wrong story.

> ### Soul Print Practice
> Here are some danger signs that might indicate if you are living the wrong story:
>
> You feel uncomfortable at social gatherings with your friends or associates. Either you don't approve of your friends and associates, or you sense they don't approve of you.

> You feel incompatible with your coworkers and alienated from your work environment.
>
> After a long day of living your life, you feel as if you are on the verge of tears. These are signs that you need to return from exile.

AFTER THE FALL

Having fallen so far and wandered so far from home, how could Jacob find his way back to his story?

Finding our way home to our Soul Print Story is not always easy. Our heartstrings are tugged by tales of people who somehow wound up in a story not their own, unsure of when, if ever, they will find their way back to the authentic inner place they started from.

My favorite singer growing up was Harry Chapin. His performance on the Hudson River pier in New York was the only concert I went to in my seminary days; I cried when I heard he was killed in a car accident on the Long Island Expressway. I was drawn to his songs in part because they were ballads. The limited lyrics of pop were a vessel unable to contain his desire to tell a story. The song of Chapin's that most captured my heart is "Taxi," a ballad about stories gone sour in a sad and desperate sort of way.

You probably remember the song's scenario. On a rainy night late in his shift, a San Francisco taxi driver named Harry picks up a woman whose fancy dress has been spoiled by the rain. He recognizes her—she's a youthful romance of his, back in the days when she aspired to be an actress and Harry a pilot. Now she's an actress in the world's shadow play, and Harry is flying in his taxi, getting stoned.

She steps out of the taxi, hands Harry a twenty-dollar bill and says, "Harry, keep the change." At that moment, we listeners are sadly far from sure that these two lost people will ever be able to find their way back to their true stories, the authentic aspirations of their soul prints. The chorus resounds in our empathetic ears. "And here she's acting happy, inside her handsome home, and me I'm flyin' in my taxi, taking tips and getting stoned."

TO DREAM ANOTHER DREAM:
THE LURE OF YOUR ALTERNATIVE STORY

Imagine Jacob's life in the house of Laban. Although he meant to sojourn there only briefly, Jacob wound up remaining for over two decades. Stories not our own have a way of growing on us. The daily patterns of our lives, the demands of our to-do lists, after a time seem to resemble the patterns of our soul print. Maybe this is my life after all, we whisper to ourselves.

Jacob was lured into Laban's alternative vision of his story. The text describes Jacob involved in complex manipulations of his flock's breeding habits as he sought to ensure the growth of his flock and his own prosperity. He entered the world of dubious husbandry with relish, breeding cattle for his own benefit. Indeed, it seems to be all he thought about. Despite a vague awareness that he must leave, Jacob did not seem able to make the move.

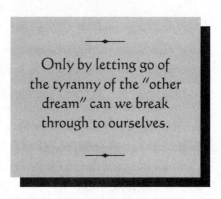

Only by letting go of the tyranny of the "other dream" can we break through to ourselves.

We all have sirens who beckon us, holding out the vision of the alternative person we could be. Only by letting go of the tyranny of the "other dream" can we break through to ourselves. This is true with ambitions, careers, vocations, relationships, and romances. Very often, a student will come to me wanting to get engaged to one woman even though he remains haunted by another woman. I always tell these students the same simple truth, one I already mentioned earlier in our journey—but which bears repeating in this context. *There are two women in every man's life: the woman he marries and the woman he does not.* It seems to help. (My female friends tell me the same is true for them in relation to men.) Of course, the difficulty is in knowing which is which. Which dream is yours and which belongs to your Laban, your alter ego, your wrong-story self? The dream that belongs to your other is the most sophisticated form of false certainty. The alternative vision is so seductive because it seems so familiar, part of you and your story, yet it is not.

My friend Keri tells the story of one of these bizarro glimpses of the other life she could have lived. Keri had just gotten engaged and was blissfully going to the bridal shop to pick out her dress. At the store, she bumped into none other than her ex-boyfriend, a man she had very nearly married. He awkwardly introduced his fiancée. They exchanged congratulations on their respective engagements, with each bride insisting that the other should come to her wedding. When Keri received the invitation, she was surprised not only to see that her ex-boyfriend's ceremony would be exactly one month before her own but that it would take place in the very same wedding hall. However, this didn't compare to the shock she had upon arriving at their wedding and, behold, the bride was dressed in precisely the same gown that Keri had ordered. She told me that the ceremony was like watching herself marry this man—having the uncanny experience of what it would have been like to walk down the path she had very nearly taken. For a few moments she was flustered—until her fiancé, late as usual, walked in, in the middle of the ceremony. As her heart leaped out to greet him, she knew she had chosen wisely.

We all have a bizarro alternative world that is familiar, comfortable, and even seductive, yet in the end not who we really are. Our alternative story actually calls us, seduces us, and seems to be connected to us. In the end, we have to give it up in order to reclaim our story. How do we distinguish between the two?

INNER-FACE

What moved Jacob to finally leave Laban? From where did he derive the strength, in midlife, to reclaim his story?

The turning point came through a subtle but important shift in perception, when "Jacob saw Laban's face, and behold it was not with him as it had been previously."

To understand the power of that seemingly simple sentence, we need to behold the fascinating image of the face, a discussion we began in chapter three.

The human face is the medium through which the invisible in us becomes visible. It is the interlocutor between the secret of our soul print and the language of our body. If we are attuned to depth and not merely beauty, we realize that as we get older and our bodies lose their polish, our faces begin to shine. *There is little more beautiful and worthy of contemplation than the face of an elder.* Indeed, there is a special biblical myth practice that invites us to perceive the *Hadar* (beauty and dignity) in the face of the elder. The face, like the name, is a symbol for the soul print. Moses, the image of the living soul print, had a face that shone. Jacob, also our soul print hero, attained the image of his face that is engraved upon the divine throne.

To be faceless is to lose the manifestation of your soul print, the primary expression of your singularity, for as the myth masters declare, "Just as their faces are different so is their essence." The word for face in Hebrew, *panim,* also means "inside." In Genesis, *panim* is a symbol indicating inner essence. How often have we said, "We'll talk about it later. It's not for the phone. Let's talk face-to-face." We are saying we want to reach a quality of communication that is not attainable by phone, fax, or e-mail. Face-to-face is not just a situational description; it means I want to talk to your inside.

In the days of Jesus and the sages, when the ancient temple still stood in Jerusalem, the high priest would approach the divine presence in the holy of holies: the inner sanctum of the Temple. It was here, in the innermost sanctum, what the wisdom masters call *lifnei velifnim,* "the inside of the inside," where priests made direct contact with God. The experience of the high priest is described by the Babylonian sages as *"cmi bifnim"*—"as if on the inside." Being holy means being on the inside.

The goal of the soul print quest is to reach the *sanctum sanctorum* in ourselves—to be *lifnei velifnim,* on the inside of the inside. Ultimately, holiness means to live on the inside of yourself. The word *lifnei,* "inside," is a daughter word to *panim,* emerging directly from the same root, *pnim,* "to be inside."

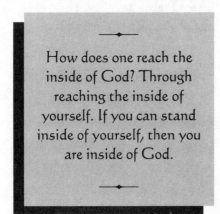

How does one reach the inside of God? Through reaching the inside of yourself. If you can stand inside of yourself, then you are inside of God.

The soul print destination is to be *lefnei hashem*—before God's name, face-to-face with what we can call the Ultimate Soul Print. If we are *lifnei* God, we are not just in front of God; we are on the inside of God. We are in God's face. How does one reach the inside of God? Through reaching the inside of yourself. If you can stand inside of yourself, then you are inside of God.

BEHOLD, LABAN'S FACE

"Jacob saw Laban's face, and behold it was not with him as it had been previously." The plain sense of the text would indicate that Jacob sensed Laban to be envious of his nephew's newfound wealth. People with recent fortunes often sense they are being perceived differently, the evil eye of envy casting darting glances. But the image of the face sensitizes us to a deeper, altogether different resonance. Jacob came to Laban's house as a young man with a dream, someone who had seen the ladder connecting heaven and earth, and he was possessed of certain earthly goals—marriage, economic stability, and not least, refuge from Esav's fury. He intended to take the first opportunity available to return to Canaan to fulfill his dream of personal destiny.

When Jacob first saw Laban's face he was taken aback. Laban's *panim* was initially repulsive to him. Laban represented corruption, complacency, and manipulation. Then Jacob married, had children, and two decades passed. His dreams waited at the gate going west.

When Laban made him an offer he couldn't refuse, Jacob wavered but gave in. He was seduced. After succumbing to Laban's business plan, Jacob found his dreams starting to fade. His accommodation to his new life was slow, gradual, almost imperceptible, and deadly. Jacob was almost unaware that he was losing himself. He no longer dreamed of "angels ascending to Heaven" but in a striking textual parallel he now dreamed of mating sheep—"sheep ascending on other sheep"! Mundane accomplishment was not only the stuff of his daily life; it had become the stuff of his dreams.

One morning after a period of feeling ill at ease with himself, Jacob woke up and looked at Laban—"and behold, Laban's face" looked . . . perfectly fine. In fact, Jacob thought, Laban looks—remarkably—like me. The notion struck Jacob like a thunderbolt. He remembered how he felt when he first saw Laban, twenty years ago as a young man with a dream, and recalled his initial repulsion, how Laban seemed to be antithetical to all he held sacred. Now Laban looked fine. "What has happened to me?" asked a middle-aged Jacob. The answer is painfully clear. He had forgotten his dreams. He had lost face.

The best way to distinguish between a false story and a true one, or between a counterfeit and an authentic call, is to compare the present experience of your story or vocation with the

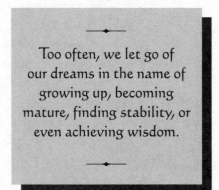

Too often, we let go of our dreams in the name of growing up, becoming mature, finding stability, or even achieving wisdom.

dreams of your youth. Too often, we let go of our dreams in the name of growing up, becoming mature, finding stability, or even achieving wisdom. If we do need to let go of dream-fulfillment because reality simply won't allow it, we must never let go of the dream-feeling. That dream-feeling is the sense of clarity and empowerment we had when our story was fresh with promise and ambition; we knew what we wanted and had a good inkling of what was right for us. The dream-feeling is our best spiritual and ethical intuition. Almost invariably, while the false dream seems to fit on the outside, it rubs against some deeply felt intuition or belief.

If we don't want our eastward exile to last twenty years—or an entire lifetime—then we need to reclaim our sense of promise. We need to retain our ability to experience the world with all the passion and clarity of youth in order to maintain our connection to that intuitive truth source. Although the face appropriately ages, we need to never lose our child's eyes.

Soul Print Practice

List three dreams of your youth.

Have they been fulfilled?

If not, take them back!

Allow yourself to meditate upon the following.

What were your dreams of who you wanted to be . . .

As a child? _____

A couple of Soul Print Hints to guide your meditation: What were your favorite toys, games, etc? What was your gut answer to the classic question, "What do you want to be when you grow up?"

As a teenager? _____

Soul Print Hints: What were your favorite TV shows, subjects in school, and extracurricular activities? Did anything come particularly easy to you?

As a college student? _____

Soul Print Hints: Was there a cause that caught your interest? Was there a teacher who sparked your passion? Was there a major that you wanted to take and didn't because you were told it wasn't practical?

Is what you are today similar to your dreams of yesterday?

If not, why not?

Did you mature . . . or settle?

If you settled . . . without rashly dismantling your life . . . take back your dreams!

How can you recapture your dreams? If you feel that the cobwebs of your life blur your vision and make it hard for you to capture your dream, then try this exercise:

What dreams do you have for your children?

Often when we give up on our own dreams we displace them onto our children. That is a dangerous practice when our unfulfilled dreams move us to subconsciously mold our children in the shape of our own soul prints—a soul print not their own. However, if our children's faces can become prisms refracting back to us our own soul print light, enabling us to see and reclaim those dreams as our own, then our children become our teachers.

COMING TO OUR SENSES

The poet Langston Hughes asked, "What happens to a dream deferred?" That is a question many of us have to face—just as Jacob did. This is the most critical juncture in Jacob's spiritual path. Will he be able to reconnect with his more authentic self? Can he reclaim his story? Can we?

The answer is we can, but only if we're willing to give something up. We need to be able to let go of some of the comfortable certainties that cloud our vision. Only if we are willing, at least for a time, to walk the path of uncertainty can we make our way back to ourselves.

Laban had not changed. It was Jacob's perception of Laban's face, of his father-in-law's true self, that changed. Jacob gained fresh eyes. For spiritual breakthroughs, however, eyes are not enough. Vision and perception involve how you perceive your external reality. You also need fresh ears.

Indeed, in the very next verse, Jacob heard a divine voice! For the first time in twenty years, a voice was urging him to return home. God was with Jacob, encouraging him in his choice to return to his story. His Ultimate Soul Print was pulling him westward, back to the truth of his story.

Jacob was finally able to recognize his self-enslavement in Laban's world. He rejected the shallow mercantile certainties of Laban and his negative model of family, and he decided to reclaim his own story. Jacob was able to break out of his old set of perceptions. His ears had become sensitive to his true inner voice: the voice of God. He began the transition from being Jacob to becoming Israel. The very name Israel means "one who sees divinity"— *shur-el,* to see God. And one who sees God in himself. Jacob, who had been lost and blind, now embarked on the path to becoming Israel, the One who Sees.

This is perhaps the subtext of that most famous of biblical myth verses, "O Israel, the Lord is our God, the Lord is One." According to the myth masters, Israel does not refer, as is popularly assumed, to any particular people. Rather, God calls Jacob to his higher name, to his soul self, Israel. Jacob has come to his senses. Jacob for the first time is able to hear. Hear O Israel. Jacob the Lost Deceiver will be called to be Israel the Seer (see-er), and Israel the Seer will be called to also be Israel the listener.

Jacob at last began the journey home, to his place, his highest name, his story, his realized soul print. Upon his return to the Land he was greeted by angels. The myth masters suggest that these were the very same angels that Jacob saw in his dream when he left the Land. Because he was able—in midlife—to reclaim his dreams, Jacob became a hero.

WRONG TURNS AND LEAKING BUCKETS

Often we feel prevented from changing course because of the sunken costs we feel we have invested in the wrong path. It seems as if changing course would be to acknowledge that we had wasted five, ten, or even twenty-five years of our lives. This seems too painful to bear. What do we do with our wrong turns, with our years of imitation? Jacob had to answer this question himself— after all, he did spend a good deal of his life in the house of Laban, invested in a story not his own.

We must understand that those years were not wasted. *All of your detours are part of your story.* You could not have realized your soul print other than by the way you traveled. Once you have integrated that affirmation, you can look back over your path, in all its tangled briars and dead-ends, and reach a sympathetic understanding of where you've been and why. *There is no place that you have been that you did not need to be.* This is true even if it takes many years to understand why this might be so.

Every morning, the water carrier of Stanislav would walk from the well at the edge of town through the same shtetl streets, toting his two buckets of water to his customers. Day in and day out, he performed his routine with a simple joy.

One day he was particularly joyous and burst out in song along the way. But his song was interrupted by the sound of weeping from one of his buckets. The bucket called up to him, "How can you sing so joyously? Are you blind? Don't you realize what a bum bucket you've got in your hand? Don't you realize that for years now I've been leaking? Look at your other bucket—he doesn't leak. I don't know why you didn't use me for kindling a long time ago. What good is a bucket that leaks!"

The water carrier gently responded to his bucket, "No, my bucket, you are the one who is blind. What good is a bucket that leaks, you ask. Well, look and see."

With these words, the water carrier made a grand motion toward the ground beneath the bucket, pointing out the same path they had walked for years. "Look, my leaking bucket, look at your side of the path—the yellow daisies, the wild red strawberries, the luscious greens. Now look at the other side of the path, the ground beneath my sturdy, leakless bucket—it is nothing but gravel and dirt. All of this beauty is precisely because of your leak. For years now you have watered this side of the path, making it the most beautiful thoroughfare of Stanislav. Your leak is what makes me sing!"

In my own life, I know my mistakes brought me to places I might otherwise never have visited. They delivered me to ideas I might otherwise never have taken seriously. I regret my mistakes, yet I love them dearly and understand that every path I walked was significant for me and was nourished by my being there. When I began my journey, I thought my calling was to be the king's irrigation system—watering the grand gardens around the palace with precisely distributed quantities of water. Today, I sometimes suspect that I am the king's bucket, or the king's gardener's bucket, or the assistant to the king's gardener's bucket—trying my best to hold my water. Leaking as I go, I am at least hopeful that I may leave behind a string of daisies to decorate the road.

For in the end are we not all imperfect vessels for the light . . . leaking illumination along the way?

Soul Print Practice

When have your mistakes led you to greater growth and illumination?

List three mistakes you have made in your life.

Try to find ways in which your leaks can be seen as advantages, as flowers.

The Leak: The Flowers:

1)

2)

3)

As I was writing this section of the book my wife, Cary, and I had a minor and somewhat funny argument about the fourth—very badly bruised—bunch of bananas that she had brought home from the market. The story that ensued resounded with the "leaking buckets" theme—so I am happy to share with you the poem Cary wrote about the incident.

I make Mistakes
(By hand/from scratch)
Homemade mistakes
All sorts and assortments
Every morning

Meager offerings
I must admit
But Somebody must do it . . .

Take the overripe bananas
Just yesterday
I bought (without thinking)
A twelve-pack, a bruised bunch
To the protest of my husband
Dissecting them from sack
upon purchase
already browned and sluggish
—to the disgust of all senses

With an echo of that odor
I would so dread as a child
Dare it seep from my discreet lunch bag

"Honey, why waste the money, the fridge space, the
strength of your arms to carry in this putrid pile of . . ."

"—oy, I apologize,
Wasn't thinking
Careless—mistake"

And this, the fifth
This morning alone
All the little misreads add up
To volumes

—Sweep me out the door—

To the bus stop
Where from my grief
I surface to find
A friend in need,
in frantic search
In corner stores
for a cure
for a mother
in the throes of labor
hospitalized next door

Sabrina
verging birth
Is screaming out
screaming screaming
for, yes, no less
than overripe bananas

I triumph home
to the scent in the kitchen
Brown bag the bananas with a note:

> *"Our mistakes can be our miracles"*
> *Yes, I make mistakes*
> *But—perhaps—*
> *Mistakes make me.*

THE STRAIGHT STORY

We often need wrong turns to test out other voices before we find our own. Other parts in our life-production—work as a camera-wielder in someone else's film, cameo appearances, a supporting actress role—all can be necessary before we become the lead character.

The Hebrew word *Jacob* means "crooked"; in biblical myth, this is interpreted in the sense of a crooked path. At the end of the Jacob *levado* story, after he wrestles with his loneliness through the dark night on the eve of his return home, he wins the name Israel. *Israel* means not only to see, but also "straight," as in the straight and narrow—or better yet, a *straight shooter. A person of integrity.*

The layered epic of Jacob calls out a wild and wonderful truth—that the nature of things is such that we can only get to the straight and narrow by going along the crooked path. *It may be true that the shortest distance between two points is a straight line. But that is only in geometry. In the higher calculus of life, we create complex equations that yield unpredictable results.*

The crooked path is sometimes the only way to the straight place. Often that place needs to be far away from mother's eyes, from the primal competition with brother, and farther still from the desperate need for the blessing of the father. Sometimes our soul print daimon trips us up, so that in the fall we land far enough away from home that we can hear his call.

Often we find ourselves in the house of a distant relative, the home of the unfamiliar uncle, where we explore our uncharted terrain in search of the real self. That uncle doesn't have to be a nasty guy like Laban; he can be at least a temporary liberator, his home not a residence but a guest house, and himself the one who points out the

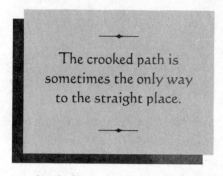

The crooked path is sometimes the only way to the straight place.

positive path. Remember the uncle of the chimney sweeper in *Mary Poppins?* He and Mary take the very stolid banker's children to explore inner worlds of laughter and tears they thought off-limits. In the wonderful children's books of C. S. Lewis, the way to the magical land of Narnia is through the entranceway in the wardrobe, and it is the strange uncle living in the attic who has the magic balls that will guide them there.

On the one hand, the uncle is a relative—in our search, we don't want to lose our bearings entirely—and on the other hand he has his own set of tensions with our parents. All of this makes him a wonderful detour where we can play-act and put on all sorts of masks that we would not dare reach for in the house of our parents. In my family, I am the designated "Wild Uncle"; and I would love to tell you some stories, but part of the Wild Uncle contract is never to reveal the secrets.

THE RITUAL THAT RECLAIMS

Let us return to the richly set table of our ritual. Our entire discussion in these last two chapters reflects the free-flowing form of the Storytelling Ritual called—you remember—"Telling the Story of the Exodus from Egypt." The Jacob story that forms the crux of the ritual and of this chapter is the mythic framework for our discussion. In what I like to call Biblical Myth Therapy, we relax by letting go of obsessive self-analysis and focus instead on the tale of the mythic hero. It allows us to be freer, more creative, and daring—and of course more honest than we otherwise might have been. All the while, however, we know subliminally that *we* are the subjects and potentially the heroes of the tale. Our life is the highest sacred text. We are Moses and Jacob and we are Buddha. The biblical myth Storytelling Ritual is no less than a Soul Print Quest.

As the night takes a bow to the first rays of day, the Ritual of Reclaiming draws to an end. The curtain closes on the stage of our storytelling; the journey and the destination have become one. The once-white tablecloth is painted with passionately spilled wine, the storybooks hang limp in our hands, the pillows behind our backs are put to good use. Our heads spin with the stories we have heard—we are imprinted by the souls who sit around us. We have spoken ourselves to freedom.

15

———◆———

RENEW YOUR STORY

THE CARNIVAL OF ALTERNATIVE SELVES

Things are rarely what they seem,
Skim milk masquerades as Cream
—W. S. Gilbert, *H.M.S. Pinafore*

In biblical Hebrew, the word for "year" is *shanah*. Wonderfully, it has two very different meanings. The first meaning is "repetition," doing the same thing repeatedly. The second meaning is "change," transformation. Indeed, the year offers both possibilities. The year can be composed of one day that repeats itself, in which case the calendar is merely a system to mark time. Alternatively, the calendar can be a system geared toward powerful growth and transformation. The biblical calendar is an expression of the latter possibility. It is actually an intricately worked system of growth exercises disguised as rituals—each one carefully developed and placed in relation to the whole. The goal of the calendar is no less than personal healing and transformation that can also change the world.

On the personal level, as we have seen, the Pe-Sach Storytelling Ritual is designed to help us tell, reclaim, and live our story. In the biblical myth calendar we have another magnificent opportunity for change and transformation, this time a chance to try out other voices and new possibilities and perspectives. The ritual expression is a carnival holiday, referred to by the Persian word *purim*. It always takes place exactly one month before the spring Storytelling Ritual that we have spent the last two chapters exploring. The timing is not accidental. In fact, the Purim Carnival experience is actually the beginning of the yearly journey that allows us the chance to test out alternative selves and possibilities—and thus not just reclaim but renew our stories.

There are three stages in the biblical timeline of transformation. The first is Purim. The second is the Storytelling Ritual. The third is the "Counting Ritual"—in Hebrew, *Sefira,* which we will investigate in the next chapter.

PURIM STORIES

In ancient Persia, King Xerxes, feeling that he has finally consolidated his power, throws a wild, six-month-long party. In the midst of the festivities, he calls his Queen, Vashti, to dance naked before his assembled ministers. Vashti, an early feminist heroine, refuses his command and is banished. Perhaps she is even executed. The King calls for a beauty contest to choose his new queen. The chosen consort is the seductive and charming Esther, the secret niece, and some say wife, of the King's Counselor, Mordechai. Mordechai tells Esther not to reveal to Xerxes that she is of Hebrew origin. In effect, Esther, masquerading as a single woman of Persian origin, has, in a strange twist of fate, become the Queen.

Meanwhile in the palace, the King's Prime Minister, Haman, is engaged in an obsessive power struggle with Mordechai and plots his execution. His hatred for Mordechai is so great that it goes beyond politics and into genocide. He wants to destroy Mordechai's entire people. The King passively supports the genocidal plan.

Esther, hearing of Haman's designs against her people, initiates a brilliant series of events within the palace walls that win her the favor of the King—at which point she reveals her Hebrew origin and brings about the dramatic reversal of Haman's designs. The tree upon which Haman planned to hang Mordechai becomes the hanging tree of his own execution. All is turned on its head. The day of intended genocide becomes a day of extravagant joy and celebration.

What characterizes the day is the sense that anything is possible. All had changed in the last moment. Radical reversal and transformation became the order of the day. Esther decrees a holiday for all future generations, which is to be marked by wine, wild revelry, and carnival—a celebration of the wide-open energy of possibility and transformation that characterized the first Purim.

The Story of Esther becomes the last tale to be included in the biblical myth canon. It is called the Purim Story. The word *Purim* means something equivalent to "lottery." Purim represents the seemingly arbitrary winds of fate to which all of us are vulnerable. Yet Purim also reminds us that this very vulnerability contains a silver lining of opportunity—the chance for renewal. Esther and Mordechai experience radical vulnerability. Initially powerful, they suddenly seem undone by fate—and yet, at the very last moment, destiny steps in and spins everything around again. According to biblical myth, Mordechai and Esther are heroes because they are able to channel the energy made available by their experience of vulnerability into a powerful force for renewal. Therefore, according to the Kabbalah, Purim is an explosive time of paradigm shift and radical change.

THE POSSIBILITY OF RENEWAL

We all have a Purim dimension to our personal stories. The trick is to listen deeply and transform what may appear to be the fate of the lottery into the destiny of the soul. It is in those times of intense vulnerability that hierarchies, false identities, pompous poses, and the external garb of status and station are cast aside. A paradoxical moment of grace is born only from the encounter with radical vulnerability. The ossified conceptions of self are shaken up. We promise ourselves that "if only" we survive the threat, we will be different in very essential sorts of ways. We promise that we will be to our own selves true. We swear an oath to authenticity. However, as we all know too well, once the threat fades we revert very quickly—like a rubber band snapping back into place—to our old and tired forms.

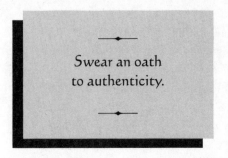

Swear an oath
to authenticity.

The goal of the Purim carnival is to reaccess the transformative energy of the very first Purim, when the fixities were loosened and anything was possible. This biblical myth carnival is designed to foster opportunities *to recapture the explosive energy set free when old identities crumble, and all is open to question, and all is up for change.*

WITH WINE AND MASK

The biblical myth masters set out a central rule for the Purim Carnival: Drink until you don't know the difference between Haman (the villain) and Mordechai (the hero). The point of this injunction is not just to leave you with a hangover in the morning; it is to allow you to escape from the strict black and white lines of definition, from the narrow straits of certain identification. Drink until you've blurred the lines between the heroes and the villians. For this state of suspension of judgment is crucial for growth and new identity formation—in small doses of course, like once a year.

Bakhtin, the great Russian writer who attempted to resist the evils of Stalinism, captured the existential essence of carnival:

The carnival involves the suspension of all hierarchical precedents. Rank, especially evident at official feasts . . . was absent at the carnival. At official feasts . . . Everyone was expected to appear in the full regalia of his calling, rank, and merits, to take the place corresponding to his position. Official feast thus is a consecration of inequality. The carnival undermines the official feast. During the carnival, all were considered equal. In the town square a special form of free and familiar contact reigned among people whom do the barriers of caste, property, profession, and age usually divide. The hierarchical background in the extreme corporative and caste divisions of the medieval social order were exceptionally strong. Therefore, such free familiar contacts were deeply felt and formed an element of the carnival spirit. People were so to speak "reborn" for new purely human relations. These truly human relations were not only a figure of imagination or abstract thought. They were experienced.

Similarly, in the biblical myth context, Purim Carnival seeks to create a safe environment to try on new roles, a place where we can tinker with the terms of our soul prints without being fully responsible for our experiments, shattering the tyranny of artifice in order to loosen the genie of the soul print. This is our trial run at ultimate freedom. The carnival helps us renew our

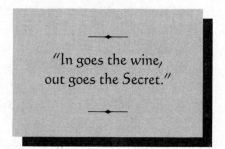

"In goes the wine, out goes the Secret."

story with fresh oxygen, water, and air. The renewal is also communal, for we reinvigorate old contexts, shaking off the cobwebs of routine and revitalizing traditions gone stale with new and fresh interpretations.

Two major Purim components are getting drunk and wearing masks. We wear masks to try out new roles with the safety and anonymity that we need in order to find out who we really are. We drink to let drop the heavy garb of habit and socialization, to liquefy the ossification of our personalities. As the Kabbalists comment, "In goes the wine, out goes the Secret." Simply understood, that means that when you're drunk you often spill your guts. More deeply comprehended, both the masks and the inebriation give us the opportunity to unfold hidden, secret parts of ourselves that we generally avoid. We can discover truer selves or discard the false selves that flirt with us, seeking to seduce us with their blandishments.

How might these masks fit our face? Are they too tight, too dramatic, too understated, or are they just right? Often we can only break the siren's song of seduction by trying them on and seeing for ourselves that they don't fit. The mask is not us. Perhaps the process can even return us to the old us whom we know and love, with a deepened appreciation of the visage behind the visor. And sometimes the mask may even fit!

This is the psychological underpinning of the "Purim masquerade." You dress up in elaborate costume, the only rule being that the costume cannot be connected to your usual life pursuit. The persona you choose should be one you want to test out. A favorite costume is drag—men dressing in women's clothes or women in men's, exploring dimensions of the other gender that they might want to access within themselves. Another favorite is to play with professions: An airplane pilot may dress as a painter, and an electrician in the flowing robes of a priest, while the priest dons the garb of the avant-garde bohemian.

PURIM MOMENTS FOR THE REST OF THE YEAR

Purim Moments are of course not limited to one semidrunk masquerade event. Life is full of Purim opportunities, which are important to take advantage of if we truly want to grow spiritually. Life sometimes cracks open a window of opportunity for expansion and experimentation—allowing us a sliver of time to slip on a mask and see how it fits without getting hurt if it does not. These are Purim Moments.

Here is a Purim Moment story I tell my students every year in the middle of the semidrunk but holy revelry of the Purim Carnival.

The Master Shmelke of Nikolsburg had become good friends with his coach driver. One day the coach driver said to him, "You know, I've driven you to many speeches. You say very beautiful things. Moreover, you say the same beautiful things every time. Not only that, but people ask the same questions all the time, and you always give the same answer. I actually know your entire speech by heart. Perhaps the next time we come to a new town where they don't recognize you, we could change clothes and I could be the master and you the coachman. I want to see how the world looks from the eyes of a master. And who knows? Maybe I shouldn't be a coachman after all."

Well, the master thought it was a fine idea, and that is what they did the very next week. Dressed as the master, the coachman gave the speech—very beautifully. Dressed as the coachman, the master watched the horses.

After the usual round of questions, a young boy raised his hand and asked a very deep question that the coachman had never heard before. Having no idea what to answer, he thought seriously for a moment. Then he looked up at the boy. "Your question appears, to the untrained ear, to be very difficult," he said. "However, it is really so simple that even my coachman can answer it. Let's call him in!"

In this story, of course, the coachman remained a coachman and the master a master. It is told as a wisdom story to remind us with gentle laughter that it is sometimes important to dress as someone else, to check whether you are living in the expanse of your soul print or merely dulled by your standard perspective and lulled by your life's routine.

A major opportunity for Purim Moments arises when you're sitting next to someone on a plane and get to tell your story over martinis and honey-roasted peanuts. There are two potential opportunities here—both important and also a lot of fun.

The first is to actually tell your companion your story. Watch, however, how you tell it. What do you emphasize, leave out, slightly exaggerate, or just plain lie about? You may want to be particularly careful to be honest. In the reflected face of a stranger and through deep listening, you may encounter your soul print in new and revealing ways.

The other option? Make believe. Try on what you would like, but haven't dared, to be. See how the story resonates. Create the wildest story you can imagine. If you do this masquerading in "real life," you should probably seek therapy. But when you're on a plane, you are allowed to soar to places beyond your usual fear of flying.

You have to be careful, though. I, for one, have run into turbulence in the past. I had been nursing a passion for new physics for a number of years. During the same week that I was making my way through a Stephen Hawking tome, I had to fly to Peoria, Illinois, to give a talk. The woman sitting next to me looked like a cross between a lifeguard and top-level business executive. At the time, I was a precocious nineteen-year-old seminary student, passionately religious, and an awkward but committed romantic. What could be safer than a public airplane ride? So when she asked me what I did, I answered in the most nonchalant of manners, "Astrophysics."

"Really?" she said without batting an eyelash. "So do I."

HIDDEN SPARKS

Luria the mystical master has much to say about the role of the Purim Carnival in helping us approach our story afresh. Remember that in the Kabbalistic creation myth there are initially vessels filled with light. At some point the light becomes too intense for the vessels and they shatter. When the vessels shatter, sparks of light remain trapped in the broken shards of the vessels.

They fall in the strangest and sometimes darkest of places. Indeed, according to Luria, this is the hidden intent of the shattering—to invite us, even force us, to look in crevices of our character that we might otherwise have never dared approach. In such a carnival atmosphere, we can grasp the fallen sparks of personality that otherwise may be too destabilizing to touch. The mystical goal of Purim, according to Luria, is to redeem those sparks of our personae—what we would call dimensions of our soul prints—that are hidden in the deepest and darkest places.

> When we pluck the string of an instrument that needs to be part of our symphony, our soul print strings vibrate back in song.

SOUL STRINGS

Following Purim is a thirty-day interlude before the storytelling ritual. In this pause we mull over and meditate what occurred there; we listen to the resonance of the carnival. For our souls, like stringed instruments, are moved by resonance. When a musical string is plucked and sends out its vibrations to the air, if there is another instrument that is strung to that same note, then its strings too will start to vibrate in song. The same holds true for our soul strings. When we pluck the string of an instrument that needs to be part of our symphony, our soul print strings vibrate back in song.

For thirty days we listen. Perhaps one of those masks we tried on will send out a song to stir our soul strings. When our spirit calls out in response, then we know we have found another part of our soul print, another note to incorporate into the symphony of our story—and just in time for the storytelling ritual.

Soul Print Practice

Make a list of five "I am" statements and five "I am not" statements. For example:

I am _____.

I am _____.

I am _____.

I am _____.

I am _____.

(This could be a dentist, a mother, hyperactive, blonde, sleepy.)

I am NOT _____.

I am NOT _____.

I am NOT _____.

I am NOT _____.

I am NOT _____.

(This could be something you don't want to be, or something you aren't but want to be . . . for example, a genius, starving artist, motorcyclist, slob.)

Let's try on a new identity for a moment, and create something of a carnival on the page. Ponder your "I am not" list. Make the most convincing argument as to why and how you actually *are* this person.

Then look at your "I am" list. Here, write the most convincing argument as to why you *are not* this person.

The point of this carnival exercise is to uncover the Haman personae hidden in your Mordechai and vice versa.

THE RISK AND THE REWARD

For Jacob, the house of his uncle Laban, with all of its intrigues and complications, was essentially a "white" sheet, a clean slate, an open venue to try on new roles, new costumes. Yes, he did get lost there. Yet, when we reapproach Jacob's story in light of the Purim consciousness, we realize that getting lost was an essential part of Jacob's finding soul print. Without the risk of getting lost, we cannot get found.

Jacob traveled eastward outside of the confines of his story in order to try on new roles and new voices. This was a part of what Jacob was doing in trying on Esav's clothes. He needed to see for himself if they fit. Before he could reach his actualized self, his name Israel, he needed to explore other identities. This was Jacob's Purim masquerade moment. Jacob, a young scholar described as "a pure man who dwells in tents" dressed in the costume of his brother, a "mighty hunter and man of the field." The moral failing of Jacob in this reading is not the fact of trying on other clothes but the deceiving of his father and theft of the blessing due his brother. Trying on new roles does not mean deceiving or destroying relations with those close to us.

The Jacob who returned to his Land and his tent was not the same man who left. The text expresses his growth by suggesting that only when Jacob returns is he able to embrace Esav. All of their encounters before he left the Land ended in disaster. In the implied reading of the Zohar he is only able to embrace his brother Esav because he has integrated his own internal Esav qualities.

Many years ago I took a memorable bus ride from Jerusalem to Tel Aviv. Those who are familiar with Israel's existential landscape know that in some ways those two cities exist on different planets. To generalize perhaps too much, Jerusalem might be called the capital of the spirit, of religion, and Tel Aviv the center of secular humanism with an ethnic overlay. Although I live in Jerusalem, and I am today emotionally and intellectually committed to both cities, back then, I was a Jerusalem man through and through. On that bus ride to Tel Aviv, my *kippah*—the head covering worn by Orthodox Jews (and Catholic clergy of a certain rank)—blew off my head. The fates were not obviously kind that day; for as I got off the bus, looking to find another *kippah* fast, and feeling rather naked, I bumped into none other than my teacher from the seminary. He looked at my bare head, smiled at my stammered explanation, and said with an enigmatic twinkle in his eye, "This is your chance to be someone else. Have fun! Just try not to do anything that would make it too hard to come back. You've lost your hat. Don't lose your head." Fool that I was, I had no clue what he was talking about and promptly went to purchase a new *kippah*. Today I am beginning to understand what he meant.

In biblical myth, the symbol of core integrity is Land. Being on the Land represents being within the purview of your story. We saw how true this was for Jacob, when he became estranged from his family's Land and his own authentic story. Much like Tara's earth in *Gone With the Wind,* the connection to the Land is something you hold on to no matter what. In Laban's house, Jacob remained lured as he was by the bait of Laban's investment plan. Yet something inside him could never be for sale. However much he tested out alternative identities and masks, he had to remain true to the ground of his own being.

Even during our occasional airplane or bus ride adventures in masquerades, we must take care not to lose the core integrity of our primary voice, even as we test out the timbre of new voices. There are parts of our story that we intuitively know are essential to our very existence. With these we can never part.

THE CUP OF ELIJAH—DRINK DEEP

After experiencing the risky but renewing alternatives offered by Purim, you recollect and reconnect to lost pieces of your story in the Exodus from Egypt storytelling ritual. You affirm the core essence of your story—the part of your identity that is inviolable, the element of your story that is not for sale. The component of the Storytelling Ritual that captures this idea of the core integrity of your story is a symbolic ritual object called the cup of Elijah.

Throughout the Passover storytelling ritual, the cup of Elijah is filled high with wine and rests as a sort of centerpiece on the table. Although inebriation does not play a role in this ritual, there are four cups of wine that are at least sipped by the participants, each cup marking a different chapter in the story of the Exodus from slavery to freedom. The cup of Elijah, however, remains untouched. It is sacred and inviolable.

The Master Abraham Joshua Heschel, the Rebbe of Opt, used to tell this story in the weeks leading up to the storytelling ritual. In his tale, a once-wealthy couple, Elkana and Penina, fell on bad times. The evening of the Storytelling Ritual was approaching and the couple had no money for the basic necessities of the festive meal accompanying the ritual. They had sold everything.

The one thing remaining in their possession was a stunningly beautiful cup of Elijah. It had been in Elkana's family for many generations. Its exquisite design, the elegant grace of its form, and the sheer power of the silver, never failed to move him. The cup's beauty, and the story of his family through the generations with which it was witness, always stirred his soul.

And yet, dejected and hopeless, Elkana decided he had no choice but to sell the goblet. His wife, Penina, fiercely objected, and after a protracted argument prevented the sale of the cup. At the very moment when Elkana, having little choice, acceded to his wife's objections, a messenger from a long-forgotten debtor mysteriously knocked on the door. He repaid Elkana an old debt, thus magically providing them with the money necessary for the festive meal.

Shortly after the meal, Elkana died. Despite his many good deeds, he was not admitted into heaven. The reason? He had been willing to sell the cup. His soul was left waiting at the gates of heaven.

A short time later, Penina also passed away. As she approached heaven, its gates opened wide with welcome, emanating light from the other side. Yet next to the gates sat her Elkana. When she realized he had been kept out of heaven, she refused to pass through the gates without him.

Though it was apparently against the rules, the angels were swayed by the depths of her love for Elkana. Elkana and Penina entered heaven together, holding between them the cup of Elijah. Love overrules even the law of heaven.

This is a strange story to hear repeated by a master on the eve of the Storytelling Ritual, especially when you realize that, according to biblical law, you would be clearly required to sell Elijah's cup in order to buy the necessities for the festive meal.

The Master of Opt challenges us to look at the tale again. Jungian psychologist Micha Ankori points out that in myth Elijah, Buddha, Brahman, Atmahn, and Shaman all represent the highest self, what we could refer to as the actualized soul print. The cup of Elijah is also symbolic of a person's core integrity. In this story, the cup of Elijah represents Elkana's deepest self. It is the expression of his soul print. It is who he is, in his most profound and real self, when all outer layers and postures are removed. We all have our own cup of Elijah, filled high with

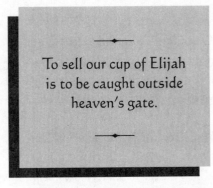

To sell our cup of Elijah is to be caught outside heaven's gate.

the story of our past, decorated with the intricately swirled patterns of our soul. Many of the cups we drink from in life are less than attractive, but our cup of Elijah is always beautiful, always precious, and unique.

To sell our cup of Elijah is to be caught outside heaven's gate. If we believe in our self enough to never sell the cup, then ultimately people will start knocking on our door with all sorts of gifts to share.

ELIJAH'S ENTRANCE

The Elijah story takes us even deeper into soul print consciousness. The magical moment that for most children crowns the Storytelling Ritual is centered around Elijah's cup.

This climactic moment was penned into the ledgers of my memory at a very young age. I recall its imprint exactly. I was about seven years old, and the evening was charged with that excitement that a child feels when he gets to stay up late to witness the mysterious goings-on and secret conversations of the adult world. My grandfather announced that the time had come to invite Elijah the Prophet to enter the house and drink from the cup we had set for him. Grandfather even invited me to be the one to open the front door to let Elijah in. With great solemnity I stepped through the alcove and grasped the great silver knob of the door.

Mind you, no one, but no one, ever used the front door. It just wasn't done. For all I knew, this door was made especially for Elijah's annual visit. With awe, and a certain trepidation about what might rest on the other side of the heavy oak, I ceremoniously opened the door to the spring wind. A gust of cold across my face made my eyes water as I scanned the front steps, the yard of wind-shaken trees, and the dark, deserted street. My limbs shivered in anticipation and fear. In a flash, I turned and ran back to the warmth and company of the candlelit table.

When I came back in, my grandfather motioned me over to him, and pointing at Elijah's goblet, whispered, "Look inside." I peered over the slope of its silver mouth, and saw it was empty. Just a moment before it had been brimming burgundy, and now it was empty! The chill caught my arms again. Elijah had entered!

Tradition understands that the experience of a child is essential to retain if we want to keep Elijah's cup. Elijah's cup is about our most personal hopes and dreams. It is about believing in miracles, about dreaming the impossible, about reaching beyond our grasp to find our heaven.

From where inside you arises your ability, and your right, to dream? Only from your deepest self, from what some thinkers have called your inner child. Beyond all of your sad and joyful temporary transformations and your wrong paths taken, that childlike part of you, capable of magic and wonder, always pure and always powerful, is your cup of Elijah.

Soul Print Practice

In C.S. Lewis's children's novel *The Lion, the Witch and the Wardrobe,* the Wardrobe is the symbol of the access point that we need to open in order to begin the journey. We need to find the right words, touch the right place in the wall, or have both halves of the ring in order for the "Open sesame" to work. This first step is essential to the journey. First steps require a combination of magic and courage.

Think of one area in which you want to make a breakthrough.

Now, list five first steps that you could take to set the game in motion.

OPEN SESAME

Why do we need to open the door for Elijah? If, like Santa, he can manage to visit hundreds of thousands of houses on this one night, then surely he can get through the door himself. Yet the magic happens only if we get up and open the door.

Magic happens only if we get up and open the door.

We need to create our own opportunities, open our own portals to possibility and transformation. Once we open the door, even a crack, the universe may open all gates for us. The first step in the soul print quest needs to be our own. In the language of the Talmudic myth masters, *"If you open for me a space the size of a needle, I will open for you the width of the sea."*

16

THE SOUL PRINT INVITATION

THE INVITATION TO BE KNOWN

Every moment in time, every encounter with a face, is a Soul Print Invitation. We were born to accept those Invitations. When we do, we engage in Soul Print Encounters. In this, our final exploration, we will endeavor to set the ground rules for the Soul Print Encounters that make up the sacred stuff of our daily lives.

I want to share with you a meditation story. Unlike the wonderful Buddhist Vipassana meditation, which is silent, biblical myth meditation happens through storytelling. The story itself becomes the meditation.

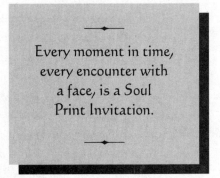

Every moment in time, every encounter with a face, is a Soul Print Invitation.

This story took place roughly around the time of the American Revolution. It is set in the Carpathian Mountains of central Europe. First, here are a few words of introduction, so that you will feel comfortable with the story you're about to read.

Today there's a lot of conversation occurring between Jews and Christians. They call it ecumenical dialogue, or interfaith discussion. I think it's a wonderful thing. There are those, however, good people, not the crazies, who are cynical about the dialogue. One religious leader put it like this: "Interfaith dialogue is when Jews who don't believe in Judaism get together with Christians who don't believe in Christianity and discover they have a lot in common." What this leader meant was that interfaith dialogue is only real if both Christians and Jews are committed to their own story. If the dialogue masks a fundamental disconnection from the story, then it is just not real.

Similarly, if the dialogue masks a Jewish desire to convert Christians to Judaism or a Christian desire to convert Jews to Christianity, then, as the Pope himself has pointed out, it is not dialogue. Dialogue begins with honoring the integrity of another story. When Pope John XXIII issued the revolutionary message of Vatican II, which for the first time affirmed the integrity of the Jewish story, he was also affirming his great faith in Jesus. He was saying, the way only a great man can, that he was so deeply rooted in his own story that he could be powerful and holy enough to live with another story by his side. Thank God for such courage.

The following story tells of a darker era, before the light of such dialogue. While it contains painful accounts of Christian-Jewish discord on several levels, it speaks also of the ultimate importance of telling a story—and having it heard.

The Baal Shem Tov, Master of the Good Name, was on his deathbed. His students gathered around him, and to each, the master revealed his particular calling in the world. To one, commerce, to the other, healing, to a third, the ministry. To his student Gabriel, the master said, "You will be my storyteller. Your job will be to travel far and wide, from town to town, from village to village, telling the stories and wonders you have seen in my company."

Gabriel hoped the Baal Shem was pointing to someone else, because the last thing he wanted to be was an itinerant storyteller. A preacher with a congregation and a stable pulpit, yes, but wandering was not the life for him. But what could he do? He had been called.

He asked the Baal Shem, "Will this be my role for the rest of my days? How will I know if and when my task is done?"

"You will know," the Baal Shem told him. "You will know."

After the death of the master, Gabriel dutifully began to wander the towns and the countryside, relating the stories and wonders of the Baal Shem. Some years went by and Gabriel longed for home. One day he heard that in Italy, in Siena, there was a wealthy man who paid fifty rubles for every new Baal Shem story he heard. Fifty rubles was a lot of money, and Gabriel had a lot of stories. After all, he was the storyteller *of the Baal Shem. "This," he said to himself, "must have been the Baal Shem's intent. I will become instantly a wealthy man and will be able to devote the rest of my life to my family and my studies."*

Gabriel traveled to Siena. Word spread quickly that the Baal Shem's storyteller had come to town, and the next day, Friday evening, the entire town gathered in the home of the wealthy patron, eagerly anticipating a rich repast of tales.

Gabriel rose to speak. He opened his mouth. Silence. Not a word came out. His face went white. He concentrated. Still silence. Three or four slow minutes inched by. Finally, Gabriel stammered, "I'm so sorry, but I can't remember a story, not a one."

The patron was gracious. "You're surely tired from your travel," he said. "Rest. Tomorrow you'll be refreshed and at the afternoon meal you will tell us your tales."

The next day the people gathered for lunch. Again, Gabriel opened his mouth and stopped, unable to remember a single story. It happened again at the evening meal—the same silence as before. The sun set upon his silence, and the patron, looking unusually sad, gave Gabriel a few rubles and sent him on his way.

Gabriel was devastated, crying bitterly. "What is a storyteller who has forgotten his stories?" he asked himself.

But just as he reached the outskirts of the city, he noticed a house whose shutters were all closed up. It provoked in him a flash of memory, a story he'd forgotten. A story he'd never told. It was the only one he could remember. Quickly he turned around, raced back to the house of the patron, and burst through the door, rushing past the servants to enter the study of the patron. Much to his surprise, he found the man slumped over his desk, racked with sobs. But Gabriel had no time for questions or explanations. He had to tell the tale. "Quick," Gabriel said. "I remember a story, a story I've never told. Let me tell it to you before it too recedes."

The patron opened his mouth to respond, but Gabriel had already launched into his tale. "It was on a Wednesday morning that the Baal Shem called me. He said, 'Hitch up the wagon. I want you and you alone to accompany me.' And we traveled what seemed like great distances in the shortest time. We arrived in the Jewish quarter of a town I did not recognize. All the houses were shuttered up. In the midst of the houses was a square and in the square people were gathering to hear the address by the priest upon a high pulpit.

"The Baal Shem asked me to knock on the door of one of the houses adjoining the square. We knocked and a voice from inside said, 'Get away from here. Don't you know? The priest is about to rile people up to commit a massacre. Any Jew found outside is fair game for the slaughter.' 'You have nothing to fear from me,' responded my master, 'Open the door.' His was a voice you could not disobey. The door opened, the Baal Shem turned to me and said, 'Cross the square and tell the priest that I, Israel son of Eliezar, would like to talk to him.' 'Are you sure?' I asked timidly. 'They'll kill me before I even take a few steps.' 'Go now,' said the Baal Shem.

"I crossed the square and the people parted before me like the splitting of the Red Sea. And I said to the priest, 'The Baal Shem Tov would like to speak to you.' You can imagine my surprise when his face paled and he began to tremble. He did not want to respond to my call, that was clear, but somehow, I don't know why, he came with me. We crossed the square together and he disappeared into the back room of the

house with the Baal Shem. They were in there for thirteen hours. Afterward, the priest came out, tears streaming down his face, and was heard from no more. That's all I remember."

Gabriel stood there like an emptied pocket, his story told.

The patron had become very quiet. He sat staring at the storyteller with an almost desperate look in his eyes. He got up, took Gabriel by the shoulders, and with his face inches away from Gabriel's, he shook him. "Don't you recognize me?" he asked. "Recognize me!"

Slowly a flicker of recognition illuminated Gabriel's face. "Why, why—you're the priest! How could it be? You're the priest!"

"I am the priest. Yes. I am the priest," the man replied, as if for the first time reconciling himself to that fact. He loosened his grip on Gabriel's shoulders, and as he spoke, his features began to relax. "Let me tell you my story. I was raised in a Jewish home, a precocious child with great aspirations. But as you know, there's not much a Jew can do to advance in the world. I wanted to get out of my hamlet and rise, to become something in the world. I thought, why don't I join the most successful enterprise around—the church. So I did. And what better way to join than to become a priest? I converted and threw myself into the priestly task. As the years passed I did so well, I rose so high, that I was considered to be a bishop. There remained, however, some faint suspicion in the Church that perhaps I had not fully left my former life as a Jew.

"And dear storyteller, I so much wanted to be a bishop that I decided to foment riots against the Jews of my town to prove to the church that I was loyal. And just as I was about to give my inflammatory speech, rousing the villagers to riot, you came to me, saying the Baal Shem wanted to see me. I had never heard of him, but there was something in your voice I could not ignore. I felt pulled. I had to come.

"The Baal Shem spoke to me for some thirteen hours. He spoke of my soul, my past, my calling. 'Return,' he said, 'Return to yourself.' And that is what I did. I committed myself to fully returning to my roots and to making amends for the enormous suffering I had caused. Before I left the house, though, I asked the Baal Shem, 'How will I know that my

return has been accepted on high, that I have been forgiven?' He answered, 'You will know your return has been received when you hear someone telling your story, and both you and the teller realize the tale belongs to you.' "

This is a story about names. It is focused around the legacy of the Baal Shem, Master of the Name. In the language of this book, we can call him the Master of the Soul Print, for name, as we have seen, is the soul print symbol. As a soul print master, he is fully living his story and responding to his call. He has fully realized his soul print and can guide others to recover the print of their own souls, which is precisely his role in our story.

This is a story about stories. Gabriel is a storyteller not entirely pleased with his calling. He would rather be someplace else. He has not embraced his story. So he must wander the world, searching, trying to tell the story right. The erstwhile priest is also a man who had fled from his story. He was driven to foment a massacre of the Jews in his town because a person living in a story not his own can be driven to the darkest places in order to maintain the disguise. He needs to prove he is a character in his foreign tale by changing his costume, accent, and religion; in the end he can only push his way into his inauthentic story by nullifying, in the most dramatic way possible, his previous story. His intended murder of his former community is really a form of suicide. We all commit small murders in order to maintain our disguise in a story not our own. Usually the people we wind up hurting the most are the people closest to us, for it is they who remind us of our impostor status.

This is a story about returning to your story. Both of the major characters in this tale can only be redeemed if they find their way back to their own stories. I once heard that there are four signs of getting old:

When you sink your teeth into steak and they stay there.
When your back goes out more often than you do.

When the old lady you are walking across the street
turns out to be your wife.
When you get to the top rung of the ladder you've been climbing and
find it is leaning against the wrong wall.

Up until number four we are in comedy. Number four is tragedy. No matter what your age, the only legitimate fear in your life should be that maybe you're living the wrong story, leaning your ladder against the wrong wall. To succeed in a story not your own is failure.

This is one of the many reasons that we cannot judge another person's failure or success unless we are intimately connected to his soul print. Even then, we don't really know enough to judge. A bishop is a beautiful thing to be, if that is your story. If it is not your story, if you are doing it for all the wrong reasons, then the church would be the first to say, "You must return to your story." Being a teacher in your hometown with stable family life and a sustaining community is beautiful—that is, unless your soul print calls you to be a wandering storyteller.

INVITATION TO THE SOUL PRINT ENCOUNTER

The meeting between the priest and the storyteller, each disconnected from his own story, becomes the model of a new and enormously exciting soul print idea. Namely, that every person we meet—in a significant meeting—possesses a piece of our story. Some people may have a sentence, others a missing word, while still others may hold a paragraph or even a whole chapter. Significant meetings involve soul print encounters.

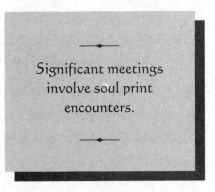

Significant meetings
involve soul print
encounters.

Of course, the ultimate soul print encounter is with your significant other in life—your soul print partner. The person you choose should be the person who can return to you a significant piece of your story that you have lost, disconnected from, or never even imagined you could possibly have. Conversely, you possess and need to share with them the missing and magnificent pieces of their story. The soul print relationship is the committed, dynamic process of discovering just what these pieces may be, and having the patience and caring to puzzle them back together.

A soul print encounter is in no sense limited to romantic partners. Your sphere of colleagues, casual friends, family, neighbors, employers, and employees all may have pieces of your story and you of theirs. Nor are soul print encounters limited to long-term connections within our fixed pattern of orbit. Often a person who is a meteor or comet in your life may leave a soul print impact of enormous significance. You may be riding an elevator with a person you have never met and will never meet again, both of you inching up to the seventy-fifth floor. And yet a Soul Print Invitation may have been extended. Inviting this soul print encounter into your life doesn't mean you need to talk about your relationship with your mother or your innermost secrets. However, it is highly likely that somewhere in your casual conversation there will be an important message for each of you. Similarly, the person who returns your lost wallet may have more to return than your credit cards. You Never Know. You Never Know.

When a soul print encounter that should have taken place does not, then we have committed a soul print misdemeanor. On a soul print level, the meeting was immoral. Of course, the morality we speak of here is very different than public morals that we often hear people getting excited about. No one can accuse you or take you to task on a soul print violation. No one will ever know—except for you and possibly the person with whom you failed to have an encounter.

Morality has two aspects. The first, upon which American law is based, is the protection of the individual from damage actively inflicted. It is immoral to steal, attack, cheat, abuse, and the like. In this sense, morality is passive and subject to public censure—don't do something wrong, if you do, you're in trouble.

The second aspect of morality is active and private. It can in no sense be enforced or legislated, yet it demands a far higher moral standard than passive public morality. We speak, of course, of soul print morality. Here the standard is simple and clear. When you have an encounter with another person, you are called upon to ask yourself, "Have I brought my unique self to the table in the meeting? If I have not given you the benefit of my soul print, then you and I both have lost something precious in the encounter."

A soul print encounter may be a wisdom encounter. Through your soul print convergence with someone, each of you may leave the meeting with a deeper understanding of your selves. The encounter may last a minute or an hour or be a two-year relationship.

A soul print encounter can also be action-oriented. You and the person you encounter may be agents of change for each other, each of you provoking the other to do something in the world you never otherwise could have done. Encounters take place between teachers and students, between lovers, among friends, in casual acquaintance, or in chance encounters.

Not long ago in Jerusalem, I had finished a lecture and stayed for a while afterward answering questions. It was raining hard outside and a student kindly offered to walk me home under his umbrella. For some reason, his gesture pressed my "Nobody-helps-me-except-for-God" button, and my "I'm independent" button. I didn't realize this at the time; I thanked him profusely as I declined his kind offer, and then walked home alone, in the rain, cold and soaked. I had allowed my encounter with this student to become an immoral meeting. I needed to be able to allow myself to be dependent and trusting of a genuine offer to help, just as he was allowing himself to seek a more intimate relationship with his teacher.

FORGETTING TO REMEMBER

The priest provokes the storyteller to remember a story he had forgotten. What is the significance of the forgotten tale?

Gabriel's forgetting has two functions. First, it shows how Gabriel is essentially disconnected from his calling, becoming a storyteller who has forgotten his story. Second, in the experience of being without the story, he realizes for the first time just how much a part of him the story really is. Sometimes the best way to find out if our occupation is truly our calling is to leave it for a time and see how our soul reacts. We may find ourselves having genuine soul print encounters in the process.

> To be redeemed, is to hear your story and recognize it as your own.

RECOGNITION

Often we hear our story but do not recognize it as our own. To be redeemed, implied the Baal Shem to the priest, is to hear your story and recognize it as your own.

INVITATIONS IN TIME

Every moment has its own revelation. The storyteller cannot remember his story initially because it is not yet time for him to. The priest needed to go through one more level of transformation before he was prepared to hear and recognize his Soul Print Story. In order to sense and receive Soul Print Invitations in their right time, we need to become sensitized to the rhythms of time itself. Developing that sensitivity is one of the primary goals of biblical consciousness.

Our soul prints unfold in time. We can comprehend tomorrow what we are not yet prepared to comprehend today. One of Carl

Jung's great contributions was an affirmation of the enormous excitement that awaits us in middle age. If you are truly living, then time is unfolding before you. You are not farther from youth—you are closer to wisdom. Each day brings its own revelation. Each day brings us closer to ourselves.

Every moment has its own revelation.

Indeed, the very word for "time" in Biblical myth, *zeman,* is layered with a second meaning as well. *Zeman* always means "invitation." The idea is elegant and simple. Time is an invitation. You can experience a month as one day that is repeated thirty times or as thirty days that grow out of each other, each day building on the one that preceded it.

Too often we miss the invitation of time, but we can learn to respond to it. We can be aware of a moment when we are making a memory; we can create a conscious practice around it that lets us accept that invitation.

Once Cary and I were sitting in Cafit, my Jerusalem writing café, working together on the text of this book. I was called to the phone, which afforded me an outsider's view of our table. It was piled high with books, making it look much more like a library cubicle than a café table. Cary was passionately crossing something out on the text in front of her, and I had been sitting across from her writing a moment before. My imagination raced forward some forty years. I saw Cary and myself, old, much closer to the end than the beginning of our journeys, sitting and recalling those days way back when we were working on that very first book. We had no idea of what the future held. We believed in our wisdom, our passion, our God, and each other. Life was a magical place. Probably a minute later, but what seemed like much longer, I snapped out of my reverie. I looked at Cary sitting there and felt overwhelmed by the joy of being able to step into that memory and live it, now.

Try to sense special moments in your life when memories are being created.

Step out of the moment, go forward in time, and visualize yourself as an old man or woman remembering the scene. Stay there for a moment. Then step out of your visualization and walk into your memory, which is now part of your present.

COLLECTING YOUR DAYS

There is a wonderful biblical myth phrase used to describe Abraham in his old age. "Abraham was old—and came with his days." All the myth masters are troubled by this phrase. What could it mean?

The mystical Zohar, illuminating this phrase, suggests that every single day brings a spiritual opportunity radically specific to it alone. There is soul print revelation anew in every day, if we can accept the invitation to encounter it. I never quite understood this idea until a soul print encounter I had with Israeli avant-garde writer Pinchas Sadeh.

I went to visit Sadeh when he was an old man dying of cancer in Jerusalem. He was in a particularly nostalgic mood that night and spun story after story of his life. I sat there wrapped in the wonder of his memories. As I was leaving, I thanked him for sharing with me from the wealth of his days. His smile turned serious as he looked into my eyes and replied, "When I was young, like you, I read Goethe but did not understand him. You see, Goethe had written that he was able to collect from his life fourteen days of happiness. How could it be, I asked myself, that Goethe, who was so successful in his own lifetime, whose wife was so beautiful, whose fame so widespread, who was surrounded by friends—how could it be that he was able to collect *only* fourteen happy days?

Was he so unappreciative, was he so insensitive and senile, that he could not remember more?

"Now at the end of my life I finally understand Goethe. But I more than understand. I am amazed by the man—that he was able to collect so many days of joy! I have tried to collect my days and have come up with a meager handful. Pieces and fragments come to me, snatches like the stories you heard tonight. But I am not sure what was real and what fantasy, imagination, or dream. A very few days remain entire and whole in my memories. The ones that do sit like gems in my hand. But they are so few. Imagine the wealth of fourteen full days of joy!"

The days that you are able to take with you are what I call Soul Print Days. These are days when you felt fully present, when you responded to your unique calling or fully lived your story. That Abraham was able to "take his days with him" meant first that he was able to collect his days; his soul print unfolded daily, becoming richer, more colorful, and textured all the time. It also meant that Abraham's days built on each other, each one giving birth to the next in a way that made aging a great joy. If you can understand your life as the process of unfolding your soul print, then the passage of time can bring great joy to you as well.

Jung writes about many of his middle-aged patients that they suffer not from any clinical condition but "from the senselessness and aimlessness of their lives. . . . I should not object," continues Jung, "if this were called the general neurosis of our age." In another passage he is even more emphatic: "Among all my patients in the second half of life—that is to say over thirty five—there has not been one whose problem in the last resort was not that of finding a religious outlook on life." This problem, he says, has nothing to do with organized religion as we know it. Rather, in the language of this book, we all seek the affirmation that the human being has a soul print—a unique calling and a special story possessing infinite value, meaning, and dignity.

KILLING TIME

Do we kill time or create holy days? Two people reading one clock
may have very different answers for what time it is. Is it late or early?
Is time slipping away or catching up? Two literary images of the clock
imply suggestively how the soul print thrives or falters. In William
Faulkner's *The Sound and the Fury,* Quentin Compson, the protagonist, is soon to commit suicide. The most startling image of his last
day is a clock that he hears incessantly chiming. The face of the clock
is broken. The hands no longer measure time. But it keeps chiming,
with maddening regularity, as time slips away. Faulkner borrowed
the title for his book from Shakespeare's *Macbeth.* Toward the end of
the play, Macbeth cries out, "Life's but a walking shadow, a poor
player / That struts and frets his hour upon the stage / And then is
heard no more: it is a tale / Told by an idiot, full of sound and
fury, / Signifying nothing." Macbeth asserts that the hour of our lives
is insignificant, merely marking time on our walk to oblivion.

Standing against Quentin Compson's clock and Macbeth's measure is the clock of the nineteenth-century myth master, Yaakov
Yitzchak, the Seer of Lublin.

*The inn was silent but for the sound of the impatient clock, the clod
of heavy boots, and the innkeeper's tossing and turning. One of the guests
at the inn, Yissachar Ber of Radshitz, student of the Seer of Lublin, and
himself a master, paced the floor of his room, unable to sleep, mysteri-*

ously animated further by every passing moment. The innkeeper, whose room was right below the master, was kept awake and unhappy the whole night by his apparently insomniac guest.

When morning finally dawned and Yissachar Ber came downstairs, the innkeeper could scarcely control himself. "Why did you dance around your room the whole night?" he demanded. "Are you mad?"

Yissachar answered the question with a question. "Tell me, where did you get the clock in that room?"

"Why does it matter! It obviously didn't work—or you would have realized how many hours you wasted pacing your floor and keeping me up!"

Yissachar tried again. "Forgive me if I disturbed you. I do apologize, but I must know. Where did you get that clock? For it must be the clock of my teacher. I can tell by the way it chimes."

The innkeeper's anger was turning to curiosity. "And who was this teacher?" he asked.

"My teacher was the Seer of Lublin."

The innkeeper was amazed, for indeed the clock had originally belonged to the Seer. It had been inherited by the Seer's son and then given to the innkeeper in payment of a debt. "But how is it that your master's clock could chime differently than any other clock?" the innkeeper had to ask.

Yissachar Ber answered him, "Most clocks chime saying, 'Another day gone, another day gone.' But my master's clock says, 'One day closer, one day closer. . . .'"

COUNTING "SEFIRA": THE COUNTING RITUAL

In biblical myth, each day of the calendar is an invitation to depth and joy. This radical sensitivity to the "invitation of time" is best revealed in the biblical myth ritual of Sefira, which, as you will see, anyone can adapt and make part of her life. Saying the word *sefira* to yourself, you'll recognize that we have encountered yet another offspring of our core soul print word *sapir,* light. *Sefira* is another sister term for *sippur,* story, and *mispar,* number. *Sefira* means "to count."

The ritual of Sefira is to count for a fifty-day period—every single day. The fifty-day sprint begins on the night immediately following the Storytelling Ritual. In an incredible chain of meaning, the *sippur* of the Storytelling Ritual is followed by Sefira, the Counting Ritual, where we count the number—*mispar*—of the day.

The Counting Ritual takes about thirty seconds a night. You say, "Today is the first day of the Sefira count." That's it—the entire ritual is just to count. The next day you say, "Today is the second day of the Sefira count" and so on. When you get into the second week, you say, "Today is the eighth day, which is one week and one day into the period." There is one catch. According to biblical myth law, if you miss one night, you're out! If you forget to count one day, you cannot ritually count the following days, you are out of the story. Until next year, that is, when you are invited to try again.

The Counting Ritual offers you an idea of an ascending pattern, where one day builds on the next. In effect, the whole point of the ritual is to collect days. Using a simple and short act of consciousness, you can prevent days from blurring into each other in a way that would make Goethe and Sadeh proud. This way, if we ask ourselves to collect fourteen days at the end of a year, it will not be well nigh impossible.

Make every day count. Whoever first uttered the axiom had it right: Today *is* the first day of the rest of your life.

Soul Print Practice

Take a soul print vacation. Pick a fourteen-day period. Every night, before you go to bed, record in a soul print notebook the day's events, feelings, and encounters. Tell yourself that after these two weeks you can revert to your normal mode of living. However, you want to give yourself a present: fourteen days that are collector's items, that you take with you. These fourteen days are your soul print vacation.

Every year pick fourteen days for your "two weeks on," your soul print vacation.

THE ULTIMATE INVITATION

At this point in our journey, we can see for the first time the grand vista of biblical myth soul print practice. We now realize that the unfolding of the soul print is a primary goal of biblical myth rituals. We can view those rituals as soul print growth seminars integrated into the calendars of our lives.

First comes the Purim carnival. There, or in Purim Moments throughout the year, we try on new personae. We explore the hidden parts of our stories in the safe environment of carnival revelry. The mask and the wine allow us to explore uncharted terrain of the self, trying on new costumes and experimenting with alternative versions of ourselves.

Second, one month later, comes the night of the Storytelling Ritual. That night, we retell our stories, and in the retelling claim what we have lost. We can even chart new directions for the future—directions that reflect more deeply who we really are. We see which of the roles we tried on in the Purim carnival are really part of our story. Those that are, we weave into our narration; those that are not, we discard.

Finally, the third ritual, the Sefira, is the Counting Ritual, where we try to collect our days, imitating the biblical myth hero Abraham, who knew how to "come with his days." This ritual begins the night after the Storytelling Ritual since they are two parts of the same process, the writing of Sacred Autobiography.

RITUAL CLIMAX

The culmination of biblical myth rituals comes at the conclusion of the Counting Ritual. For seven weeks, we have counted every day. Every day, we have responded to the unique invitation of time folded into that specific two dozen hours. The excitement builds. Day by day, the intensity increases until we reach the ultimate moment, on the fiftieth night after the storytelling ritual, when we stay up an entire night to receive the Sefer.

The word *sefer* means "book." As I am sure you have already noticed, it derives from our *sefer-mispar-sapir-sefira* root family. According to Hayim Vital, a mystic from Tsfat and the most impor-

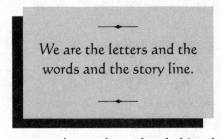

We are the letters and the words and the story line.

tant student of Isaac Luria, the goal of life is to write your own letter in the biblical scroll. The biblical scroll is called the Sefer Torah, the book of the Torah. Now you are ready to take up the ultimate cosmic invitation,

one that we have already hinted at earlier in these pages. You are now ready to be a letter in the Sefer.

In the Bible we have inherited a sacred text, yet there is another book and second Bible that is written anew in every generation. This second Bible is by far the more sacred of the two. In this Bible, we are the letters and the words and the story line. This book is also called a *Sefer—Sefer Hachaim,* the book of your life. Our lives have become the sacred text. Our words have become the words of God. Now we have realized our soul.

IF ONLY . . .

There was once a disgruntled stonecutter. All his life he spent toiling at the rock face, the sun beating down on his back as he chipped away in the quarry. He hated his job and he hated his life, and more than any-thing he hated his foreman.

He hated the foreman not only because the foreman would always shout at him to work faster, and not only because the foreman rarely paid him his wages on time, but chiefly because the foreman made him feel so envious. There the foreman would strut, handing out orders left, right, and center with not a care in the world, venturing nowhere near a hammer and chisel. What a life! "If only," thought the stonecutter, "if only I could be the foreman!"

Well, strangely enough, some power was listening to the unhappy stonecutter, and before he could say "I wish," he was suddenly transformed into the foreman. What a joy! No more work on the rock face. He could walk around all day giving orders to everyone. He was happy—until one day when the King came to visit. The foreman had to give over all his profits to the King, and had to serve on him hand and foot, and laugh at his stupid jokes. "If only," he thought, "if only I could be the King!"

Shazam. Suddenly he found himself transformed into the King. What a delight! He was carried around the kingdom on his palanquin, with servants to cater for his every needs and with worshipping crowds to be waved to in every town. Life as a King was great. Of course, it was a little hot to be moving outside because the sun was rather strong— indeed the sun was very bright. And indeed his crown and robes were hot and heavy, and soon the heat and the sweat became unbearable. "If only," he thought, "if only I could be the sun!"

In a flash there he was, up in the sky, beaming and shining all around. It was fun being the sun. See that green field? One beam and it gets yellow. That white nose? Red in an instant. Beaming here, beaming there, until—a cloud suddenly appeared and stood right in front of him, blocking his beams. "If only," he thought, "if only I could be a cloud!"

Life as a cloud was lovely. Fluffy, floating around at leisure, with his back warmed by the frustrated sun, the cloud found life a pleasure. Until a vicious wind blew in and violently flung him away from the sun. He was blown hot, he was blown warm, he was blown so cold he even began to drip water and rain. "If only," he thought, "if only I could be the wind!"

Whoosh! Sweeping here and sweeping there, his life as the wind was wild and free. Whistling through rafters, rustling through trees and knocking off hats—being the wind was a joy. He swept down a valley and then—a mountain stood in his way. He could go over it, and he could go round it, but he wanted to go straight ahead and this obstinate mountain simply wouldn't let him. "If only," he thought, "if only I could be a mountain!"

Mountain. Rock. Been here for ages. Going to be here forever. Rock hard. Rock steady. Solid as. But then he heard a knocking sound at his base, and slowly, ever so gradually, he felt himself being diminished. Looking down, he could see a little man in a quarry, chipping away at his sides with hammer and chisel. Ah. Ah yes. "If only," he thought, "if only I could be a stonecutter."

And there he was, stonecutter once more, at last at peace.

FOR ME WAS THE WORLD CREATED

Biblical myth consciousness does not demand that we obliterate the self and merge with the divine. Quite the opposite. Biblical spirituality calls for us to fulfill and sing out the music of our own self. Only through fulfilling the whole of ourselves, celebrating the flaws in our jewels, collecting the lost notes, do all our pieces come together in symphony. Whether we are king or stonecutter, living another person's melody results only in fragmentation, a cacophony of blind noise.

The biblical mystic Abraham Kuk says it well.

> *Every person needs to know*
> *that he is called to serve*
> *based on the model of perception and feeling*
> *which is unique to him,*
> *based on the core root of his soul.*
> *In that root,*
> *which contains infinite worlds,*
> *he will find the treasure of his life.*
>
> *A person needs to say:*
> "Bi-shvili nivrah ha-olam,
> *the world was created for me."*
>
> —(R. Kuk, Orot ha-Kodesh, "Sacred Lights," section 3:221)

We must not allow ourselves to be swept up in stories from "strange places" but focus instead on our unique stories. Each of us needs to value ourselves to the extent we each can say, "The world was created for me." The word *shvil* in Hebrew means both "for" as in "for me" as well as "path." Thus the Hassidic masters read this last verse both as *bi-shvili,* "for me," and *bi-shvil sheli,* "in my own unique path." To be connected to your soul print means to get up in the morning and know that your story is sufficiently important, significant, and wonderful that the entire world was created for its sake. We must each of us be able to say that the world was created for the sake of our own unique way, for our own particular story.

THE SNAKE'S OPINION

We return at the end to the beginning—the first story of biblical myth. According to Abraham Kuk, our struggle to gain certainty of being is an echo of the original sin in the Garden of Eden. Kuk maintains that the notion of original sin—eating the forbidden fruit—has nothing to do with betraying God in the old way of thinking. The original sin that resulted in humanity's exile from paradise was a betrayal of self. The fundamental sin, according to Kuk, is that when Adam ate of the fruit of the Tree of Knowledge, he accepted the opinion of the snake rather than holding firm to his inner convictions.

The first man sinned.
He became alienated from his own personhood,
for he accepted the opinion of the snake
and lost himself.
He did not know how to give a clear answer
to God's question, "Where are you?"
for he did not know his own soul,
because his "I" had perished
in the sin of bowing to a foreign god.

In Kuk's words, Adam "lost himself." To lose himself was to lose his story. In failing to affirm his authentic self, Adam failed to respect and affirm his own calling and divinity. As the juice flooded into his mouth upon the first bite, Adam tasted the loss of his certainty of being. According to the Zohar, the Tree of Knowledge is the tree of uncertainty. In effect, when man ate the fruit of the tree of good and evil, he brought the uncertainty of his story into his very being. He did not believe he had a uniquely valuable story.

BLESSINGS

Books are important only if they spark us to be more than we already are. If in some small way, *Soul Prints* becomes part of the consciousness of your life, your communities, and ultimately our planet, then our journey together will have been wildly successful. If the concept of a unique soul print resonates with your soul strings, then I urge you—share it with a friend, around the table, in a group. Make a "live your story" bumper sticker, or pass on the book. You will know what to do; the key, as we have learned, is "Do something." The soul print is in the details.

Finally, I want to thank you from my heart for taking the time to go on this journey with me. Writing from my home in Jerusalem, I thought of you on every page. Your life, your meaning, your memories, your joy, and your fulfillment are infinitely important to me. I would be privileged in my short life to do you some small service. I hope this book is the beginning of that service. I would be honored to hear from you personally.

I leave you with a blessing and a prayer.

My prayer has been that each page be a point of light. A book is nothing but bound light. Like the biblical scroll, which is written with "black fire words" upon "white fire parchment," this book is sown with the light of my own soul print. My deepest hope and intention is that in these pages we have had a soul print encounter.

My blessing is for the blossoming of your soul print. May every day bring a new revelation of your own unique beauty, as well as the fathomless beauty of every soul around you. May such revelations help bring you a delicate balance between peace and passion, patience and expectation, care for self and care for other. May you be the hero of your life and in so doing further the heroic story of the world. May you hear your calling and courageously respond. May you know the glorious fulfillment of telling your story and having it received, and hearing deeply the stories of the ones you love.

> *I pray each page has been a point of light*
> *To illuminate the mind*
> *Or if not the light*
> *At least the wick*
> *That holds the fire in line*
> *And if not the wick then may it have been*
> *The oil to anoint the eye*
> *And if not the oil then at least the branch*
> *That brought the olive to life*
> *And if not the branch then single seed*
> *To plant the point of light.*
> *I pray there's been a single seed*
> *within each page I write.*

SCHOLAR'S PAGE

This book is—God willing—the first in a series of books on what I call Personal Myth. Personal myth seeks to unpack the implicit structures of Biblical and Kabbalistic thought on our inner emotional and imaginative lives. Topics include laughter, tears, eros, dance, silence, uncertainty, anger, joy, fear, Lillith and loving. On these topics I have written, or hope and pray to write, monographs or books that will form part of the library of the School of Personal Myth. Some of the books will be more formally scholarly in nature, others will be academic, and still others will use the more accessible style of this volume. There are a number of other scholars who are doing pivotal work in various arenas of personal myth. I benefit almost daily from conversation and interaction with them.

My core belief is that the pathways of personal myth form the high road toward the growth of the spirit for which we're born. It is in the living of our personal myth that we realize our soul print.

In terms of intellectual history, Personal Myth is a reformulation and expansion of the classic Hasidic ideal of *devekut*—the realization of and merging with the indwelling divine spirit in man.

This book in particular and the specific soul print philosophy it describes finds its roots in a particular strain of Hasidic thought— namely, the path of Pschisca, Lublin, Kotz, and Ishbitz. And let the hint be sufficient for the wise.

ABOUT THE AUTHOR

Rabbi MARC GAFNI has emerged as one of the important new voices in Israeli religion, culture, and spirituality. He is the Dean of the Public Culture Study Initiative, a division of Melitz Educational Institutions. The American-born philosopher has developed an ever-increasing following of ardent enthusiasts who consider him to be one of this generation's most insightful and exciting teachers. Lecturing to consistently overflowing houses throughout the country, Gafni is known to combine intellectual acumen with profound spirituality. Gafni, a unique blend of academic, mystic, and philosopher, has proven himself to be a thinker of great depth and sensitivity, a man who teaches from the mind as well as the heart.

Together with colleagues and students, Gafni is developing what he terms The School of Personal Myth. Focusing on the inner depths of the soul, Gafni's work explores dimensions of the individual's story, probing experiences ranging from laughter, tears, silence, and creativity to eros, uncertainty, and anger. While rejecting fundamentalism, Gafni's work explicitly seeks to reweave the fabric of biblical myth that forms the core of the Western democratic tradition. Gafni is seen by many of his students as a passionate and committed *Rebbe*—"spiritual master." In his own self-description, Gafni calls himself "a flawed human being, forever striving." Who passionately loves all people.

Gafni's latest venture is a weekly, hour-long television program on Israel's highest-rated station. The show offers a creative and passionate glimpse at the depth of biblical ideas. It speaks powerfully to secular and religious Israelis together. The show has become an important inspirational force for religious pluralism and personal growth among all sectors of Israel.

Rabbi Gafni is also a visiting member of the Advanced Institute of the Hartman Institute and a contributing editor to *Tikkun* magazine, where he writes the "Kabbalah/New Theology" column.

Born Marc Winiarz, he adopted the Hebrew name Gafni upon taking up residence in Israel twelve years ago, as a symbol of identification with the spirit of biblical myth. He is married to Cary, a poetess, and is the father of three children.

Rabbi Gafni can be contacted at info@soulprints.org

Continue Your Journey of
Mystical Discovery with the
Companion Home Video Release

SOUL PRINTS
Your Path to Fulfillment

with Marc Gafni

As Seen
On PBS

Available March 2001 on VHS
and April 2001 on DVD

To order, call 1-800-414-1690 or order on-line at
www.winstarvideo.com

Soul Prints: Your Path to Fulfillment with Marc Gafni is a Co-Production of Winstar
Productions and MPI Media Productions International, Inc.

WELLSPRING
MEDIA